THE
Magick of Lenormand
CARD READING

Kalliope

ILLUSTRATED BY
YASMEEN WESTWOOD

REDFeather™
MIND | BODY | SPIRIT

4880 Lower Valley Road, Atglen, PA 19310

Designed by Danielle D. Farmer
Type set in Desire/Ainslie Sans/Minion Pro
Images of the Lenormand cards are from *The Lenormand of Enchantment* © by Yasmeen Westwood (Enchanted Soul Art)
Cover design image reproduced from *The Lenormand of Enchantment*

ISBN: 978-0-7643-6772-4
Printed in China

Published by REDFeather Mind, Body, Spirit
An imprint of Schiffer Publishing, Ltd.
4880 Lower Valley Road
Atglen, PA 19310
Phone: (610) 593-1777; Fax: (610) 593-2002
Email: Info@redfeathermbs.com
Web: www.redfeathermbs.com

For our complete selection of fine books on this and related subjects, please visit our website at www.redfeathermbs.com. You may also write for a free catalog.

REDFeather Mind, Body, Spirit's titles are available at special discounts for bulk purchases for sales promotions or premiums. Special editions, including personalized covers, corporate imprints, and excerpts, can be created in large quantities for special needs. For more information, contact the publisher.

We are always looking for people to write books on new and related subjects. If you have an idea for a book, please contact us at proposals@schifferbooks.com.

MIX
Paper | Supporting responsible forestry
FSC
www.fsc.org
FSC® C104723

Every generation, the nine daughters of Zeus are reborn, and with their rebirth are also nine Guardians. They will be marked by the gods, and given gifts to protect his treasure. Their abilities will only be unlocked when they find their muse.

—Lisa Kessler

Contents

Acknowledgments 6

Welcome 7

Introduction 9

How to Use This Book 10

Practice Makes Perfect 11

Tips and Tricks 15

The Magick of the Cards: Magickal Moments 20

How to Read the Cards 35

The Magickal Combinations of the Cards 41

1. Rider 42	19. Tower 165
2. Clover 49	20. Garden 172
3. Ship 56	21. Mountain 178
4. House 63	22. Paths 184
5. Tree 70	23. Mice 190
6. Clouds 78	24. Heart 196
7. Snake 86	25. Ring 202
8. Coffin 93	26. Book 208
9. Bouquet 100	27. Letter 215
10. Scythe 106	28. Man 222
11. Whip 113	29. Woman 228
12. Birds 120	30. Lily 235
13. Child 127	31. Sun 241
14. Fox 133	32. Moon 247
15. Bear 139	33. Key 253
16. Stars 146	34. Fish 259
17. Stork 153	35. Anchor 265
18. Dog 159	36. Cross 271

Acknowledgments

When I set out to write the guidebook of *The Lenormand of Enchantment*, the cards spoke to me; what I didn't know at the time is that they would *never* stop talking . . . and clearly had more to say. That is when Chris McClure from REDFeather gave me the green light to continue writing book 2; that is how *The Magick of Lenormand Card Reading* came to be. A big thank-you to Chris for the opportunity and the title of this creation, for the Lenormand is all wordplay.

To my council of spiritual beings that continue to leave droplets of sunshine in my life: I revere all your continued wisdom and honor your teachings through words encased in this book.

And finally to my Muse Kalliope, who continues to whisper words of love and wisdom, inspiring me to share her pretty words with the world.

Welcome

Welcome to the *The Magick of Lenormand Card Reading*—the living book of lore, offering vital information and guidance in understanding the way the cards speak. The divine knowledge imparted in this book will transform your life, while navigating this earthly classroom by giving insight into life's everyday situations, allowing you to experience your creations physically through thousands of unique combinations. The combinations I have created spring from the source of many decades of sitting face to face with clients, as the cards use my frame of reference to speak combinations into existence on a wide array of topics and subjects. There is something for everyone pressed into these pages—an entirely new culture is born in this book; using my own vernacular phraseology completely shifts aged combinations, bringing modernization and clarity into this antiquated system.

The Lenormand keeps growing and evolving with the times; while holding on to the traditional framework of the cards' original meanings, you will come across some combinations with terminology you might not currently comprehend but will become very relevant in a not-too-distant future. It will offer you a peek into the modern world as we are ushered into a new age. I write things that are channeled, words that touch every aspect of the soul, things inspired by my muse, things that make me feel deeply, since writing is cathartic and affected by my macrocosms and microcosms perspective.

I welcome you to experience the lore seen though the kaleidoscope of life, as its energy vibrates out into the world of Lenormand through words, thoughts, and meanings, and as they materialize into being. A truly magickal experience that has the transformative powers with the ability to transmute pain into art, fears into strength, and passion into love; you will embark on this journey finding your way back to your soul's highest expression of itself.

So here we are, years later, still feeling the effects of the world's turmoil, since these are challenging times for most sentient beings on Earth, and yet, the most exciting times teach humanity a lot about themselves and others. May this book help you embark on a magickal journey of fulfillment by finding purpose and seeing the magick in everything. May your days be filled with freedom and unity as you carry love in your heart for yourself and others, remembering that sometimes things have to get worse before we herald in a new golden age. May your eyes be open, your words be powerful, and your hearts always full.

All my love,
Kalliope

It was the best of times, it was the worst of times, it was the age of wisdom, it was the age of foolishness, it was the epoch of belief, it was the epoch of incredulity, it was the season of light, it was the season of darkness, it was the spring of hope, it was the winter of despair.

—*Tale of Two Cities*, Charles Dickens

Introduction

The Purpose of the Magick of Lenormand Card Reading

Today, the Lenormand is slowly regaining momentum and seeing a resurgence in popularity, mostly due to artful decks being created after losing favor to other modernized and flexible systems of divination. This loss of favor is largely due to many of the Lenormand's outdated meanings and difficulty of use, whereas the reader tries to make sense of meanings created hundreds of years ago by trying to fit them into a modern world. So, here we have beautiful innovated decks being used with standardized meanings included in "the little white book." I have been successfully using the Lenormand, reading clients, and using my own personal style, showing me there was a need for modernization. Sharing this method of reading fills the gap and synchronizes relevant meanings to match the modern decks being produced; this is how the series of books came to be. The system outlined in this book is my personal tried-and-true method that works and can be easily applied to any life situation. This current volume is written with the professional reader in mind, with expanded meanings and new combinations, allowing you to foster an even-deeper, more magickal relationship with the cards. The Lenormand is a verbal system, using a play on linguistics, nuances, idioms, and syntax to find meaningful phrases sprinkled with intuition; when the cards are combined and kept within the context of the question is when the magick happens and the language of Lenormand is born. The mystery is the ability to hear what the cards secretly talk about when standing next to one another, making readings even more insightful—full of relevancy with the ability to specifically answer all kinds of questions. This is what I impart in this volume: changing the way you interpret the cards, thus enhancing accuracy when reading for clients or yourself, bringing the Lenormand into the forefront to rival any divination system out there, and to win the hearts of the masses. This is my gift to the world.

Creating this book has been a true labor of love; the time spent writing this book has allowed me to dive even deeper into the rabbit hole, and I am forever grateful for this experience.

Oh, since we are talking about bunnies, I have hidden multiple Easter eggs within this book that will take you to a whole new level of understanding the cards . . . happy hunting!

The best and most beautiful things in the world cannot be seen or even touched. They must be felt with the heart.

—Helen Keller

How to Use This Book

The Lenormand is a verbal system where cards are read in pairs to produce a combined meaning in relevance to the question asked. I provide many diverse combinations covering a multitude of topics; this lexicon, being extensive, is by no means complete but provides a generous jumping-off point limited only by your own command of language and wit. The most important part is understanding the cards' energy and applying the keywords to interpret what the cards are saying. By mastering this piece, you will never be at a loss for words, because the Lenormand always has plenty to say. The poem will give you a snapshot of the card; if you memorize these mnemonics, you will always have enough keywords to interpret the cards. The imagery used in this book is from the *Lenormand of Enchantment* deck; this is where artistry and writing blends, making the cards come alive with magick. Each card will tell a story, since the keywords are woven throughout the description. If inclined, you can highlight the keywords in the text for a great visual. Included under the cards are many subheadings to give you even more references, including timing, numerology, and various categories of life and modern-day meanings. Using the pips adds a layer of cartomancy, which sprinkles an extra bit of magick and enhances any reading. This book has a distinctive and purposeful touch of magick, providing an additional tier to complement your craft captured in magickal moments.

In its simplest form, this book can be used when a question is presented; throw two cards, turn to the relevant page, and read the subheading section for relevancy of timing, then choose an applicable meaning from the combinations listed.

Practice Makes Perfect

Journaling

Next, I would like to introduce you to journaling; this is an art form unto itself, an invaluable tool, and I cannot stress enough how it has changed my life over the years and honed my skills. I personally have many journals going at once with different themes, bringing incredible insight and clarity into my life. Here we will discuss how using a journal will help you become a better reader through personalization and personification of the cards. As you delve into a more symbiotic understanding of the Lenormand, you will in turn be lead into a deeper sense of self-discovery.

How to Begin?

1. Start with a notebook, something that inspires you; grab some of your favorite pens. I am a big fan of putting pen to paper versus typing, since I find that there is more of a connection from heart to hand this way. Although, ultimately, if you find it more comfortable to journal electronically, that is up to you—as long as you are journaling; that is what matters most.

2. Before reading the book's meanings, start with a card and just write; do not censor yourself. Record any impressions, thoughts, and intuitive flashes that you may receive. Ask yourself: How does this card feel energetically, and what is it saying? By listening closely, the cards will begin to "speak" to you; take your time and go through each and every card, trusting the process. You will actually be surprised at how much you can tell from a card by looking at the image and using your common sense.

3. Keep adding to your living record as you continue with your Lenormand journey; revisit your journal often, making adjustments or adding new insights as you go along.

4. On a final note, journaling is a tool that will help you get acquainted with the Lenormand system. Whether you are a novice or a seasoned expert, journaling will hone your skills and deepen your practice. Your accuracy in interpreting the cards will get better, and the flow of information will come easier as your understanding of the cards and how they relate to each other evolves.

Journaling Can Do the Following:

1. Create a deep bond between you and your cards, facilitating a sacred space where you can express yourself freely.

2. Certain cards carry similar connotations as another card, but the slight nuances are where the magick lies; this may cause confusion, making learning the

Lenormand a bit challenging. First let's look at the Snake and the Fox: the Snake represents lies, cheating, and betrayal, and the Fox deception, manipulation, fraud, scam, and trickery. Both meanings are *similar*, but when you look up the meaning in a dictionary, they differ.

There is also the point I want to make about certain cards being assigned different meanings. Let's take this one example of the theme of work/job/vocation. There are two different systems: the French traditional style and the German traditional style, which assign *different* cards to represent work. The French style assigns work to the Fox, and the German style assigns work to the Anchor; there is no right or wrong—this is where your journaling will help you deduce what feels right for you. Once you assign a meaning to a card that resonates with you, stick with it. In this book, I use the Fox as work/career; that is how I was taught, and it resonates with me in this way, since the Fox is diligent and purposeful but always practical and gets the job done.

3. Eventually, your journal will become your own custom guidebook that you can refer to and contribute to at any time—the key is to just keep writing!

4. Your journal will become a treasured record of growth, and as time goes by, your own personal style will develop and yet continually evolve. For we are all students of the universe as we progress toward enlightenment, and when you understand this, you will be rewarded with much insight and wisdom.

Practice Exercise

Context of the question is key to the Lenormand system, and practice makes you a more accurate reader. Now that you have gotten to know the cards better through journaling, you can move on to the next steps of developing your *Mental Lexicon* to increase your fluidity and flexibility when reading for yourself and clients.

Remember, when reading the cards, they must be interpreted while kept within the context of the question.

For example: A client asks, How is my relationship going? And you flip over the Fox + Mice.

Sure, this can definitely mean less work, pertaining to your job, but does that answer your client's question? So, when kept within the context of the question, the answer would be Fox + Mice = Destroyed by manipulation. The answer to your client would be that your relationship is being destroyed or eaten away by manipulation, so beware!

I teach this exercise to my students and call it the *Mental Lexicon*. It is the ability to construct sentences by using all your senses, including facets of syntax, nuances, play on words, literal meanings, idioms, and semantics.

The Mental Lexicon Example

Once you have gone through each individual card and recorded them in your journal, create a special section for combining each of the cards with another. Lay the two cards side by side and write down what you think they would be saying to each other in each of life's categories.

EXERCISE

1. Draw two random cards; write them down on the top on your page in your journal section.

2. Under the two cards, write down possible questions in all the areas in general categories that a Seeker might ask. (Look to the description of each card for what is meant by categories.)

3. Next, write down potential answers that would make sense, keeping within the context of the question.

4. Repeat the practice exercise often by choosing two cards at random, honing your skills, and building your *Mental Lexicon*; use this book for assistance for keywords to spark your imagination.

Example:

Let's continue looking at an example of the Fox + Mice combination:

Question: How will my relationship progress?

Answer: Eaten away by guilt, one of you is stressed by carrying around guilt—Guilty! Or gaslighting, wearing you down slowly with the intent to manipulate you.

Question: What do I currently need to pay attention to in my business?

Answer: Theft! These two are as "thick as thieves." Watch out for theft happening right under your nose, over time, little by little. Major fraud could be committed if not caught sooner rather than later.

Question: Is there anything I should be aware of on my upcoming vacation?

Answer: Pay close attention to being constantly whittled away at and tricked into a fraudulent timeshare opportunity; also pay attention to theft, scammers who will take your possessions or rob you.

Question: What do I need to do to take better care of myself?

Answer: You are feeling worn down by working too hard. Try to leave the stresses of work at work, and don't bring them home.

Question: What will my finances look like in the next month?

Answer: Your savings are depleting; review your accounts regularly and watch out for fraudulent transactions or little service charges.

Question: What can I add to my spiritual practice to take me to the next level?

Answer: Each day, be intentional and opportunistic to incorporate spiritual practices, such as shadow work, meditation, and journaling, to achieve your goals.

Question: How can I experience a better sense of well-being in my life?

Answer: Become aware of stress, and work on triggers that are causing you to feel this unwanted emotion, and try to facilitate more of a "work-life balance."

Question: What news will I hear?

Answer: You will hear that a coworker is losing their job, or your place of employment is reducing jobs.

These are just a few examples by using the same card combination of Fox + Mice and applying the meaning to a multitude of topics. Keep pulling two cards at random and keep practicing!

Tips and Tricks

* **Sometimes** one card can have two very different meanings or even be contradictory. For example, let's continue looking at the Fox, where it has both positive and negative qualities attached to it, such as work, employee, practical, and it also carries the meaning of scam, guilty, clever, instinct, and underhanded. Here again you have to remember to work within your context of the question to see where this is leading; looking at the surrounding cards will always point you in the right direction in applying the correct or relevant meaning.

* Most Lenormand cards have a timing attached to each card, some more poignant than others, by using the numerology or the generally accepted timing of that card. You can find reference of this under each card description. Example: the Stork. Generally accepted timing is using the card number of the card: 17th day, the 17th of the month, or 17 months, if the Mountain is near. I was taught to use the Stork card to indicate within nine months, due to the fact that the Stork is the baby card and gestation takes nine months. Also, many livestock birth babies in the spring. To substantiate this, the Stork card bears the pip of the Queen of Hearts; she denotes spring coinciding with the Stork and specifically the month of April; so as you can see, by using common sense and qualities of the card's pip, you can come up with a timing that works for you. Keep in mind that timing is always tricky with any system of divination, and some feel comfortable skipping it all together, which is perfectly acceptable.

* *The Red-String Method*
This method appears like a spiderweb when I visualize the interconnectedness of the cards and how they relate and speak to each other. This works well when you have a multitude of cards laid out, such as the Grand Tableau. Picture or actually put a red string on the focal card; now, keeping the string stationary with your finger on the main card, pivot the string around your spread, noting each card the red string crosses, since all these cards have an effect on your main card. The closer a card is to your main card, the stronger the influence; the farther away the card is to your main card, the more the influence diminishes. If the string does not touch a card, there is no influence and it should not be used in your interpretation, for it carries no weight.

* Cards are ***always*** read within the context of the question, and common sense is key when interpreting the Lenormand. At times, cards come up that just don't fit at all within the context of the question. Here you have two choices: pick a clarification card or utilize your intuition. With the Lenormand, clear and concise questions will result in clear and concise answers. If clarification is required, feel free to pull another card or two. Sometimes, when you find yourself pulling out multiple clarification cards and not getting a clear answer, the problem is with the wording of your question, so rephrase.

* The cards are metaphoric and to be read literally at times. Sometimes they present themselves as a humorous play on words and often speak bluntly with a kind of in-your-

face attitude. Example: Bear + Ship = Seafood; the Bear represents *food*. Then, look to the second card and ask, *What kind of food?* Ship means the *sea*; therefore, the combination would be read as *Seafood*. We can also look at Ship + Dog = Friendship. This is how specific you can get with the Lenormand. Let's look at another example: Letter + Cross = To-do list. The Letter means *list*, and the Cross means *obligation or duty*. When you write things down on your to-do list, they are things that are important and must get done; when done with an item, you *Cross* it off. All it takes is a good command of language, imagination, a dash of humor, with a sprinkle of common sense, and in no time the Lenormand card will be "speaking" to you.

* Order matters! What comes before and after? It is in this nuance that makes all the difference of the interpretation of the cards. Here, in this example, Ship + Tower = Restricted travel (with this combination you cannot travel). Now let's switch the order of the cards to Tower + Ship = Travel restrictions (in this combination you *can* travel, but with restrictions outlined by an authority). However slight this seems, the meaning is quite different. Here is another example: Birds + Clouds = Think before you speak (this person is careful before speaking).

Clouds + Birds = Speaking before you think (this person just blurts things out with--out thinking).

Mic drop . . .

* Categorical spreads are not common with the Lenormand system. The *House Method* used when reading the Grand Tableau would be the closest to using categories. This is where you lay the cards out in the Grand Tableau style and read each card by using the *natural house* as card 1 and the card that turns up in this spot as card 2. Then, combine both of them. Example: in position 1, the first house is where the Rider lives, and let's say the Coffin lands here, resulting in the interpretation as *Bad News*. This is my go-to method for an in-depth reading with clients who want a "general" type of reading, with no theme or question.

* The Key and Coffin Cards
Most people read the Key as open/closed. I read the Key *only* as open and the Coffin *only* as closed. This makes the Coffin and the Key opposite to each other when speaking of open and closed.

This way it avoids confusion: Is it an open/closed meaning? *A casket is always buried closed and a door is always meant to open . . . that is my logic behind it.

* Conversation = Birds (verbal) Communication = Letter (written). Slight difference, but a biggie.

* Understanding Loss/Losing/Lost
Coffin = Loss (gone, final; there is no coming back from this). This is usually permanent.
Cloud = Lost (could be temporary, could be found, not quite so final yet). This is usually referring to a mental state, because the Clouds symbolize the mind or thoughts, so feelings lost would apply here; or if inquiring about a physical item, what is lost could be gone for now and may be found later or permanently lost—really depends on the surrounding cards, especially if the Coffin is hanging around, or the Scythe.
Mice = Losing (it's happening gradually, slowly getting eaten away over time and usually undetected); the process of . . . making its way to loss (Coffin), which is permanent. The Mice

card gives you a chance to notice something happening and reverse it, like a warning, which if caught in time might be preventable.

* The Bear is actually a neutral card but strengthens the proceeding card, making it bigger or more. When you are at a loss with a combination and the Bear follows, you can always throw in the word *very* and then say the meaning of the first card. Works like a charm every single time. Example: Birds + Bear = Very talkative, Mice + Bear = Very stressed, Tower + Bear = Very tall.

* The Mice card eats away at the preceding card, making its effect weaker, or the opposite. If unsure of a combination where the Mice comes second, use the prefix *un* or put the word *less* in front. Example: Bouquet + Mice = Unattractive, Heart + Mice = Uncaring, Whip + Mice = Less sex, Letter + Mice= Fewer text messages.

* The prefix *mis* works really well with the Fox card when combined.
Example: Book = Information, and adding the Fox card becomes Book + Fox = Misinformation.
Stars + Fox = Misguided, Woman + Fox = Misogyny.

* The Tower represents ego. By looking at the tower's phallic shape, we understand it is single (alone) as opposed to the Garden, which refers to many people. In a romantic context, the Tower (single), Garden (available, playing the field), Ring (married or committed), Heart (dating/relationship).

* The Birds refers to a pair (couple) of something.

* The Snake: Just because it carries the keyword enticing/desire doesn't mean it's a good thing; it's looked upon negatively, because at the end of the day, a Snake is a Snake. Sure, you are enticed or feeling desire, but when the snake is slithering about, it might be best to just walk away!

* For the Paths I have assigned the keyword *between*, because it's neither here nor there . . . undecided, in between two paths. The term *between* can also show up as Tree + Paths = Between trees, literally, which is useful for finding missing items/people, or Fox + Paths = Between jobs, House + Paths = Between houses.

* Spirit uses your frame of reference. Here is a good example of how this happens: if I am not used to living in a place with droughts or tornadoes or earthquakes (which I am not), I wouldn't have these things in my frame of reference, so when combining cards for a client, which could be relevant to someone who resides in a different part of the world where these are genuine concerns of theirs, I would be missing key information—that the cards may be referring to as a warning. So the moral of the story is . . . the more worldly and wordy you are, the better and more accurate your readings will be.

* No stone left unturned. I have covered a multitude of categories and possible questions/ queries or concerns that one could possibly want to know: everything from job to health, relationship, death, mediumship, magick (occult and divination), science, sex, pop culture, politics, hot topics, current affairs, predictions, jumping-off points, and investigations, to

mention only a few. These versatile combinations can be applied to a wide range of topics affecting people's daily lives, and all things that the human spirit is so curious about. There is something for everyone here; regardless of experience level, you will never be at a loss for words or answers.

* How much thought went into creating these combinations? A whole lot. Let me show you an example: Garden + Tower = Background. Not only is this a perfect example of two cards, one word, but here is how I came up with this: The Tower refers to something in the past, but it also can indicate the *back* as a body part . . . so it's not only a play on words, but back and past make sense together. Your back is always behind you; so is the past. Now let's bring the word *ground* in as in reference to culture. A keyword of the Garden includes people and land and culture; thus the term *background* is not only fitting but actually makes a lot of sense. It can be used within the context of a question; for example: What do I need to know about this person? Answer: look into the person's *background*, and it will give you clues as to what their intentions are toward you. (If the Fox is hanging around, or the Snake, well, you have your answer on the person's background right there and then.)

* Intuition is most welcomed but not necessary; with the Lenormand system, the cards have a very straightforward approach, since the cards are read semantically. Intuition brings another layer where you can elaborate on the initial combination or specific question asked, offering more in-depth information, especially if you are like me, an intuitive reader.

* The Lenormand is a great system when you need straightforward answers to questions. When you are too close to the situation and invested in the outcome, the Lenormand gives you an objective view when reading the card as is, versus reading *into* the card's picture symbolically as with other styles of divination (such as the Tarot). With the Lenormand, "It is what it is!"

* The KISS method (Keep It Simple, Sweetheart/Stupid) really embodies the spirit of the Lenormand cards—less is more with the Lenormand.

* The Lenormand combinations are truly endless; all you need is a good command of language, a great frame of reference, and creativity.

* To dive even deeper, don't ignore the Pips (Hearts, Spades, Diamonds, and Clubs). Find ways to incorporate their meanings for an additional layer of detail. Since I was taught to read playing cards by my great-grandmother, I have incorporated the Pips' meanings to complement the Lenormand cards, for there was a reason that certain cards carried certain Pips.

* The Lenormand cards follow one another, so the second card will always influence the first card because that's what is coming up next in its path. The second card describes what is happening to the first card; always look to the second card and ask yourself the five Ws (and H): Who/whom, what, when, where, or why, and sometimes how. Example: Whom is it happening to? What is happening? When will it happen? Where will it happen? Why did it happen? How did it happen?

* Pay close attention to clusters and groups of cards; some of these characters are always hanging out together. Example: Heart, Ring, Star, and Moon. This grouping would suggest there are a lot of positive cards surrounding the Heart card (relationship), also noting that they are celestial bodies grouped together. Opposite to that, if the Scythe, Coffin, Whip, Mice, and Snake are grouped together, take note that these are a bunch of nasty cards in proximity. Let's look at the Sun, Star, Clover, and Bouquet combination. Here we have fun and a happy group all hanging out. When you pay attention to these clusters, you receive a general impression of the tone of the reading, or the answer or probable outcome to the question with just a glance.

* Mix and match methods and styles of reading the Lenormand. At the end of the day, if a system does not work for you, switch it up. If you constantly have to struggle to try to remember a meaning that just does not resonate with you, change it! Always go with what gives you a visceral response to the card and its meaning; just remember to stick with it to avoid confusion.

* Directional interpretations of the cards are very dependent on the imagery of the deck. Traditional decks make it very obvious when looking at the Rider, Scythe, Book, or Clouds that they are used to provide another layer to your interpretation. There are many wonderful modern decks that have not taken directional imagery into consideration while creating the artwork, and that is perfectly acceptable. As a reader, you should be flexible enough to just roll with it and not get hung up looking for a dark or light side of the Clouds. I personally do not look for directional meanings when I read, and I have not included that angle in this book, but if they are there and find me . . . I take notice.

* This expanded book with all new combinations will really challenge you to stretch your mind and vocabulary, giving you the opportunity to perfect your craft. Remember, it's always important to (Birds + Paths) that fit, and you will (Rider + Key).

Turn to page 279 to see the answer to the above riddle.

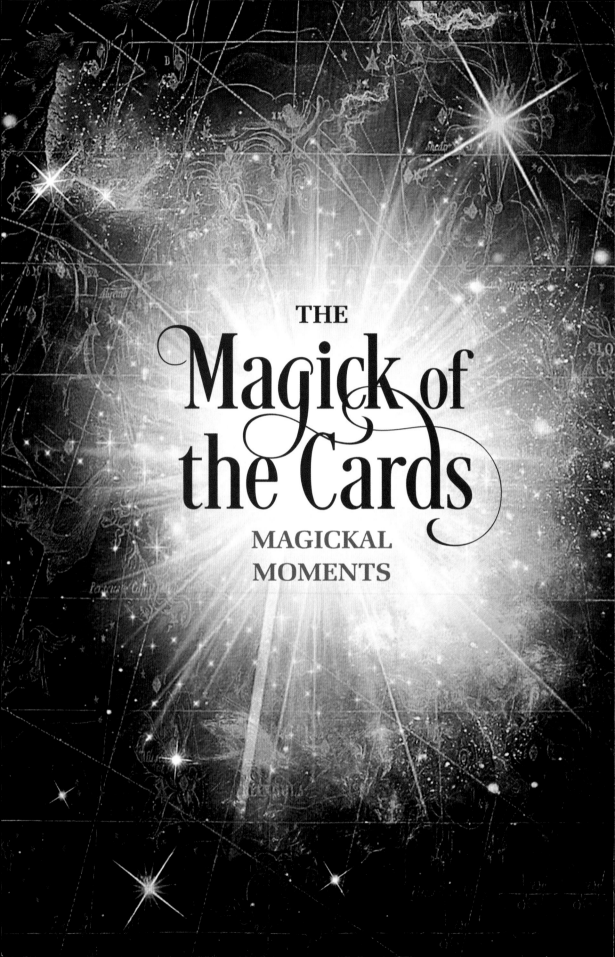

THE
Magick of
the Cards

MAGICKAL
MOMENTS

36 Magickal Moments

These spells and rituals will take you even further into *The Magick of Lenormand Card Reading*. When performing the intentions that follow, remove the corresponding card and have it near you while performing the spell. If you want to match the images, you can always use the cards that came with the first volume of *The Lenormand of Enchantment*, but any lenormand deck can be used. If possible, it is best to use a new lenormand deck and to keep the deck for this purpose only so that it is "magickally prepared." You can perform the spells as many times as you want, using the same card or any other spells keeping within the theme of the card.

RIDER

Summon Someone or Something
Write on a piece of paper something that you would like to *arrive* into your life, and then use Drawing Powder to facilitate that. If it's a specific person, sprinkle a bit of powder on a photo of the person.

Drawing Powder
Icing Sugar / Confectioners' Sugar / Powdered Sugar

During a new moon, write the name or thing of your desire with a red pen on a piece of parchment, making sure to state that it will come to be only if it is for your highest good. Whisper your intention onto the paper, put it in an envelope, and seal it with a kiss. Slip the envelope into your pillowcase and release it by burning it on the next full moon.

CLOVER

Lucky Charm Oil
In a 5 ml glass vile, add:
1 drop of basil
3 drops of bergamot
2 drops of vanilla
1 drop of cinnamon

Add enough jojoba oil to fill to the shoulders of the vile.
    For an extra pinch of magick, drop in a citrine chip to keep the mixture fresh, and make the potion on a waxing moon.

To Use:
Rub a drop of the prepared potion between your hands while focusing on luck; fortune will transfer onto any object, such as chips, clothing, lotto tickets, cards, slot machines, dice, or talismans and amulets, or anything else you want to magickally enchant.

    When you need to change your luck, chant the following three times:
    "Bad luck turn away, time to flee. Good luck is welcome come onto me."

Travelers Charm

Put a piece of malachite or a holed stone on the Ship card and set your intention; leave the stone on the card for three days.

Malachite

Tuck a piece of malachite in your pocket or wear it on your person. It is renowned for being a guardian stone of travelers. Its mesmerizing, swirling pattern will trap any negativity within and shatter when extreme peril is imminent. Malachite also helps soothe jet lag. Remember to cleanse malachite often, since it is a great absorber of all energies.

Holed Stone

If you are really lucky to find a holed stone or hag/witch stone, these naturally occurring holed rocks are the most precious and rare treasures you can find in nature. They are protective stones safeguarding you against negative energy and malevolent spirits. Great protection for travelers or carried when traveling on the road, by air, or by sea; carry one of these stones on your person in a pocket, put it on a chain, using the natural hole, or keep one in the car.

Household Houseplant Magick

1. Purchase a new houseplant.
2. Gather one of each of these crystals:

Citrine: prosperity and abundance
Rose quartz: love and affection
Smoky quartz: protection
Amethyst: health and well-being
Clear quartz: happiness and Joy

3. Charge the crystals in the light of the full moon for three days (one day before, during, and after the full moon).

4. Take each crystal individually, blow three times with the corresponding intention, and press each one into the dirt in the shape of a five-pointed star, starting with the clear quartz at the top.

5. Repeat the process for the remaining crystals in a clockwise manner, letting your intuition guide you on which crystal should be next.

6. Place this potted plant at the entrance of your home so all who enter will see it. This magickal plant will cover all the areas of life, enabling everyone who resides within the home to thrive. A snake plant, commonly referred to as mother-in-law's tongue, is the perfect choice.

Not only is it a stunning specimen, but it's easy to care for while improving the air quality in the house.

Tree of Life-Chakra Healing Meditation

1. Lie in a comfortable position and begin by taking deep centering breaths while focusing on your body. You can put on some soft music in the background if you choose.

2. Imagine a prism of light shaped as a sphere, sparkling and alive with healing energy. Slowly take this sphere up through the bottom of the soles of your feet, gently moving it up your legs until you reach the first chakra.

3. As the sphere reaches the *Root Chakra*, see this area being flooded with various shades of reds, healing and relaxing every cell, tissue, muscle, bone, and organ.

4. The sphere returns back to the iridescent ball as it moves up to the second position of the *Sacral Chakra*, flooding the area with shades of orange, healing and relaxing healing energy, protecting and calming every cell, tissue muscle, bones, and organs.

5. The sphere returns to its iridescent shape as it moves into the third position of the *Solar Plexus*. You see that area being encompassed by various hues of yellows, healing, protecting, and relaxing every cell, tissue, muscle, bone, and organ.

6. The sphere returns to the iridescent ball as it moves into the fourth position of the *Heart Chakra*, as you see that area being filled by vivid hues of greens, healing, protecting, and relaxing every cell, tissue, muscle, bone, and organ.

7. The sphere returns to its iridescent spherical shape as it moves into the fifth position of the *Throat Chakra*, and you see that area being filled by cool hues of blues, healing, protecting, and relaxing every cell, tissue, muscle, bone, and organ.

8. The sphere returns to its iridescent spherical shape as it moves into the sixth position of the *Third Eye Chakra*, as you see that area being filled by majestic hues of purples, healing, protecting, and relaxing every cell, tissue, muscle, bone, and organ.

9. The sphere returns to its iridescent spherical shape as it moves into the *Crown Chakra*, the seventh and final position, as you see that area being filled by spiritual hues of indigo, healing, protecting, and relaxing every cell, tissue, muscle, bone, and organ.

10. The iridescent sphere now keeps moving upward until it comes out from the top of your head, as it is cascading multiple colors around your body, shimmering and healing and relaxing every part of your body. Sit in this energy for a while and continue accepting the regenerative properties of the light. Express your gratitude for the healing you are receiving, and trust that all is as it should be. Sit in this state as long as you feel necessary, letting this light work its magick as it radiates all around you, filling your body and aura. Repeat as necessary.

CLOUDS

Releasing Depression

1. Do this on a gray, cloudy day.

2. Write on a piece of paper what you need to release, using black ink.

3. Roll up this piece of paper.

4. Insert the rolled-up paper into a gray or blue balloon.

5. With every breath you use to blow up the balloon, blow your depression into that balloon.

6. Once done, tie a knot with the intention, trapping what you are releasing within.

7. Go outdoors with your balloon.

8. Take three deep grounding breaths.

9. Pop the balloon, releasing all the energy within, allowing the universe/spirit to dissipate it.

10. Discard the balloon and note in whichever way you desire, for the energy has been neutralized when the balloon was popped.

SNAKE

Perform this spell when feeling betrayed in all its forms; it removes feelings of humiliation or treachery and eliminates any attachments from you and the one who betrayed you.

Cleansing after Betrayal

1. Get a photograph of the person who betrayed you.

2. Soak the photograph in a bowl filled with salted water.

3. Remove the photograph when it's thoroughly soaked.

4. Let air-dry.

5. Safely light a censer with white sage and lay the photo on top, letting the embers either smoke or ignite the photograph (the amount of smoke or fire you use will tell how much of an energetic effect they have over you).

6. Use the smoke to smudge yourself to remove any energetic attachment from the betrayal and the one who betrayed you.

COFFIN

* Best done on or between October 31 to November 1; this can be made in large quantities and kept indefinitely.

Black Salt

Repels any negativity—very protective or used to cast away any enchantment or spirit and works great for magickal barriers as well. Black salt is so versatile: it can be spread on thresholds, sprinkled in shoes, or put in a vessel by an entrance or in any room you wish to protect. Black salt is easy to make and is a cornerstone of many spells.

1. Choose a container to store your black salt.
2. Pour in some kosher/rock salt.
3. Take the ashes or charcoal from the remnants of a fire or use the scrapings of a cast-iron vessel; break into tiny pieces if necessary.
4. Mix well and use or store for future use.

BOUQUET

White sage is one of the most powerful and effective magickal cleansers. Burn white sage and smudge the area or item to banish stagnant, unwanted, or negative energy of spirits.

House

Using proper burning techniques, light the sage stick or loose sage in a censer and waft the smoke around, using the stick, hand, or a feather, paying special attention to thresholds, windows, mirrors, and corners when doing a house starting in the north, east, or south and ending in the west.

Person

Have the person standing in a star shape symbolize the five-pointed star. Sage all the limbs, with the head last.

Object

Waft the smoke around the object.

SCYTHE

Use when you feel that you have been targeted by a spell, have immense negativity in your life, or are having a really negative string of bad luck.

Breaking a Spell / Removing Negativity

1. Purchase a small glass beverage bottle; dump out the contents at a crossroads. The bottle can now be brought into the home, rinsed out, and dried.

2. On the waning moon, fill the bottle with 80% water and 20% vinegar.

3. Use a piece of toilet paper to write what you wish to be rid of from your life, being very specific.

4. Roll up the piece of toilet paper and place it into the bottle, then put the bottle outside your home, checking daily and giving it a good shake.

5. When the paper within is dissolved into a pulp and you can no longer make out what was written, the negativity or spell will have been dissolved.

6. On the next full moon, go to a crossroads and break the bottle, taking care not to injure yourself, by using protective gear.

7. Collect all the pieces possible and discard the bottle away from your home in a safe manner.

WHIP

Breaking a Bad Habit/Pattern
With this spell you will need a double-terminated crystal (two pointy ends). Try to use a crystal in correspondence to what you wish to break.

Carry this crystal on your person, and every time you are tempted or get consumed with this thought, hold the crystal in your right hand between your thumb and pointer finger and press on the points as hard as you can stand.

Keep repeating this as often as needed.

If the crystal gets lost or breaks, know that the job is done.

BIRDS

Words carry the power of intent and can be used to create profound manifestations. This spell is very useful to stop or prevent gossip, rumors, or any problems or situations you want to stop.

Chill Out
1. On a piece of toilet paper, write in black ink either the person's name or the specific situation that is causing the problem.

2. Place this paper in a freezer-safe vessel or in an ice cube tray. Then and water and freeze it either in the freezer or outside in the winter; by doing this, you are putting this person or situation on ice.

3. When the gossip or situation ceases, remove the vessel from the cold and allow it to naturally thaw out.

4. Dump the water with the paper into the toilet and flush as you say, *"Good riddance."*

CHILD

Poppet Magick
This can be used to manifest healing, love, or fertility. There is a darker side to using poppets; it is to inflict the opposite.

1. Using a muslin or white material, cut out two equal shapes, like a gingerbread man.

2. Use white thread; sew around the poppet, leaving an opening at the top of the head.

3. Fill the poppet with cotton balls and corresponding crystals, herbs, coins, hair, or a secret note. Infuse the poppet with your intention and sew the top of the head shut.

4. On the front of the poppet, using various colored markers, write empowering words, statements, or a quote. Decorate it in a way that inspires you, keeping within the theme of your intention.

5. Keep the poppet as a reminder, so when you look at it, you remember.

6. When you feel what you intended has come to pass, dispose of the poppet by burying it into the earth, away from your home, or by burning it.

FOX

This versatile oil can be used in many ways: retain employment or find a job, promotions, personal achievements, and career success. Use this potion by wearing it on your person when having an interview, or anoint a job posting or résumé.

Career Oil
1 drop of frankincense
3 drops of sandalwood
2 drops of vetiver
1 drop of patchouli

Add all drops into the 5 ml glass vial and fill to the shoulders with sunflower oil.

BEAR

Use these waist beads to bring beauty and awareness to your body; by making them yourself, you will be putting your energy and intent to every bead you string. When the beads sit higher or become tighter, it allows you to become aware that you are gaining weight—this allows you to take quick action. If the beads become loose and sit lower, you are achieving your weight loss goals. Every time you feel these beads against your body, you will feel a sense of empowerment, beauty, and body-positive vibes.

Belly Beads for Weight Loss
1. Purchase glass beads of your color of choice from a craft store or online.

2. Using a strong string or heavy-duty fishing line, measure your waist.

3. Thread your line on a needle.

4. One by one, thread your beads onto the line, focusing on your goal with intention.

5. When done, fasten these beads to your waist while tying a secure knot. For extra protection against it loosening, you can add a dab of strong glue.

6. Wear these beads at all times—no need to take them off; you can perform any activity while wearing them.

STARS

Using the power of the Stars card for manifestation by performing the Wishcraft spell; remember to be careful what you wish for!

Wishcraft Spell
Write your wish, goal, dream, or message clearly onto a bay leaf and light it; using the same flame of the bay leaf, light a birthday candle (you can use a color corresponding to your wish) and make the same wish as you light it. Allow both to burn down in a fire-safe vessel. The smoke is carried out to the universe; all you have to do now is let it go and forget about it.

STORK

Fertility Spell
Brew yourself a cup of basil tea; it encourages fertility both physically and symbolically. While brewing the tea, you are incorporating all the elements. Earth is the basil, Fire is the flame used to boil the water, Water is the actual water, and Air is the steam when the kettle brews.

  While sipping your tea, envision that you are with child. Repeat this once per month, after your menstrual cycle ends, on every full moon until you achieve your heart's desire. Surround yourself with potted basil plants within your home or grow basil in the garden; remember to incorporate fresh basil whenever you can in your food to reinforce your intention.

Alternatively, or accompanying the above spell, once a month when the moon is full, take a bath (even better in moonlight) filled with rose petals, basil, rose quartz, moonstone, and clear quartz—put all the items in a drawstring sachet for easy cleanup. Repeat every month on the full moon until you achieve your heart's desire, using fresh rose petals and basil.

DOG

Sometimes the best therapy is writing out your feelings. There is something to be said about the connection among your hand, heart, and head—it is very cathartic. Purchase a beautiful journal, buy some pretty pens, and begin your journey one word at a time. Remember that this is just for you, a way to sort things out in your life. Journaling can become an invaluable magickal practice, helping you through tough moments and sticky situations.

Magick Court Case Crystal
Hematite crystal protects and aids in all types of legal cases.

1. Charge the hematite either in the moonlight for litigation involving a female or in the sunlight if involving a male.

2. Take the crystal into your palms and put your intentions into it, blowing three times.

3. Wear or carry it on you person during court proceedings.

4. Cleanse and recharge as necessary.

Justice Is Served
1. Hold a purple taper or chime candle in your hand and infuse it with your intention.

2. With a sharp pin, etch out the words "Justice is served." Do not envision how or when; just trust that it will be so.

3. Light the candle and let go of any outcome, knowing that the universe will find a fair and just way for all involved; let the candle burn all the way down in a fire-safe vessel.

4. Keep the remnants of the candle until "justice is served," then dispose of it by burying it in the ground.

GARDEN

When in a public place or crowded venue, or when feeling overwhelmed, use this visualization exercise to bring about peace and protection.

Magick Diamond Mirror
1. Imagine a sparkling white light surrounding you.

2. Then visualize many small diamond-shaped mirrors stuck on the outside of this sphere, reflecting outward, that will move with you.

3. Anything directed at you energetically will be reflected back to the person(s), whether positive or negative.

4. This will become second nature to you, and once you have established this and do it often, it can be activated at any time by saying, "Shields up."

MOUNTAIN

To Charge (Program) a Crystal

1. Choose a crystal to correspond to your intention.

2. Cleanse your crystal.

3. Hold the crystal in the palm of your hands.

4. Take three deep, cleansing, centering breaths.

5. When you feel your energy is in tune with the crystal's energy, clearly state your intention, repeating it three times.

6. When the charging is complete, blow three times into the crystal.

7. Place the crystal in the desired location and detach your attention from it, letting it work its magick.

PATHS

The crossroads is a very magickal place; here you can leave behind anything you want to be rid of—a place where the energy gets transmuted, rendering it neutral. Therefore, the crossroads is a very powerful and neutral place. Remember: you can leave anything at the crossroads, but never take anything into your home—not dirt, item, or stone. If you are leaving an item behind, bury it at the crossroads and don't look back.

MICE

Antitheft Protection

Wear an amethyst on your person or leave a crystal in your car, home, or anyplace of value that you wish to protect. Amethyst is a strong and natural theft deterrent.

HEART

Use this spicy intoxicating oil to enhance or draw love into your life. You can anoint your body or items or put a few drops into your bath water. Remember, as with all essential oils, to be aware of sensitivity when placing undiluted oils near or directly on the skin.

Love Potion of the Nine Muses
1 drop of bergamot
1 drop of cedarwood
2 drops of nutmeg
2 drops of cardamon
3 drops of patchouli

Add all drops into a 5 ml glass vile and fill to the shoulders with almond oil.

Get-Engaged Spell

1. Do this spell on the first day of June.

2. Buy a new pack of playing cards and remove the Ace of Diamonds; discard the rest of the pack.

3. Make a circle out of red thread and tie the knot with the intention.

4. Write your name and your intended's name on the card in red ink.

5. Hold the red circle that symbolizes the ring in the center of the card. Get a sprig of rosemary and poke it through the center of the card and the circle while reciting your intention three times.

6. Leave the card on your bedroom's windowsill where it sees the sun and the moon for the full month.

7. On the last day of June (June 30), take the card and go outside at midnight; safely light the card on fire, letting the ashes either fly away or discarding them at a crossroads.

8. This can be repeated once per year until you achieve your heart's desire.

BOOK

The BOS (*Book of Shadows*) is a very important tool of any magickal journey. This book is for you to fill with potions, spells, journals, incantations, quotes, herbal remedies, ideas, poetry, deck catalog, beliefs, rituals, family traditions and celebrations, dreams, teachings, recipes, and much, much more. Anything can be written in your *Book of Shadows*; there are no rules except that it is a personal account of your magickal journey. This book grows with you as you walk the magickal path.

Book of Shadows (BOS)
A blank, black book, or a black binder with sections.

LETTER

Return to Sender
A form of magickal writing is ink on paper. If a situation or someone is weighing heavy on your heart, write it all out with black ink on paper. Take your time and be as specific with as many details as possible, making sure to write it in first person. Get an envelope and address it to the person or spell out the situation. On the back of the envelope, write RETURN TO SENDER. Seal the envelope with the intention of returning whatever it is back to the sender, then safely burn the envelope in a fire-safe vessel. The ashes can either fly away in the wind or you can discard the ashes at a crossroads or in a body of water. In a pinch you can always flush the ashes down the toilet.

MAN

Empowerment Spell

The divine masculine thrives in the presence of a living basil plant. This can be grown in containers around your home or in the garden. Whenever you have need of empowerment, bruise a leaf between your fingers and inhale three deep breaths of the aroma.

WOMAN

Empowerment Spell

The divine feminine thrives in the presence of a living rosemary bush. Grow it in containers around your home or in the garden. Whenever you have need of empowerment, rub a sprig of rosemary and inhale three deep breaths of the aroma.

LILY

This has all the proprieties you need to alleviate all the age-related ailments. For extra power, tie the sachet to the spout or tap under running water.

Magickal Bath Sachet

In a muslin sachet, put a handful of natural, freshly picked pine needles; to this, add a tumbled amethyst stone and a few drops of lavender essential oil and enjoy.

After your bath, remove and discard the pine needles, keep the amethyst crystal, and let it recharge on a windowsill for future use. Dry out the muslin sachet well to reuse. Repeat once per month; this is best done when the moon is full.

SUN

Choose any intention or something you would like to manifest into your life; with this very versatile spell, working with the sun is especially potent when performing a truth spell.

Candle Magick

1. Choose the appropriate corresponding color of candle for your intention.

2. Charge the candle by holding it in your hands and, using three breaths, blow your intent into it.

3. Using a sharp pin, carve out sigils or power words, names, or symbols onto the candle.

4. Dress the candle, using moon water or corresponding oil to anoint it, which then can be rolled into herbs or sparkles or decorated with objects for more of a magickal punch.

5. Safely burn the candle all the way down and dispose any remnants at a crossroads.

MOON

Moon Water
During a full moon, fill a vessel with clean water, place the vessel outside in the view of the moon, and let it sit there for three days: one day before the full moon, on the full moon, and one day after the full moon for maximum power. This moon water is now charged with the properties of that particular moon and can be used to cleanse, charge, or protect, for any type of spell or anointing items. Don't forget to label your vessel with the date for future reference. To keep the water fresh and cleansed, put a citrine crystal into the water.

KEY

This spell is done to protect your home from anything seen or unseen, not allowing anything negative to cross the thresholds of your home.

Keys of the Kingdom
1. Count the number of doors or entrances that lead into your home.

2. Find or purchase the same number of keys; random keys or antique keys from old doors are great for this.

3. Touch each designated key to each designated door in your home while reciting the following:

> Key of protection, key on guard
> Protect my home, including my yard
> Stand sentinel and watch over where I reside
> And protect my family and everything inside

4. When finished, use a beautiful red ribbon to string all the keys together; tie a knot on top to create a circle. Hang this above your front door or near the front door of your home.

FISH

Prosperity Oil
1 drop of lavender
3 drops of bergamot
2 drops of patchouli
1 drop of peppermint

In a 5 ml glass vile, add the drops and fill with almond oil to the shoulders.
    Make this potion on a full or new moon.
    Use to anoint money, wallet, business documents, home or business doors, mirrors, and candles.

Knot Spell

This is one of the most ancient forms of magick. Intentions put into a knot can be used to bind anything. Focus your intention as you tie each knot; in good magickal practice, use only an odd number of tied knots. Materials that are commonly used include ropes, strings, threads, ribbons, or hair. This type of spell can be used both for benevolent or malevolent magick, so choose wisely.

1. Choose a material in the corresponding color of choice.

2. Center and focus your intention by blowing three times into the material.

3. Incant (speak) your intention each time a knot is tied.

4. When done, wrap your cord in a fabric and put it away, out of sight, for safe keeping.

5. When what you have intended has manifested, get rid of the spell by burning or burying the spell; there is no more power left in the object, so you can release/discard it any way you choose. Note: If hair is used, it must be buried.

CROSS

If you feel that you or someone else, a place, or object has a spiritual attachment, this method can be used to rid of the attachment. This spell is to be done on a sunny day.

Removing an Attachment

1. Purchase a small mirror.

2. Peer into the mirror, looking at the reflection over your shoulder, capturing an image of the entity, place, or thing with the attachment.

3. Once the image is captured, cover the mirror immediately with a black cloth; do not look into the mirror again.

4. Take the mirror outside and expose it directly to sunlight, capturing the sun's image within the mirror for no more than nine seconds.

5. Cover the mirror back with the cloth; using a hammer, safely smash the mirror.

6. Take the remnants with the cloth and bury it off your property; dig a deep enough hole so it cannot be easily unearthed.

NOTE:
Once this spell is performed, the shards are rendered safe, for there is no more attachment left.

How to Read the Cards

The difference between the almost right word and the right word is really a large matter. 'Tis the difference between the lightning bug and the lightning.

—Mark Twain

* This quote perfectly sums up the Lenormand. It's all in the applied linguistics of semantics, nuances, idioms, and syntaxes—coupled with your vernacular native tongue used to interpret the card combinations, while using your frame of reference, dotted with a dab of intuition that takes your skills to the next level, and *that's* how to read the Lenormand.

A Few Pointers to Remember First

* Positional spreads are not common with the Lenormand as they are in Tarot, due to the fact that Lenormand cards are always read in pairs. If using the Lenormand cards in the same way that you would lay out Tarot cards in a spread, it would leave you with very little relevant information, rendering the spread useless; however, there are structured ways to lay out cards in the Lenormand, as I will outline below.

* There are many ways to combine and interpret the cards. When first starting out, choose one method and stick to it until you can explore other ways to combine cards. You will eventually settle on one method that works for you as you gain experience. You can string together as many or as few cards as you feel necessary or comfortable reading.

* At the end of the day, just get in there and start reading. There is no method that is written in stone, and no one person's method is the "authority" on reading the cards; with practice you will develop your own style and rhythm when reading the Lenormand.

How to Cast the Cards

Begin in the way you are accustomed to: by setting the mood, shuffling the cards, and laying out the cards framed in the methods below.

THE YES OR NO METHOD

Shuffle the cards while thinking about your yes/no question. Draw five cards and lay them out. Look how many positive vs. negative cards come out, and take note of any neutral cards. If there are more *positive* cards, the answer is *yes*; if there are more *negative* cards, your answer is *no*. The neutral cards are just that, *neutral*. If you receive all neutral cards, it means you will not receive an answer at this time and should not be privy to this information. Then go ahead and read the five-card string to acquire additional details and insight to your query. If the Key comes up, it's an automatic *yes*; if the Coffin comes up, it's an automatic *no*. If both the Key and Coffin show, they cancel each other out, or you get a strong *maybe*. You can do the Yes/No Method with three cards as well.

Key + Coffin = Maybe. * Why is this? Even though the Coffin follows the Key (which is a very positive card), you cannot treat the card as a stand-alone . . . you must combine the Key card, which falls in the first position with the Coffin that comes next, so when you blend the Key = Yes and the Coffin = No, you get a maybe (leaning on the no, because that is next in its path). Now let's reverse it . . . Coffin + Key = Maybe, still a maybe . . . but leaning more toward a yes.

If the Book comes up in the five cards, there is an element that is unknown or secretive in nature at play.

TWO CARDS

All the combinations are derived from reading the card from right to left, so the first word will be card number 2, then combined with card 1. I find that using this deconstructed method makes the most sense, since the first card is always being influenced by the second card's energy, demonstrating what is coming up next in its path, essentially reading the pairs "backward," opposite to how we read English from left to right. I find that two cards are usually enough to answer a question; if needing more clarification, you can pull another card or ask a supporting question and throw an additional two cards.

THREE CARDS

When reading three cards, read the pair as usual and use the third card as the outcome or further clarification.

FIVE CARDS

When reading five cards, you have two options: The first option is to read both cards 1 and 2 as a pair, and cards 3 and 4 as a pair; then use card 5 (the last card) as the outcome or theme. The second variation in reading five cards is to read cards 1 and 2 as a pair and cards 4 and 5 as a pair, leaving the center card number 3 as the outcome or theme. Use whichever method works best for you, but a word of caution here: pick one method and stick to it to avoid confusion or second-guessing yourself when reading, and a different structure looks more favorable.

THE NINE-CARD BOX

Cards 1 + 2 + 3 on top (future)
Cards 4 + 5 + 6 in the middle (present)
Cards 7 + 8 + 9 on the bottom (past)

Card 5, in the center, will be the outcome, subject, or central theme; some like to choose the center card as the theme or use the man or woman card as the significator.

With this Box method, you can read the cards up and down, from left to right and diagonally, or combine the corners together. When you understand this nine-card box, the Grand Tableau will be easier to grasp because you can find many boxes of nine cards in the Grand Tableau.

THE GRAND TABLEAU
(My Method)

So, do you have all day to play?
Pull out your journal, take a picture, and let's go!

Let's tackle the Grand Tableau. Lay out all 36 cards in four rows of eight cards in each row, lining up each card underneath each other. The last four cards should center in the middle under the last line (under numbers 27, 28, 29, and 30).

Here are some tips on my method of reading the Grand Tableau. Listed below I have included some great pointers to help get you get started, but with practice you will soon add many more of your own. The Grand Tableau is made up of many nine-card boxes within the grand spread; when all connected, it forms a bigger picture.

Here are some pointers on how to read the Grand Tableau:

  * Carefully lay out the cards in the Grand Tableau style as shown above.

  * Take a moment and look at all the cards, as one would when looking at a painting. This is the "big picture." Just take in the impression of all the cards and pay attention to any groupings.

  * Take a peek at the first card, number 1, since this sets the tone. Then look to the last card, number 36, since this is how it ends: Does it end on a high or low note?

  * Look at the cards right in the center, cards 20 and 21; this is "the Heart"; combine those two cards and see what is in the seeker's heart.

  * Next, find the Key card; this card will provide more insight. Take a good look around the Key and feel out all the cards in proximity, like a mini nine-card box spread, if possible. This is what's going on in their life, the key issue.
  Find what *natural house* the Key is sitting in, and combine (Key being card 2). This will identify how open the seeker is to receiving the information—come up with a word or sentence; this is Key. Example: if the Key card is sitting in position 18, the house of the Dog, it would be read something like as follows. Dog + Key indicates that the Seeker is open and trusting, ready to receive help and support. Using the same example, but moving the Key card over just one position to position 19, the Tower + Key would indicate that the Seeker is open and wanting to hear what you will say, but will have a rigid attitude and probably think they know best, especially if it's not what they *want* or *expect* to hear. This is information just for your own insight and points to how best to navigate the reading. The Key Card is very important; it will often indicate a theme, since it is a card of karma.

  * Now find the Clouds card; this is what the Seeker's mind is on; look at the nine-card box around the Clouds. Next, take note as to what *natural house* the Clouds are sitting in, to see specifically what's on their mind. Example: Let's say that the Clouds are sitting in house of the Fish. With Fish + Clouds, you automatically know that the Seeker's mind is on their finances. This is a good jumping-off point to begin any reading.

  * Next, take a closer look at groupings/clusters of cards that are gathering: who are all the characters hanging out with and why?

  * Find the significator (Man or Woman card) and look at the surrounding cards.

Start combining the cards near the significator on the same line. Use the *Red-String Method*; start combining the three cards and then move to the nine-card box spread, with the significator in the middle. This is a wonderful snapshot of what's happening around the Seeker. (If there are no cards above or below the Significator, take a note of that.)

* Then look back to the Significator and draw an imaginary X (or use the red string) through the Significator and note what cards are in the upper arms of the X above the Significator. The left arm of the X represents the past that they are aware of and what still affects them today, and the right arm of the X is the probable future, where they are heading, as they carry themes of the past. (Sometimes there are no cards above the significator, and that is okay; it shows that they are really not putting too much thought into anything from the past nor are too concerned about the future at the moment.) Now look at the bottom arms of the X; first, the left arm below the Significator represents the past and the effects that they are not aware of, and the right bottom arm of the X shows where they are heading and forces they are not aware of yet but are in the process of becoming. (These forces can be negative, positive, or neutral—just take a note of this.)

* Next, look to the card of the opposite sex of the significator (if the Seeker is a Woman, we are looking at the Man, and vice versa). This is an important step; when looking at the opposite card, it represents the most significant person of the opposite sex in their life. The opposite card is always someone important in the Seeker's life, such as a significant other, boss, boyfriend, husband, brother, father, and so on . . . it will always be someone the Seeker "knows." Example: Let's say the Seeker is inquiring about her husband, and the Man card is clear on the other side of the Grand Tableau. That in itself speaks volumes that they are definitely not on the same page, and their communication could be better.

* Next, look at the four corners of the square (exclude the four cards on the bottom). This gives you a frame, like a picture of what's going on inside the Grand Tableau as it sets the overall tone of the reading. Combine card 1 with 8 and card 25 with 32 and read them accordingly.

* Starting at the beginning and combining the first two cards, continue right through 1 to 36 as if telling a story and letting it flow. If there is a focus to the Grand Tableau, such as relationship, keep this theme in mind as the story unfolds.

* Next, look to see what interesting strings of three or five cards are hanging out together, and read them, adding more depth to your reading.

* Next, focus on themes in the Seeker's life: finances, relationships, career, spirituality, home, friends, wellness; find the coinciding card in the spread, regardless of where it landed, and read it like a nine-card box around that topic.

* Another way to dig a bit deeper is to locate the *natural house* for the themes the Seeker is asking about. Example: For finances, look to position 34 and combine it with the card that showed up in that house, to see what the underlying energy is on this topic. Let's say the Bouquet is in position 34. This would indicate that money is used for enjoyment and a bit of a showing off, depending on the cards next to it, which will indicate the effects of the spending. This is great for a *general* type of reading and adding details.

* Last, look to the last four cards (33, 34, 35, 36). These four positions represent the cards of karma / fate / destiny / final outcome. This string is out of the Seeker's control and left in the hands of Fate. Pay particular attention if the Key card falls in any one of those positions, because the Key is the card of karma; Fate and Destiny definitely denote that karma is at play. You can additionally read the last four cards as the probable outcome by combining 33 + 34 and 35 + 36, especially if a specific question was asked at the beginning.

* Observation is key in the Grand Tableau. Look, listen, and relay what the cards are saying. The possibilities and combinations are endless.

On your journey through the 36 cards, I wish you blessings bright.
Take my hand as your earthly guide; we claim this sacred rite.
We'll start at the very beginning, where the Rider takes the lead.
Together traversing life's tapestry, with magick threads we weave.

THE
Magickal
Combinations
of the Cards

1. Rider

As a young Suitor I arrive, atop Jack my nimble steed.
Everything I bring comes fast, going at a racing speed.
Coming in quick as I ride, just on the horizon I loom.
News and announcements move fast; I'll be visiting soon.

DESCRIPTION

Upon a majestic, gray elephant, a stunning silver-haired woman in her crone years rides in on the ebb and flow of life-heralding announcements. As the embodiment of the Moon, the Rider delivers news with expertise and wisdom garnered throughout her years—traveling swiftly among the immortal thickets, a place of serenity where the balanced forces of the divine feminine and the divine masculine combine in between realms. This magickal place is where the unknown resides while everything hangs within the first breath of creation, and bewitching, sparking, golden orbs come and go, filled with tidings from afar.

Befitting her station as the messenger, she wears a crown adorned with pheasant feathers symbolizing speed; it is in this way the Rider makes her deliveries fast and quick. When delivering difficult news, she exudes discernment and compassion, demonstrated by the red roses growing profusely on the forest floor beneath her feet.

Under the mantle of the great cosmos, the Rider sits dignified upon her steed, sheltered and protected under the shade of her red umbrella, making her stand out so everyone sees her coming and going. Potential suitors looming in the horizon see this passionate color from afar, and it attracts them and draws them in for a closer look.

When the Rider comes a-calling, she brings the possibility of a special someone waiting for just the right divine timing to enter your life. The Rider has chosen the elephant as her trusty steed; these gentle giants are kind, earning them the title of the Rulers of the Forest, being special messengers to the gods. These beloved animals will quickly move through anything blocking their path in order to reach their destination and complete their task. Revered as the bringers of news and announcers of visitors makes them very sympathetic to the Rider's mission. Embellishing the elephant's third eye is a beautiful piece of cinnabar named after the Roman god Mercury, who is charged as the messenger to the gods, further solidifying the card's message. In the Far East the elephant is revered as the "Opener of Ways." As with every announcement brought forth, it is an opportunity to bring about a potential new way to proceed.

The Rider appears, foreshadowing the effects and staying power that announcements or news can have, leaving lasting impressions that may reside within your psyche for a very long time. Remember, everything is in the delivery! Follow the lead of the Rider, ensuring that messages are received with the intended energy.

The number 1 graces the first card of the Lenormand, standing tall and strong, always being a force to be reckoned with, for it leads the way for all other numbered cards to follow suit.

KEYWORDS

News, announcements, coming and goings, delivery, mobile, visit, speedy, arrival, the other man, young man, a suitor, a broadcast, mail, parcel, movement, fast, quick, active, first, messenger, action, race, rushed, notification, visitor, guest, looming in the horizon, on the way!

TIMING

The first card in the Lenormand deck denotes the number 1, which is associated with one day, one week, one month, or the month of January. This is a card of swiftness, indicating soon or the connotation of first in order.

MEANING

The Rider is a card traditionally indicative of a young man, but today it can also be read to signify a young woman. The Rider arrives with a feeling of quickness, since this card is one that denotes movement, especially something coming into your life. The Rider brings the premise of something looming on the horizon, such as the arrival of a potential suitor or caller—someone who is interested in pursuing a romantic connection with you. You can also pay attention to the direction that the Rider is facing, since this will give you further insight as to what the Rider is looking at, depending on the artwork. This first card has a general feel of something incoming and viewed upon as the "bringer of something." What the Rider brings can appear in the form of news, mail, a parcel, a delivery, an announcement, or even the arrival of a visitor. The Rider is a welcome sight, and usually a good omen, for when the Rider appears, it's indicative of movement to a stagnant situation.

RIDER IN LOVE

A new romantic situation could be on the horizon when the Rider approaches, often meaning a new love or romantic opportunity coming your way. Sometimes the Rider can lack maturity and commitment, but he has the potential to be molded into a strong, faithful lover.

RIDER IN CAREER

When the Rider comes galloping in, it may be a new role or movement in your existing job. The Rider can also represent the hustle and bustle of the workplace or the daily work commute. If unemployed, have patience, because something is in the works, since the Rider could bring news of employment. As a project or task, the Rider indicates progression. As a career, the Rider symbolizes a messenger, a delivery driver, a newscaster, or a career involving equines.

RIDER IN WELLNESS

Traditionally, the Rider governs the legs, knees, feet and joints, ligaments, and tendons, signifying the need for movement in order to keep limber. If you are waiting for news regarding health, you may be hearing something soon.

RIDER IN FINANCES

Money coming and going, transactions whizzing in and out, trading stocks, transfers, and day-to-day movement of money. News regarding finances is on the way.

RIDER IN MODERN DAY

Traditionally, a card denoting a young male, but in modern day, this card can depict either sex or persons identifying as queer or gay or fluid in nature. It represents news in a fast-paced, modern world, and you can be sure to have the most up-to-date, minute-by-minute news flashes at your fingertips since it moves at a very rapid speed.

AFFIRMATION

I will show up for myself every day, and with my energy I announce my presence.

CARTOMANCY: 9 OF HEARTS

Traditionally observed as the **Wish Card**! The 9 of Hearts is a card of hope, dreams, aspirations, fulfilled desires, and positive outcomes. When the 9 of Hearts appears, it signifies an affluent social status of wealth and importance. Nines always represent a completion of a cycle or an ending of some kind. As a mature card, it represents the kind of wisdom that comes with age and experience. Being connected with the Moon, the 9 of Hearts also possesses a dark side of overindulgence; here, the shadow is thick when falling into the clutches of vices deemed taboo.

LENORMAND RIDER COMBINATIONS

2. Clover: brief encounter, wild young man, temporary visit, quick bet, happy-go-lucky young man, lighthearted visit, luck is on the way, lucky young man, opportunity looms in the horizon, brief encounters with the other man, fun ride, wild movement, easygoing

3. Ship: "Your ship comes in," car race, leaving quickly, foreign suitor, going away, exploring a suitor, leaving the country, going far from home, leaving a suitor, going, leaving the other man, leaving first, distant other man

4. House: homecoming, comfortable speed, relative visits, household activities, real estate activity, comfortable young man, family announcement, property moves quick (real estate), sheltered young man, family arrives, home page activity, indoor visit, related young man, familiar suitor, comforting news, indoor activity

5. Tree: at a medium pace, slow delivery, vigorous movement, spiritual connection with the other man, medical announcement, extended delivery time, healthy young man, slowly making way, healthful visit, systematic announcements, growing fast, natural movement, living life in the fast lane

6. Clouds: misplaced mail, passing go, lost parcel or package, transient visitor, lost race, storm is looming on the horizon, lost young man, unstable suitor, scary news, uncertain movements, passing through, troubles incoming, troubled young man, addicted to "the news," addicted young man, thoughts racing, insecure young man, uncertain actions

7. Snake: dark-haired woman visits, cheating suitor, evil young man, complicated young man, enticing news, constricting other man, toxic news, betrayal looming on the horizon, evil suitor, complications coming, enticing young man, complicated suitor, complex news, constricted mobility, problematic news, toxic guest, problems on the horizon, need to hurry, cheating young man, toxic suitor, lying broadcaster, toxic young man

8. Coffin: negative activity, dark young man, dark horse, denied movement, death of a suitor, let go the suitor, death rider, ill young man, obituaries, last visit, no go, nonexistent other man, immobility, loss of a suitor, death comes, letting go the other man, negative news

9. Bouquet: gay, wonderful visit, attractive young man, surprise guest, flower delivery, polite guest, pleasant other man, artistic young man, surprise visit, pleasant news, sweet other man, handsome suitor, special announcement, presenting the suitor, stylish other man, show-off, gift horse, polite young man, invitation arrives

10. Scythe: unexpected movement, cutting news, unexpected delivery, urgent announcement, splitting up with the other man, cutting off broadcasts, urgent delivery, sudden movement, wounding announcement, abruptly cutting off visits, removing a guest, urgent visit, separated/divorced other man, cutting off the suitor, danger incoming, emergency broadcast, urgent news, threatening movements, cutting off deliveries

11. Whip: hurtful news, abused young man, going back and forth, aggressive other man, sex with the other man, intermittent visits, competitive race, sexual young man, back and forth with a suitor, argumentative young man, aggressive guest, pattern of coming and going, sexually active, repetitive announcements/news, back-and-forth visits, intermittent announcements, aggressive speed, virile other man, sexual act, hurt other man, aggressive suitor

12. Birds: discussing news, talking about the other man, anxious movements, couple arrives, excited young man, two suitors, couple of announcements, conversing with the other man, vocal young man, musical young man, hectic activity, rumor mill, nervous young man, calling the other man

13. Child: inexperienced young man, small parcel, childish suitor, new guest, shy suitor, immature other man, vulnerable suitor, fragile young man, childish young man, short suitor, playful young man, little announcement, younger suitor / other man, little action, small movements, shy young man

14. Fox: working with the other man, suspicious news, calculated visit, scheming young man, practical young man, job announcement, avoiding the other man, sneaky visitor, employment looming on the horizon, suspicious young man, slick move, avoiding a suitor, stealthy visit, sly young man, slick suitor, cautious movements, pseudo news/announcements, one-trick pony, suspicious movements, avoiding an announcement, suspicious visit, sneaky other man, suspicious coming and goings, avoiding a visit, calculated young man

15. Bear: food delivery, very rushed, more news, intense guest/visitor, more movement, bold suitor, assertive other man, bold announcement, major news, very fast/quick, increased coming and goings, assertive actions, increased activity, increased announcements, more mobile, assertive young man, more suitors, increased visits, more action, very active, increasing speed

16. Stars: harmonious visits, exposing the other man, great announcement, amazing race, best news, great visit, high-speed internet, great young man, best suitor, future action, great things looming on the horizon, headliner news, potential suitor, you will see it coming, vast broadcast, unlimited action, exposing the media, enhanced activity, inspirational young man, expand your horizons, seeing beyond the news, future announcement, great action

17. Stork: returning suitor, trending news, baby delivery, changing announcements, returning guest, long visit, a move is looming on the horizon, baby is coming, changing news, evolving news, returning other man, move quickly!

18. Dog: supportive other man, investigation looming, friendly guest, service announcement, following the news, therapeutic friend, investigating a young man, following along, stalking the other man, following a young man, loyal young man, friendly young man, following the action, stalking a suitor, reliable news, helping a young man, friendly gesture, supporting a young man, investigating the news/announcement, submissive young man, faithful other man, watch the horizon, helpful actions, trusting the news, therapeutic visit, friendly race, following the activity, helpful announcement, investigating a suitor

19. Tower: single visit, city news, officially on the way, government action, registered mail/delivery, established other man, traditional suitor, past other man visits, official race, government broadcast, legal announcement, past visitor, legal action, formal visit

20. Garden: social movement, meeting in a hurry, group activity, gathering quickly, meeting notification, social media broadcast, popular young man, general broadcast, meeting the suitor, group visit, public broadcast, meeting the other man, average suitor, group arrives, people's movement, outdoor activity, social media news, guests arriving

21. Mountain: restricting movement, interrupted visit, obstacles ahead, challenging visit, limited mobility, delayed arrival, hard announcement, stubborn young man, limited suitors, delayed news/announcement, permanent guest, delayed guest, restricted visits, interrupted broadcast, tardy/late, interrupted announcement, limited visitation, delayed visit

22. Paths: strange broadcast, choosing between suitors, unusual other man, strange visit, wandering, between visits, on the way, decision looms, strange young man, unusual news, many visits, unusual guest, choices ahead, between deliveries, going separate ways / parting ways

23. Mice: losing momentum, ruined visit, rat race, damaged delivery, draining rapidly, spreading quickly, fewer announcements, decreased comings and goings, losing mobility, fewer visits, losing steam/speed, corrupt other man, less mail, dwindling activity, less notice, unhurried, sluggishness, corrupted news/broadcasting, sabotaging a visit, diminishes activity, damaging activities, destroyed package, ruin awaits, dwindling quickly

24. Heart: compassionate young man, considerate other man, romance is coming, romantic suitor, love incoming, lovely guest, favorite suitor, intimate visit, tender young man, cherished young man, heartfelt news, relationship is coming, lover arriving, a suitor, love comes in a hurry, favorite guest, cherished visit, admiring a young man, passionate suitor, caring young man, flirty suitor, interested young man, generous other man, forgiving a suitor, pleasurable visit, kind guest, caring young man, romantic suitor, giving news, lovely visit, favorite young man, intimate announcement

25. Ring: married other man, ongoing action, proposal coming, married quickly, entire visit, wedding guests, ongoing announcement, continuous broadcasts, ongoing deliveries, surrounded by action, committed suitor, promised announcement, married suitor, ongoing visits

26. Book: historical news, information arrives, educated young man, historical movement, remembering the other man, informative visit, secretive other man, informative announcement, secrets move quickly, information comes quick, secret announcement

27. Letter: sending an announcement, text message sent, results announced, sending a parcel, newspaper, message/text notification, reading text message notifications, message incoming, scheduled visit, message delivered, written notice, texting the other man, messaging a suitor, text messages coming and going, communicating with the other man / suitor / young man, text notification

28. Man: flamboyant man, male visitor or caller, man arrives, the other man, news about a man, male suitor, young man, male admirer, first husband, acting manly, male guest, gay man, queer man, male suitor, attractive young man

29. Woman: colorful lady, female visitor or caller, woman arrives, news about a lady, female admirer, female suitor, young lady, first wife, acting feminine, female guest, gay woman, attractive young lady

30. Lily: older suitor, conservative announcement, calm actions, privy news, father/grandfather visits, private broadcast, aging quickly, old guest, cold other man, discreet other man, private suitor, peaceful movement, old announcement, "slow your roll," going along for the ride, discreet delivery

31. Sun: good visit, abundance incoming, victory lap, daily visit, annual ride/race, annual announcement, daily news broadcast, annual visit, happy news, confident young man, real news, truthful other man, actual visit, real suitor

32. Moon: night rider, creative young man, emotional announcement, nightmare, emotional young man, skilled horseback rider, monthly visit, nightly activity, manifesting a suitor, influenced by the news, influential guest, monthly visitor, skilled young man, nightly visit

33. Key: privileged news, affluent guest, key announcement, privileged other man, VIP guest, revealing news/announcement, honoring a young man, well-respected suitor, important news, karma delivers, fate awaits on the horizon, important delivery, answers on the way!

34. Fish: getting drunk quickly, money incoming, market/stock news, wealthy guest, financial announcement, business delivery, budget announcement, resources arrive, flowing fast, business mail, wealthy other man, commissions on the way, water rushing in, investing in a young man

35. Anchor: lingering visitor, arranged visit, staying active, keep going, staying ahead, still interested (suitor), keep racing, routine announcement, still moving quickly, saving a young man, still coming, enduring the visit, saving the other man, enduring the news, hanging on to the other man

36. Cross: tax notice, painful news, difficult young man, disappointing visit, regretting actions taken, crisis looming in the horizon, difficult guest, cursed other man, disappointing suitor, difficult other man, disappointing young man, exhausting visit, intolerant young man, miserable other man / suitor, shameful announcement, miserable visit, exhausting other man / suitor, crossed notification, unethical action, disappointing race, obligated other man, regretful news, painful joints/knees, difficult news, regretful young man

You have brains in your head.
You have feet in your shoes.
You can steer yourself any direction you choose.
You're on your own.
And you know what you know.
And YOU are the one who'll decide where to go.

—Dr. Seuss, *Oh, the Places You'll Go!*

2. Clover

Lady Luck gives a smile, with a mischievous glint in her eye.
Coaxing you to take another chance; just give it one more try.
Quickly place your bet before the opportunity becomes too late.
All in, kiss for luck, roll the dice, in this spontaneous game of fate.

DESCRIPTION

Washed in lush hues of greens, an enchanted scene unfolds; a thick energy of laughter fills the air. The happy-go-lucky Clover is seen swinging at the tip-top of a twisty vine of ivy, being a quintessential symbol of luck spreading a bit of joy and opportunity everywhere he goes. It is said that Clover attracts the wee folk by promising fun and shenanigans, so, of course, wherever you find Clover, be sure the fairies are close by. At the base of the vine's thick stem is a small fairy door, serving as a doorway between this world and the realm of the Fae. If you are ever lucky enough to spy a tiny door like this, leave a little offering of milk and honey and be quickly on your way for fear of getting trapped in their realm, where time stands still and the years quickly fly on by. On the ground appears a profusion of fragrant flowers representing many of the Clover's endearing qualities. The deep-red roses bring gratitude for blessings bestowed, as the shy daisies humble themselves in honor of the riches begot. The precious, petaled dame's rocket grows in the wildest thickets and foreshadow the fleeting nature of the Clover, for they are nearly odorless during the day but in the evening release an intoxicating spicy aroma, only to be gone by morning as if never existing at all. The Clover wears an Irish hat atop his head to bring about luck, hoping to lead him to the fields of gold with riches beyond his wildest of dreams, and where the game is almost always surely afoot.

An old Irish legend says fairies bury their gold in pots at the end of a rainbow; it is here they keep a watchful eye, charming all those approaching to keep trying their luck and taking gambles. Once the treasure is discovered, the Fae quickly call upon the leprechauns to hide their pot anew, continuing the game and eluding the treasure seekers once again. Fairies are known for their comical antics; what fun they have frolicking among the fields of Clover, laughing at the unsuspecting humans playing their games.

Being superb at accumulating vast stockpiles of riches, the Fae live a very opulent life, sparing no expense, illustrated by the Fairy house decorated with dripping strands of diamonds boldly displayed for all to see. The diamonds, at first, appear colorless, but once a shard of light hits these precious, brilliant stones, the observer is rewarded by a dazzling prism of colors that make a beautiful rainbow. Buzzing around this cheerful scene is a busy little bee, harnessing the magic of the sun and bringing copious amount of good luck, prosperity, and wealth. The other little creature supporting the message of the card is the ladybug, which is said to be the manifestation of Lady Luck herself. The carefree Clover swings with ease while watching the spontaneous games unfold, making him roll in laughter, for it never gets old. The humans always think they will win and get to keep all the gold for themselves, but every single time they come up empty handed, as the Leprechauns hide the pot of gold once again.

Rich in symbolism, the Clover is a very lucky card to appear heralding in good fortune, opportunity, and luck into your life. But remember, just as fleeting as the rainbow is, so is this little streak of luck; so plan accordingly. The thrill is in the gamble in hopes of winning the game, so have fun, count your blessings, take nothing for granted, and ALWAYS know when to stop and walk away.

KEYWORDS

Luck, short term, small opportunity, chance, gamble, informal, small gain, small happiness, spontaneous, quickness, ease, carefree, lighthearted, fleeting, temporary, casual, comical, fun, cheerful, games, green, brief, serendipity, betting, wild, happy-go-lucky

TIMING

The Clover's timing can be shown in a couple of ways, the first being the month of February, two days, two weeks, and two months if the Mountain is around—this would indicate a delay. The other way the Clover is viewed is as quick, brief, and immediate, right now! (If the Scythe is nearby, it can mean sudden and unexpected.)

MEANING

The Clover always brings luck, but it's fleeting. When the Clover appears, it can bring a surprising twist of fate, or an unexpected opportunity. It is a positive card that is light and carefree. The Clover fills you up with excitement and puts you in the spirit of the expectation of *What if?* Now is the time to pay attention to things, situations, or people who appear in your life; like synchronicities or coincidences, these serendipitous events are not as random as they seem, for they are a part of the tapestry of grand design. At best, the Clover reminds you to lighten up and laugh a little; don't take life or yourself too seriously. It's fun to believe that amazing things do happen to those who take a chance once in a while and bet it all on life.

CLOVER IN LOVE

This is a card of chance meetings, brief encounters, and having a good time. A small shot of happiness comes into your love life. It can denote a brief relationship, a whirlwind romance, or even a second chance at love.

CLOVER IN CAREER

This card describes someone who is a risk taker and is attracted to lighthearted careers, even if the employment is brief. Any job that involves a casual, fun work environment is best for this type of worker. Careers as a professional poker player, a casino employee, a carnival worker, or a comedian are just some examples of jobs that have the feel of the Clover card.

CLOVER IN WELLNESS

The Clover speaks of minor issues; because of the positive nature of the Clover, it's indicative that whatever aliment is present will be brief, or at least improving. Pay attention to the order of the cards, and the surrounding cards, to give you more insight and details. This card brings attention to feeling the rush of adrenaline flooding your system, so take care and slow your roll.

CLOVER IN FINANCES

A lucky small opportunity presents itself, a lucky investment, a small gain, a small sum of money.

CLOVER IN MODERN DAY

March 17 (St. Patrick's Day), a gold digger, luck of the Irish, or someone of Irish decent. A talisman or a lucky charm.

AFFIRMATION

I am a lucky magnet and attract all good things into my life.

CARTOMANCY: 6 OF DIAMONDS

The 6 of Diamonds represents wheeling and dealings that are risky but usually of an advantageous nature. This can imply money invested, financial responsibilities, and receiving an unexpected small sum of money. As a final outcome, it is frequently viewed upon as a positive card. The 6 of Diamonds always brings improvement to any situation and clears a path to your desired destination. Sometimes the 6 of Diamonds refers to a vehicle or the garage area where vehicles are housed.

LENORMAND CLOVER COMBINATIONS

1. Rider: going green, first chance, acting quickly, incoming luck, moving easily, arrival of happiness, speedy bet, super quick, bringer of a small opportunity, acting casual, coming in quick

3. Ship: car rental, boat (full house), distant opportunity, car games, driving quick, travel luck, leaving it to chance, adventurous gamble, leaving happy, departing from spontaneity, leaving quickly, traveling casually, international game

4. House: real estate gamble, house bet, indoor game, family games, indoor fun, real estate opportunity, comfortable, familiar surroundings, domestic opportunity, branding opportunity, real estate games

5. Tree: growing luck, growing pot (gambling), slowing down briefly, vigorous fun, spiritual serendipity, naturally easy, medical gamble/chance, growing opportunity, spiritual happiness, natural luck, growing spontaneously, naturally fun, organic greens, vital game, living green

6. Clouds: lost chance, temperamental luck, hidden opportunity, lost a bet, confusing game, passing opportunity, transient, lost the game, doubtful chance, confusing humor, pathetic luck, misunderstanding the game, it's a gamble, obscured luck, vague opportunity, storm is fleeting, insecure bet, desperate chance, mind games, troubling luck, addicted to gambling/gaming, obscured bet, behaving like a clown, lost sense of humor, thought it was funny, desperate games

7. Snake: evil game, constricted luck, tempting gamble, toxic game, tempting small opportunity, enticing opportunity, enticing game, twisted sense of humor, deception comes with a smile, complicated game, need to take a chance, a bluff, seduction of the game, lying effortlessly, envious of luck, problematic opportunity, deceptive bet, evil laugh, cheating comes easy, cheating luck, affair is brief, twisted games, needing luck

8. Coffin: empty laugh, deleted game, no luck, dark sense of humor, denied opportunity, bad game, last bet, final game, dark games, final chance, no dice, denied happiness, out of luck, end game, closed bet, morbid sense of humor, no fun, ending happiness, deadpan humor, bad bet

9. Bouquet: gift for the occasion, sweet bet, wonderful small opportunity, show-off, enjoying the game, happiness, joy, surprise luck, sweet laughter, special opportunity, enjoying the occasion, having fun, blossoming quickly, showing your/their hand, colorful sense of humor, perfect opportunity/chance

10. Scythe: dangerous bet, risk taker, break (draw), cutting your chances in half, dangerous games, chop (splitting the pot), cutting the deck, risky, disqualified (removed from the game), broken chances, cutting sense of humor, decimating fun, killjoy, cut off from gaming/gambling, cut off from happiness, obliterating luck

11. Whip: hurtful games, sexual bet, intermittent luck, habitual gambler/gamer, sexual gamer, intermittent fun, competitive game, aggressive bet, sexual games, intermittent opportunity, back-and-forth games

12. Birds: song game, musical laughter, call (matching a bet/raise), nervous laugh, talking quickly, couple of chances, talking casually, rumored opportunity, double the fun, nervous bet

13. Child: small bet, child's play, new game, slight chance, small gain, a little bit of fun, childish games, weak bet, immature sense of humor, weak game, fresh chance, weak player, childlike joy, simple game

14. Fox: faking happiness, work opportunity, calculated bet, clever gamble, sneaky games, survival games, avoiding fun, tricky gamble, suspicious bet, elusive luck, cautious bet, pseudo opportunity, bluffing, avoiding the game, mischievous sense of humor, fake laugh, suspicious opportunity, mistaken for fun, running a game

15. Bear: very short term, large gamble, big bet, jackpot, increased gambling/gaming, major opportunity, big game, fat chance, intense laugher, eat more greens, major player, strong bet, more fun, very lucky, increasing your chances, hilarious, very funny, more games, increased gains, increased happiness, very easy, strong chance, increased luck, "They have game!"

16. Star: see beyond the laughter, amazing luck, clear bet, best chance, great gamble, positive game, improving your chances, clear opportunity, wishing for a chance, stellar luck, seeing beyond the opportunity, harmony, seeing a chance, happiness, wishing for luck, lucky game, showing their hand, greater chance, shinning opportunity, best of luck, great opportunity, of great ease, great fun, e-gaming/gambling, unlimited fun, vast opportunities, improving luck, online opportunity

17. Stork: changing a bet, seasonal game, returning luck, changing the game, slim chance, changing quickly, baby shower games, long shot, getting pregnant easily, altered sense of humor, evolving opportunity, trending quickly, seasonal opportunity, shifting spontaneously, returning quickly, progressive jackpot, long game

18. Dog: familiar game, friendly bet, submitting quickly but temporarily, following the game, trust your luck, following along quickly, familiar game, relying on chance, investigating a small opportunity, submitting to chance, supporting a gambler/gamer, investigating a gambler, therapeutic gaming/gambling, watching the game

19. Tower: one chance, official bet, old-man games (cribbage/bridge), past opportunity, formal chance, official opportunity, arrogant laugh, corporate opportunity, official game (lotto)

20. Garden: average luck, public bet, social games, public park, common gamble, recreational games, average bet, social gaming/gambling, popular game, recreational opportunity, cultural game, social media opportunity, outdoor games

21. Mountain: hard luck, interrupted lucky streak, limited chances, blocked luck, limited bet, hard game, remote chance, restricted gambling, interrupted opportunity, delayed fun, restricted games, limited opportunity, interrupted fun, challenging game, restricted bet

22. Paths: multiple bets, strange opportunity, unusual chance, adventurous gamble, unusual laugh, many chances, strange/unusual sense of humor, unfamiliar game, many laughs, strange games

23. Mice: losing the game, dirty bet, costly bet/game (not money), stressful game, diminished fun, dwindling opportunity, worried gambler, reduced chances, dirty games, less luck, low chance, jinxed, losing your chance, dirty stack, dissolving opportunity, dwindling luck, sabotaging fun, fewer opportunities, deliberate (less casual), extended (less temporary), prevailing (less fleeting), worried (less lighthearted), apprehensive, stressed (less carefree), struggling (less ease), clumsiness, strategic (less spontaneous), cheerlessness, losing, perpetual (less short-term), inopportune, unlucky, decreased gambling/gaming, contaminated fields

24. Heart: dating game, flirting with luck, generous bet, relationship luck, interesting game, favorite game, interested in a small opportunity, considerate gambler, interesting stakes, heartfelt chance, infectious laughter, given a chance, relationship games

25. Ring: Ongoing gamble, entire game, continuous chances, all in (betting it all), ongoing fun, engaging sense of humor, entire pot, surrounded by clover, continued laughter, marriage opportunity

26. Book: informed gamble, logical bet, expert gambler, knowledge game (*Jeopardy*), secret games, educational game, hidden opportunity, learning the game, learning to gamble, teaching opportunity, secret bet

27. Letter: sending luck, communication opportunity, deck of cards, something reviewed casually, word game, messaging opportunity, card game, sending a text is a gamble, results are fleeting, texting/messaging doesn't last, communication is brief, results are spontaneous, advertising opportunity, something written casually, results are in, text brings happiness

28. Man: the gambler, a lucky man, a risk taker, an Irish man, a casual man, a happy-go-lucky man, a lighthearted man, a funny man, an exciting man, betting man, casual boyfriend, wild man, spontaneous man

29. Woman: lady luck, a gambling woman, a risk taker, an Irish woman, a casual woman, a happy-go-lucky woman, a lighthearted woman, a funny lady, an exciting woman, betting woman, casual girlfriend, wild lady, spontaneous woman

30. Lily: wise gamble, conservative bet, restrained laughter, old bet, private park, old games, discreet opportunity, private bet, retired quickly, resting easy, private game, retirement opportunity

31. Sun: good bet, winning the game, golden opportunity, really fun, very happy, confident gamble, real chance, actual opportunity, really quick, winning the bet, truly happy, successful bet, good game, confident bet, winning the pot, really easy

32. Moon: manifesting quickly, emotional bet, manifesting a small opportunity, appearing causal, fantasy game (Dungeons and Dragons), emotional ease, skilled gamer/gambler, magickal luck, emotional gamble, creative bet, appearing fun, nightly game, manifesting luck, magickal games, appearing happy, influenced bet, mystical laugh, feeling lucky

33. Key: significant gamble, defiantly brief, opening games (Olympics), privileged opportunity, key chance, uncovering a small opportunity, respecting the game, definitely temporary, privileged bet, unlocking a game, significant chance, open field, definitely happy, karmic luck, distinguished laugh, destined opportunity, answered spontaneously

34. Fish: a small business opportunity, small financial gain, a fish (weak player), cash game, bankroll, bank (the house in a casino), financial gamble, drinking game, expensive game, financial bet, stock market, expensive gamble, wager, money games (poker)

35. Anchor: long-lasting game, still lucky, arranged opportunity, still betting on it, fixed game, down on your luck, keep betting, remaining chances, keep it short term, still gambling/gaming, keeping it casual, constant gamble, keeping it spontaneous, still easy, remain carefree, keep it lighthearted, still temporary, still funny, serious sense of humor, saving the game, there's still a chance, "stay" (on a bet), enduring the games

36. Cross: difficult game, testing your luck, disappointing game, desperate games, disappointing opportunity, cursed luck, regret playing games, difficult gamble, intolerant of games, terrible-luck "gremlins," obligated gamble, regret taking a chance

For years, kids have been asking me what's the greatest superpower. I always say luck. If you're lucky, everything works. I've been lucky.

—Stan Lee

3. Ship

Sometimes there comes a time when you need to say goodbye.
Leaving far-from-home briny tears, the sea begins to cry.
A journey always happens when adventure begins to take hold.
Follow the navigation of your heart, a destination of the bold.

DESCRIPTION

The warm glow of the setting sun splashes this enchanted scene with briny hues of blues as the day departs to usher in yet another anew. Just over the horizon, a Ship appears with full resounding sails, navigating the surging waters as it travels in what seems an erratic direction. The sails represent freedom and potential, encouraging you to take the helm and steer through the tumultuous waters of life's unpredictable nature. The billowing white masts empower you to harness the strength required to say goodbye and change directions, while embarking on an adventurous voyage far from home, keeping aligned with the journey of your soul's path. Brimming with anticipation of exploration, this sturdy Ship is very capable of sailing in rough seas, since the rust on her body indicates that she's been in use for a long time and has proven herself time and time again as a seaworthy vessel. This Ship is a good guide, since she can effortlessly cruise through life's many ups and downs by fearlessly riding the waves with exhilaration.

As you peer out of the Ship's portholes, it's reminiscent of having tunnel vision, but the time has come to open the porthole, let in the salty cleansing air, and look at the situation from a different perspective. The Ship travels through surging waters, demonstrating personal struggles of trying to get to where you want to go, while the sea keeps destroying and creating your path anew. Nothing remains stagnant; similar to the continuous movement of the Ship, life keeps coursing forward, leaving everything in its wake; it's now up to you if your vessel will be fighting against the tide or moving along with it, since this is your trip, and the destination is always yours to choose.

In the distance behind the Ship, we see a map of the ancient world, plotting out your life purpose, enabling you to see the direction that you are currently heading and providing the insight to chart out an even-grander course. A ladder displayed on the side of the Ship is symbolic of hard work and great effort that's required to climb the ladder of success, enabling you to reach your goals.

Seagulls soaring above from lofty heights embody the qualities of independence and purpose. Always being carefree, they find a unique way to survive in every situation. By having a bird's-eye view, the seagulls endeavor to instantly spot an opportunity in all things—just as the most clever of merchants had to do, as they would seek out international trades in foreign lands abroad, not only for survival, but to thrive and prosper overseas. The Ship card bears the mystical number 3, full of abundant energy and a spark of creativity. The number 3 is the bringer of change in the flux of expansion and loss, always creating and expressing life in a robust and daring manner, just like the sea. The number 3 is an entrepreneur and increases abundance everywhere they go, with promises of adventure, success, and riches beyond wildest dreams.

KEYWORDS

Travel, movement, goodbye, distance, transportation, journey, direction, trade, adventures, international, trip, overseas, near the sea, abroad, voyage, cruise, far from home, departures, foreign, navigation, leaving, moving on, exploration

TIMING

As the third card in the deck, timing is connected to three days, three weeks, or three months. With the Mountain or Anchor present, it could possibly mean three years, but usually within months.

MEANING

The Ship, being a card of movement, is indicative of something leaving in your life and creating the distance needed for you to embark on a new journey filled with adventure. This is a card of travel by means of transportation from one destination to the next, representing all types of vehicles. While exploring all the angles of any situation, you are able to see that life is one big adventure, since you are always heading toward your final destination, but who says you can't have fun along the way? The Ship card gives off an exotic feel of foreign lands and wayward souls.

Bohemian lifestyle, where freedom and exploration are always tied to some kind of rewarding experience and outcome. The Ship is generally viewed as a positive card associated with Sagittarius the traveler.

SHIP IN LOVE

A long-distance romance may present itself; look to other cards surrounding the Ship for details. Another, more personal meaning could be that it is time to start transitioning away from an old flame by truly leaving that relationship behind. When the Ship describes a person, it could represent someone from a different country or with a foreign background. On more of the adventurous side, the Ship can be indicative of exploring a relationship with someone you met on your travels. When the Ship comes floating into a love reading, it might just mean that someone travels to meet up with a lover due to physical distance. At times, the Ship shows up warning that a love interest is not ready to settle down and drop anchor, for the lure of dating adventures and exploring others is far too strong.

SHIP IN CAREER

When the Ship appears, it shows up as movement in your career. Maybe it's time to say goodbye and to look for something new that will stir that feeling of adventure as you explore a new job/career. As far as actual careers, the Ship can be indicative of anything in the field of transportation or logistics, shipping or foreign trade, international business, travel and tourism, a pilot, a driver, joining the navy, a captain of a ship, a job on a cruise ship, import/export—or even employment abroad or working for a company whose headquarters are in a different county.

SHIP IN WELLNESS

The Ship can indicate feeling nauseated, homesickness, or travel sickness. Sometimes the Ship implies that an illness is passing or moving around within the body. Traveling internationally for a medical procedure or even trying out a foreign mode of healing is possible.

SHIP IN FINANCES

Your Ship is coming in! Your funds are in transit, creating movement in your finances. Sometimes there are indications that fortunes will come from some form of international source.

SHIP IN MODERN DAY

Making waves, by creating a movement. Progress is being made in some aspect of your life while you continue on your soul's journey navigating through life. The Ship can also indicate a fiancé coming overseas or from another country for marriage. Companies that do a lot of shipping such as Amazon, Wayfair, or eBay.

AFFIRMATION

I navigate my life's ups and downs by trusting the journey, as I ride the waves of adventure.

CARTOMANCY: 10 OF SPADES

When the 10 of Spades comes up, it's indicative of a large body of water or a journey of some kind. This card highlights the setbacks and fears that block you from reaching your goals. In the body, it represents the digestive track, and for timing, the 10 of Spades denotes the winter season. In the home, it represents an actual floor or that the house is haunted. Traditionally, this card is a telltale card of negativity and problems with many challenges ahead, foreshadowing illness, loss, and tears. A dark night of the soul amplifies emotional distress, anxiety, sadness, disappointments, depression, and grief with tears like the salty waters of the sea. In a shroud of mystery, the 10 of Spades uncovers disharmony, untruths, and darkness, evident that negative forces are at play. The 10 of Spades also gives a nod to having mastered the craft and being adept to the occult by applying those teachings in everyday life.

1. Rider: going away, quick trip, speedy passage, fast car, horse and buggy, news from afar, first trip, race car, acting distant, mail/post truck, rushed visit, news that they're leaving, speedy departure, runaway train, in route, Other man/suitor is far from home, delivery truck, regatta, going abroad, first exploration, quick goodbye

2. Clover: small opportunity to travel, ciao (casual goodbye), fun destination, wild ride, green vehicle, temporary goodbye, fun trip, fun ride, casual trip, clown car, see you later, lucky departure, joy ride, gambling boat / casino boat, brief trip, temporary passage

4. House: familiar destination, family car, home abroad, family member leaves, house hunting, family trip, house overseas, local trip, house directions, brand departure, familiar goodbye, small building abroad, property overseas, comfortable movement, familiar direction, home page navigation, domestic travel, place far from home, domestic cargo/freight, family member is far from home

5. Tree: spiritual destination, slow movement, ambulance, living on a boat, slow to depart, medical leave, growing distant, extended departure, branching out, healthful movement, natural departure, medical transport, healthful travel, living abroad, extended goodbye, life's adventures, living near the sea

6. Clouds: passing ships, confusing goodbye, lost direction, passed on by, sailing yacht, sad goodbye, chaotic movement, lost soul, fear of leaving, confusing departure, unclear direction, unsettling movements, addicted to travel, bad weather at sea, vague direction, lost (navigation)

7. Snake: constricting travel, wanting to leave, enticing journey, complicated goodbye, the liar leaves, other woman is far from home, constricted movement, needing distance, running a tight ship, the other woman leaves, toxic goodbye, cheating abroad, tempting trip, deceptive movements, problems during travel, attracted to foreigners

8. Coffin: denied departure, death at sea, last goodbye, Black Sea, denied travel, hearse, final passage, last trip, let go and move on, nonexistent travel, funeral procession/cortege, burial at sea, died far from home, no direction, died on a trip, dreadful journey, making a bad move, buried far from home

9. Bouquet: wonderful trip, special goodbye, Volkswagen Beetle (flower car), surprise destination, beautiful car, showboating, pleasant goodbye, beautiful departure, souvenir, special trip, appreciating the journey, easterly direction, invited to a trip, surprising goodbye, gifting a car, showing off a car, beautiful movement, pleasant trip, gifting a trip, traveling in style

10. Scythe: dangerous destination, emergency travel, dangerous passage, unexpected departure, broken car, dangerous trip, sudden departure, unexpected goodbye, dangerous car, urgent departure, cutting travel, removing a vehicle, decimating travel, cut off from traveling, obliterated vehicle, emergency vehicle, urgent trip, cutting off someone (caused car accident), threatening to leave

11. Whip: back-and-forth trips, opposed to travel, intermittent departures, aggressive movements, sports car, sex drive, repetitive travel, pattern of leaving, aggressive departure, angry goodbye, battleship, waving goodbye, rocking the boat, intermittent travel, aggressive driver, habit of leaving

12. Birds: discussing travel, flying car, partnership, talks about leaving, flying ship, a flight (plane), anxious goodbye, partner left, anxious traveler, talking about a trip, rumors of someone leaving, couple's trip, sibling far from home, partner is far from home, "honk, honk," saying goodbye, flying plane

13. Child: new destination, short bus, slight movement, school bus, childish goodbye, new driver, short distance, weak movement, small car, short goodbye, child is far from home, insecure movements, child leaves home, playful goodbye, inexperienced driver, trust the journey, slightly distant, vulnerable traveler

14. Fox: plotting a course, suspicious trip, sneaking away, calculated goodbye, practical trip, avoiding travel, fleeing the country, work vehicle, pseudo goodbye, calculated trip, work leave, avoiding a trip, misdirection, avoid leaving, work trip, suspicious departure, stealthy movements, careful goodbye, pseudo trip, escaping, guilt trip, pretending to leave, avoiding a goodbye

15. Bear: assertive movements, intense goodbye, big truck (18-wheeler), assertive driver, grand adventure, forced goodbye, mega yacht, powerful car, assertive goodbye, big adventure, forced to leave/go, more travel, mighty journey, intense trip, lorry, big car, major trip, big departure, mother/grandmother is far from home, restaurant far from home, obese foreigner, dominant move, leadership

16. Stars: UFO/UAP, space exploration, great trip, spacecraft, astral journey, space travel, great journey, electric vehicle, at a great distance, harmonious journey, on a great adventure, space shuttle, electric bike, inspired journey, astral travel, great goodbye, best direction, great trade, best car, *Star Trek*, unlimited travel, vast distance, very far from home, extensive travel, upgraded travel, technologically enhanced vehicle, see beyond the distance, future travel, great exodus

17. Stork: seasonal destination, return trip, long holiday/vacation, moving truck, long distance, changing direction, long departure, maternity leave, moving far away, long goodbye, long trip, changing cars, seasonal traveler, long journey, baby stroller/pram, moving away, returning a car, moving overseas, spring departure

18. Dog: self-reliant, friend's leaving, followed at a distance, trust the journey, familiar destination, observing movements, familiar trip, investigating travel destinations, friend overseas, servicing a vehicle, reliable direction, friendly departure, friendship, assisted travel, reliable transportation, friendly trade, helpful direction, navigation, familiar journey, therapeutic travel, trust the direction, friends trip, watching from a distance, guided movements, familiar vehicle, guided travel, following a car, guided journey, friend is far from home, service truck

19. Tower: authorized leave, defensive move, solo travel, past trip, self-directed, city trip, solo journey, corporate vehicle, official leave, formal departure, isolated far from home, traditional goodbye, lonely trip, withdrawn and distant, controlling movement, consulate

20. Garden: public transportation, socializing far from home, membership, bus, cruise ship, in a general direction, citizenship, meeting far from home, event abroad, recreational travel, group trip, online travel group, festival overseas, socially distant, public departure, meeting abroad

21. Mountain: blockade (vehicle), hardship, blocked passage, delayed departure, remote trip, rough journey, far away, interrupted goodbye, distant trip, stalled car, immovable, challenging/ hard goodbye, very distant, limited transportation, restricted vehicle, challenging journey, delayed cruise, restricting movement, off-road vehicle, interrupted trip/travel, interrupted departure, distance, limited travel

22. Paths: unfamiliar destination, strange trip, unusual car, unfamiliar car, road vehicle, multiple departures, strange goodbye, multiple trades, many adventures, directions, between trips, walk away, road far from home, choosing to say goodbye, strange foreigner

23. Mice: losing steam, fewer trips, low tide, stolen vehicle, damaged boat/ship, closing the gap (eating away at the distance), damaged vehicle, stress leave, decreased travel, reducing the distance, stressful goodbye, derailed, domestic (eats away at international), sabotaged travel/ trip, scurvy, decreased movement, leaving, damaged car, jeopardizing a trip, losing your bearings

24. Heart: romantic destination, passionate goodbye, a lover leaves, dating far from home, lover overseas, romantic trip, love escapades, lover says goodbye, pleasurable journey, flirting with a foreigner, loving goodbye, generous trade, flirty moves, heartfelt distance, giving directions, lover far from home

25. Ring: a wheel, entire trip, the whole distance, agreeing to say goodbye, ongoing travel, surrounded by foreigners, ongoing journey, roundabout, wedding destination, surrounded by ships/boats, committed to travel, marital distance, circular movement, agreeing to travel

26. Book: secret destination, informative trip, memorial trip, educational leave, secret departure, remembering a goodbye, educated abroad, school far from home, secret goodbye, booking a trip, secretive movements, smart direction, unknown travel date, expert traveler, memories of a trip, researching travel destinations, secret passage

27. Letter: message in a bottle, scheduled travel, sent away, pen pal, communicating a goodbye, scheduled trip, paper boat, advertising travel, newspaper from abroad, authorship, message/ text in transient (sent), advertising internationally, sent away far from home, scheduled departure, reviewing a trip, writing about travel, documented foreigner

28. Man: foreign man, male traveler, worldly man, vagabond (male), male ship's captain, male gypsy, jet-setter, male who works in travel and tourism, driver (male), man is leaving, distant man, male far from home, international male, bohemian, saying goodbye to a man

29. Woman: foreign woman, female traveler, international woman, worldly woman, ship's captain, female gypsy, jet-setter, bohemian, female who works in travel and tourism, driver (female), female is leaving, distant female, female far from home, saying goodbye to a woman

30. Lily: peaceful trip, private jet, cold goodbye, seasoned traveler, cold destination, old car, geriatric movements, winter vehicle, discreet movements, peaceful goodbye, lifetime traveler, experienced traveler, classic car, father/grandfather is far from home, peaceful trip, private goodbye, calm movement

31. Sun: sunny destination, really leaving, good passage, day trip, good car, convertible car (summer car), yearly trip, annual vacation, real adventure, goodbye, light traveler, confident direction, actually traveling, actual departure, vacation/holiday far from home

32. Moon: creative direction, skilled foreigner, creative journey, monthly trip, appearing far from home, manifesting travel, nightly passage, intuitive movement, reflecting on a trip, feeling distant, magickal adventure, appears far away, aware of every move

33. Key: free trade, first-class travel, affluent foreigner, VIP travel, key trip, open passage, definitely leaving, free transportation, karmic travels, distinguished traveler, open travel dates (open ticket), passport, free ride, fated goodbye, destined to leave, free car, answers abroad, fated direction

34. Fish: expensive trip, business vehicle, boat, ship, expensive car, resourceful trip, fishing vessel, money leaving, exchanging a vehicle, purchasing a car, buying a boat, leasing/financing a vehicle, business far from home, purchasing a trip, commerce abroad, exchanging goodbyes, shopping destination

35. Anchor: moored ship/boat, enduring travel, anchored vessel, armored car, coastal destination, secure passage, staying far from home, keep a safe distance, safe car, routine trip, remaining abroad, keep traveling, routine trade, parked car, safe vehicle, still leaving, staying away, still navigating, staying the course, rescuing a vessel, tow truck, enduring a goodbye, parked far from home, routine goodbye

36. Cross: difficult passage, a lemon (car), disappointing goodbye, miserable trip, exhaust of a vehicle, regret leaving, cursed trip, a spirit moves on, regret saying goodbye, difficult trip, miserable goodbye, intolerant foreigner, regretful trip, exhausting travel, ghost ship, difficult goodbye

Twenty years from now you will be more disappointed by the things you didn't do than by the ones you did do.
So throw off the bowlines.
Sail away from the safe harbor. Catch the trade winds in your sails. Explore. Dream. Discover.

—H. Jackson Brown Jr.

4. House

Family comes together, within these four walls I reside.
People I can count on, whom will always be on my side.
Home is my sanctuary, my refuge, my shelter, my place.
Familiar surroundings comfort me, in this domestic space.

DESCRIPTION

In the starry night, a mysterious glow is cast upon a whimsical House in the shape of a shoe as it sits nestled in a lush colorful meadow. This is the magick of the House, which keeps the family housed within this indoor sanctuary among familiar surroundings, safeguarded from all elements. The House is situated among the cheerful daisies representing the month of April, which corresponds to the number on the card. In Victorian times, the daisy represents trust and loyalty, the way we feel about our loved ones, and those we welcome into our home.

As in all fairy tales, the fly agaric mushroom, with its quintessential red cap that is associated with the yuletide season, stands sentinel by the stairs. Fireflies flit around the shadows, bringing light, magick, and nostalgic memories of your childhood home to mind. The pretty twinkling string of colorful lights hung on the roof portrays the promise of the returning light, which is the essence of the winter solstice, as the House card traditionally also represents the month of December.

The Fae lie hidden behind the mushroom caps, and unbeknown to you, the wee folk bestow good fortune and blessings upon the house and all those who dwell inside. The shoelace, done up partway, describes the family's easygoing nature, while the missing roof tile is symbolic of their openness and welcoming hospitality. It is considered very lucky to move into a new house when the moon is full, for it will bring good tidings and positive transformation to the family, mirrored by the white butterflies. These winged beauties represent change, the very essence of their transformational medicine, as they are drawn to the illumination of the lantern perched at the tip-top of the roof acting like a beacon to all those wayward souls who have lost their path and can once again find their way home.

The number 4 is structurally sound and represents the four corners the House card. Each one of these pillars strengthens family bonds by providing refuge, a comfortable sanctuary of familiar surroundings with the comforts of home. Wrapped within the arms of the number 4, one is sure to feel loved.

KEYWORDS

Home, family, real estate, property, comfortable, relatives, sanctuary, familiar surroundings, domestic affairs, indoors, brand, home page, small buildings, refuge, shelter, a place, family members

TIMING

The House card has two timings associated with it: the winter solstice, yule season or April (fourth month), four days, four weeks, or four months. If the Mountain is in proximity, it fortifies the duration of the delay and could mean up to four years. I personally use the House card as the season of yule; there is something comfy and cozy about the winter season that floods me with memories of family and the smells of smoke in the fireplace, and food cooking on the stove reminds me of the nostalgia of my childhood home.

MEANING

The House card represents any place of familiar surroundings that brings comfort and the nostalgia of home—a place where you are surrounded by family, friends, familiar people, loved ones, and relatives. It represents the interior hustle and bustle of domestic life, and a perfect indoor sanctuary that welcomes you home with open arms, soothing your soul after a long day. The House card pertains to any kind of building or dwellings of a smaller stature.

HOUSE IN LOVE

A relationship that feels familiar and comfortable, with the intention of moving toward settling down and setting up house together. This card can also denote love and loyalty you have for your family and relatives.

HOUSE IN CAREER

A family-owned business, a home-based business, or a work-from-home situation. As a vocation, the house can indicate a realtor, contractor, maid, handyman, domestic worker, architect, or stay-at-home parent.

HOUSE IN WELLNESS

Usually indicative of stability and well-being, given the solid four corners.

HOUSE IN MODERN DAY

A home page or your social media page, a brand, what represents you online.

In familiar surroundings I find comfort, as I retreat into my inner sanctuary.

CARTOMANCY: KING OF HEARTS

King of Hearts is the archetypal family man. With a sweet and affectionate temperament, this great King prides himself as being a benevolent protector of his family clan. This devoted gentle giant is generous and fair, with an empathic heart of gold. His home is his castle, and he relishes all the comforts that his sanctuary provides. At times, due to his sensitive nature, the King of Hearts finds himself feeling uninspired and can easily slip into one of his moods. But don't fret; it won't be long before this loving man snaps out of his melancholy and finds his passion once again. In a reading, he can also represent a male who is close to you and well loved by all.

LENORMAND HOUSE COMBINATIONS

1. Rider: going home, first visit, guest room, suite, first place, acting domestic, first home, first family, news regarding family, launching a home page, visiting home, quick real estate (deal, sale, listing), young man at home, active real estate (deal, sale, listing), visiting a place, young relative, moving comfortably

2. Clover: greenhouse, lucky house, betting the house, happy-go-lucky family, country home, green space, temporary place, *pied-à-terre*, wild family member, green room, lucky in real estate, temporary home page, briefly moving in, the other man lives close to home, greenery, temporary shelter

3. Ship: overseas relatives or family, foreign family/relative, leaving home, distant relation, distant family member, faraway place, mobile home, boathouse, leaving familiar surroundings, leaving the family, saying goodbye to a family member

5. Tree: ancestral home, wooden house, blood family, slow real estate market, blueprints (house), extended family, architectural building, medical building, living at home, natural place, living with a family member / relative, wooded property/place, deep family roots, spiritual place, blood related

6. Clouds: misplaced, unstable family, chaotic place, lost family member, not sure about a house, unstable real estate market, depressed family member, addicted family member, sad house, troubles at home, doubting a real estate deal, misunderstanding in the family, disturbed family member

7. Snake: evil place, toxic house, problematic property, constricting family, toxic family, tight space, toxic place, complicated family member, pipes/wires (indoors), lying family member, cheater under this roof, desiring a place of your own, enticing property, complicated real estate

8. Coffin: empty house, dark home, coffin, denied shelter, dark place, sick/ill family member/ relative, no one's home, death in the home, last place, final home, let go the property, loss (death) of a family member / relative, skeleton's in the closet, funeral parlor, delisted/terminating (real estate), dead house / mort house, a dead space, bereaved, gravesite

9. Bouquet: fashion house (Versace, Chanel, Gucci), wonderful family, charming house, beautiful property, polite family, pretty house, special place, fashion brand, beautiful space, inviting family over, sweet relative, designing a brand, grateful for family, show home, east of the property, beautiful surroundings, pleasant family, east-facing house, gifting a house/ property

10. Scythe: dangerous house, divided/broken family, west-facing house, cutting off / removing family / family member, severing a property, separated/divorced family member, demolished house, operating/theater room (hospital), decimating a family, obliterating a small building, cut off from family, threatening family member, splitting up the family, wounded family member, vaccinated family member, risky real estate, west of the property, emergency room (hospital), danger zone

11. Whip: questionable property, hurtful family member, exercise/workout room, arguing over a property, questioning a family member, active family, aggressive family member, fitness/ sports facility, aggressive real estate (deal, market, listing), arguing with family, sex room, exercising at home, angry family member / relative, conflicts at home

12. Birds: discussing a family member / relative, musical family, conversations about real estate, restless at home, anxious family member, nervous about moving in, gossip/rumors about a family member / relative, siblings in the family, conversations within the house, talking to family, noisy household, cohabitation, negotiations (real estate), call home/family, curious place, music room/studio

13. Child: small property, shy family member, weak branding, small space/place, weak family member, vulnerable family member, childish family member, children in the family, a little familiar (place), simple family, small building, immature family member, inexperienced in real estate, short building, childhood, new place

14. Fox: scheming family member / relative, practical household, pretending to be related, sneaky relative, avoiding family, sneaky family, workplace, escaping the house, practical family, suspicious property, sneaky relative, stealthy family member, cautious family, pseudo family, escaping the family

15. Bear: grand home, assertive family member, big property, matriarchal home, strong family, large family, very domesticated, strong mother/grandmother, very familiar surroundings, big space, intense family member, strong branding, big house, more properties, very comfortable, den, kitchen, dining room

16. Stars: famous house, great room, astral plane, north-facing house, famous family, astral family, amazing property, famous family member, inspiring family member, harmonious family, great family, high property (situated), vast property, expansive home, north of the property, great house/place, smart home (technology), improving real estate (market), guiding you home, beyond the property, seeing family, future family

17. Stork: returning home, changing houses, quiet family member, longhouse, dance studio, born and raised, birth family, baby's room, seasonal room, moving, change in the family, spring cleaning (house), returning family member, progressive branding, birthplace

18. Dog: smell of home, protect the family, dependent, protect the property/house, dog crate, helpful family, familiar, relying on family, loyal family, watch a family member, searching for a house, familiar house, friendly family, animal shelter, supportive family, dog/animals in the house, following a family member, searching for family/relatives, trust family

19. Tower: defensive family member, city house/property, single-family home, past home, established family, defending a family member, defending your property/home, jail house, city dweller, head of the family, withdrawn family member, tall building, controlling family member, official residence, defending your family, courtroom, isolated place, city hall

20. Garden: common household, group home, populated small building, common area, average family, the garden (house), common brand, popular place, together at home, public room, community house, virtual tour (house), public space/place, family network, everybody in the family, meeting family, clubhouse, popular room, common room, public gardens, crowded house, neighborhood, meeting place

21. Mountain: brick/stone house, remote property/place, delayed house, challenging family member, stubborn relative, limited real estate, challenging property, restricted property (off-limits), blocked home page, distant place, permanent place, remote place, rough housing, restricted space, permanent shelter, interrupted real estate (deal/sale), hilly property, "between a rock and a hard place"

22. Paths: decision about the family, between properties, strange family, eccentric relative, unusual property, many relatives, multifamily dwelling, multiple family members, strange surroundings, unfamiliar relative, many places, strange house, multiple small buildings, between houses, unfamiliar surroundings, roadhouse

23. Mice: scattered family, crumbling house / small building, low property (situated), undomesticated, dirty place, losing family, less room/space, dissolving brand, dwindling family, uncomfortable, filthy family, infestation (mice in the house), spread out family, discomfort, contaminated property, messy house, dilapidated house, damaged property, jeopardized real estate

24. Heart: compassionate family, loving home, considerate family, affectionate family, loving the house, generous relative, favorite room in the house, forgive a family member / relative, passion for real estate, favorite place, interest in a property, favorite place, kind family

25. Ring: close-knit family, bonded family, offer (real estate), surrounded by houses, central place (location), entire family, the whole place, surrounding the property/house, entire household, inside, united front, matrimonial home, surrounded by family, whole house/property

26. Book: logical family, unknown place, secretive family, remembering a place, booking a house (Airbnb, Vrbo, Homestay), historical house/property/place, unknown house, secret place, remembering a house, student dorms (dormitory), memorial place, remembering family/relative, booking a place to stay, information on the property/house, unknown family member

27. Letter: address (house), certified home, texting family, reviewing a place, blog (family), advertising (real estate), sent internally, sign (real estate), blog (housekeeping), sent home, letter to family member, posting (home page), blog (real estate), advertising a brand, documents (house/family), reviewing a brand, brochure (real estate), filing a title (real estate), results for a family member, communicating with family

28. Man: family man, man of the house, male family member, male relative, man with strong family values, lord of the manor, male homeowner, homeboy, handyman, houseboy, male homebody, domesticated man, male real estate agent

29. Woman: nurturer, the lady of the house, female family member, housekeeper, landlady, female relative, female with strong family values, lady of the manor, female homeowner, homegirl, female homebody, domesticated woman, female real estate agent

30. Lily: conservative family/household, winter home, cold room / cantina / cellar, reserved family member, ice hut, igloo, private family, cold space/place, patriarchal home, private residence, homely, private household

31. Sun: light-filled home, fireplace, real property, south-facing house, happy family, actually related, confident family member, real family, bright place, really comfortable, truthful family member, really familiar surroundings, actual brand, real place, south of the property, sunroom, actual house

32. Moon: feeling at home, creative family member, bedroom, magickal space (indoor), feeling comfortable, creative space, creative brand, emotional place, month-to-month house rental, intuitive family member, magickal room, emotional family member, it feels like home, craft room, influenced family member, spelled household, talented family

33. Key: privileged family, distinguished brand, karmic houses, defiantly related, significant place, important family, definitely a family member, karmic family, a way out of this place, access to the house/property, keys to the kingdom, destined house, free family

34. Fish: expensive house, a bar, lake house, waterfront property, wealthy family, income property, fluctuating home prices, valuable property, investment house, rich relative, shopping for a house, investing in real estate, resourceful family, pool, washroom / toilet / bathroom / loo / water closet, laundry room

35. Anchor: solid house, staying put/home, keeping the house/property, safe space/place, grounded family, saving the house, beach/coastal house, suspended (real estate sale), dependable family, hanging on to a house/property, stable family, holding on to family, staying comfortable, keeping it familiar, staying indoors, saving a family member, keeping it in the family, basement of the house, stuck at home, safe room, beachfront property, settling in, reserved room

36. Cross: hallowed ground, cursed family, sacred space/place, church, religious place, sacred indoor space, cursed place, testing real estate, disappointing family member, cursed house/property, hellhole, disappointing property/house, intolerant family member, shameful relative / family member, scandalous family, regretful family member, miserable place, terrible house

There is a magic in that little world, home; it is a mystic circle that surrounds comforts and virtues never know beyond its hallowed limits.

—Robert Southey

5. Tree

Ancestral blood ties that bind, essence deeply rooted in the earth
Vital spiritual connections that took place, way before your birth
Healthy boughs growing, slowly coming alive "as above, so below"
Anchoring the body in this lifetime, while spiritually you grow

DESCRIPTION

Standing tall and strong, proudly displaying its beautiful colors, this flourishing Tree has captured our imagination since the beginning of time. The Tree is synonymous with well-being and is the embodiment of eternal life—a true hallmark of immortality, survival, growth, and rebirth. Even though the Tree is rooted onto one spot, new offshoots and branches emerge to ensure the continuance of legacy, as seen in the very blueprint of the Tree's DNA throughout the passage of time.

Nestled in the Tree's majestic canopy of lush green foliage is a plethora of colorful butterflies that mimic the life cycle of the leaves that display the power of immortality. The leaves are in constant flux of life, death, and rebirth—as the seasons change and the old life withers and dies, but not before a promise of tomorrow and eternal life is given. Resilience is the key to the Tree's survival, the belief that even though the end is nigh, human spirit and the will to survive will always prevail. This energy empowers the butterflies as they eloquently dance to express the joyful celebration of their own endurance through transformation and the completion of their metamorphosis. The butterflies survive by accepting the change of total liquefaction of a former life, and they reemerge and rejoice in the knowledge of immortality, celebrating their new way of existence in the dawning of a new day.

An enchanted fairy ring of brown mushrooms forms at the base of the Tree trunk, reinforcing the theme of the card: out of chaos and destruction in the pits of decay emerges something new and beautiful. The very life force of the Tree is in the labyrinth of the root system, which is encapsulated in the protective womb of Mother Earth. Magickal sparks of light fly around, showing you that just beneath the surface lies powerful root magick. This magick will assist you on your journey, only if you can learn to harness the power and yield this obscure gift. In the backdrop of the Tree, dignified majestic mountains stand as silent, but vigilant, watchers representing the ancestors—always observing and protecting you from forces seen and unseen, demonstrating that no matter what we encounter on our path, there is always a way to overcome any obstacle simply by rising above and getting closer to nature to hear the spiritual messages that fuel the song of our soul.

Often overlooked is the green grass, which is plentiful and lush surrounding this mystical tree. Grass grows together harmoniously and is the quintessential embodiment of community, since you never see a single blade of grass growing alone. This symbolizes the need for human contact and connectedness in order to thrive in our lives. Grass roots have a very elaborate and intricate system, just like the systems in our bodies and the roots of the Tree.

The Tree card bears the number 5, traditionally associated with health and the body. This number denotes the marriage between heaven and Earth and suits the symbolic imagery of the Tree card, as it digs in its feet into Mother Earth and reaches up its arms to embrace Father Sky. The number 5 is also representative of the five elements of Earth, Water, Fire, Air, and Spirit. Characteristically, the explosive 5s demonstrate someone who is an adventurous freethinker, who seeks truth and knowledge above all.

KEYWORDS

Health, system, an extended time, ancestors, living, well-being, vitality, natural, medical, spirituality, blood ties, growth, deeply rooted, essence, vigor, DNA, life, the body, spiritual connections, slow

TIMING

Reference to the summer. The tree is very slow growing, so the effects of the Tree card are long lasting. If using the cards, number 5 would represent five days, five weeks, or five months and, dependent on the cards surrounding, may even be up to five years if the Mountain is present.

MEANING

When the Tree card shows up, it is most likely connected to health and well-being. When the inquiry is in regard to a situation, the Tree is indicative that something has taken root and has been steadily growing for some time.

When looking at the Tree from a spiritual perspective, it demonstrates the spiritual connections you carry with you in this human experience, while bringing forth the DNA of our ancestors and creating blood ties that carry on for generations.

Anyone who feels a natural infinity for trees is adapting a more spiritual life, looking for deeper meanings. This card also reminds you that everything takes time; have patience to see through whatever you are experiencing, while knowing, like the tree, that you are an immortal being, for you will live on throughout future generations.

TREE IN LOVE

The Tree is hallmark when feeling a familiar spiritual connection toward someone, especially when a serendipitous event brought you together. The Tree carries qualities of a long-lasting love that nourishes and grows over time. It can also represent a connection that starts off as a budding infatuation and steadily grows to a fulfilling, flourishing love of a lifetime. If the Tree appears between the Man and Women cards, watch out for a lack of passion or excitement, where complacency has taken root. It is indicative of boredom that has been growing for a while.

TREE IN CAREER

The primary meaning of the Tree is health; this card would indicate a career in healthcare or in any field in medicine. In business, it can denote branching out or healthy and steady growth, or that sound ideas are taking root. It's a great card to see when asking career questions denoting a viable job or career choices.

TREE IN WELLNESS

This is the primary meaning of the Tree card and, by paying close attention to the surrounding cards, will show you the nature of the issue at hand. Attention is to detail, and discernment is paramount here; be open to all the possible interpretations, taking care when consulting the seeker unless you are a qualified healthcare professional.

TREE IN FINANCES

Steadily growing finances. If unsatisfied with a current financial situation, look to decisions and spending habits of the past that have taken root that are manifesting today.

TREE IN MODERN DAY

Tree of Life, ancestry and DNA, blood ties, and natural medicine.

AFFIRMATION

I focus on my breath and ground myself as I plant my roots deep into the ground.

CARTOMANCY: 7 OF HEARTS

When using the 7 of Hearts for divination, it pertains to the circle of life, and within the body it could manifest as an issue with the circulation or the reproductive system. The 7 of Hearts has a peaceful nature, filled with ethereal healing and pleasant surprises. This Heart is all about second chances; but, as with everything, beware of self-doubt, for it can seep in over time, causing stagnation. At best, the 7 of Hearts is a positive card to see, for no matter what the situation may be, it heralds improvement.

1. Rider: acting natural, fast growth, young man's life, the other man's moving slowly, news takes awhile, active system, coming in slowly, delivery system, announcement is slow coming, suitor keeps you waiting, fast diagnosis, active growth, visit extended, overextending a body part, active life, young person's well-being, arrival of vitality, moving naturally, announcement about health, quickly growing

2. Clover: country life, brief life, a wild life, nature, green living, evergreen tree, lucky life, gallbladder (small and green), wild tree, natural life, temporary system, natural living, brief spiritual connection, gambling with your life, spontaneous living, easy living, casual diagnosis, bet on life, natural medicine

3. Ship: transportation system, cruising slowly, exploring ancestry, direct bloodline, distant ancestor, navigation system, exploring life, adventure of a lifetime, exploratory drugs/medicine, journey through life, exploring a spiritual connection, foreign living

4. House: family roots, the skin (because your skin houses your body), sheltered life, family life, familiar system, yule tree (indoor tree), family/relatives, finding sanctuary in a forest, house systems, family member diagnosis, family doctor, small medical building, familiar spiritual connection, family ties, garden/backyard tree, domestic life, home health, family medicine

6. Clouds: lost spiritually, mental health disorder, unstable health, lost spiritual connection, shade tree, sad life, respiratory system (lungs), the mind/brain, chaotic life, fearing diagnosis, troubled life, hidden medical issue, vague diagnosis, weather system, doubting healthcare system, addiction, fearful of doctors (white-coat syndrome), insecure about your body, uncertain medical treatment, scared to take medicine, hidden life, confused spiritually, mental health, head in the clouds

7. Snake: toxic spiritual connection, problematic life, constricted healthcare system, tunnel system, problematic growth, elimination (bowels) system, malignant, plumbing system, poisonous roots, complicated life, constricted growth, caduceus, constricted body (arthritis), need more time, poisoning, complicated diagnosis, lying about a medical condition / health, issues with health, cheating the system

8. Coffin: dark forest, bad blood, underground healthcare system, deathly ill, no cure, dark spiritual connection, bad blood circulation, denied healthcare, loss of life, grave illness, deadwood, musculoskeletal system, letting go of life, buried alive, ill/sick body, buried roots, dead body, empty life, bad diagnosis

9. Bouquet: wonderful health, surprising diagnosis, herbalism, beautiful spiritual connection, enjoying life, beautiful body, celebration of life, flowering tree, the face, beautiful bouquet/ flowers, grateful to be alive, beautiful tree, pleasant diagnosis, herbal medicine, special tree, beauty of nature, gift of life, plant medicine, a specialist (medical)

10. Scythe: cutting a tree, broken system, severing blood ties, cutting cords (spiritually), risking life and limb, broken healthcare system, fall/autumn tree, decimated body, removed from the system, dividing/splitting DNA strands, divorced life, surgery, emergency medicine, wound/

cut (on the body), broken body, removing a growth, severing a spiritual connection, risky surgery, decimating healthcare, taking a life, decimating forests/trees/nature, split system, broken DNA sequence, splitting logs, broken spiritually, sudden/unexpected diagnosis, broken life, emergency system

11. Whip: sex life, aggressive growth, reproductive system, aggressive medicine/drugs/therapeutics, back-to-back treatments, pattern of growth, athletic body, aggressive medical treatment, sexual health, exercise the body, intermittent medical treatments, sexual diagnosis, questioning a medical treatment, conflicting diagnosis

12. Birds: nervous disorder, talking to trees, double life, throat/esophagus, discussing life, talking to a medical/healthcare professional, anxiety, hypochondriac, nervousness, anxious about a diagnosis, restless life, two diagnosis, talking to ancestors, calling the doctor, couple has a spiritual connection, rumored ailment

13. Child: small tree, capillary system, growing, shallow roots, short life, weak medicine, new spiritual connection, weak DNA strands, feeble body, minor health issue, small growth, weak immune system, weak blood, short lived, small life, sapling, weak spiritual connection, new diagnosis

14. Fox: avoiding doctors/healthcare, faking a medical condition, fraudulent system, practical life/living, suspicious medication/drugs, avoiding medication, fake medication/drugs (placebo), stealthy medical issue, caution with medicine/drugs, careful with medical treatments, cautious living, pseudo diagnosis, avoiding a medical procedure, surviving, scamming the system, faking spirituality, suspicious of doctors, avoiding life, cautious diagnoses

15. Bear: big life, digestive health, strong medicine, strong health/vitality, muscular body, huge growth, strong blood, powerful body, intensive care, strong DNA strands, more time, strong tree, gastrointestinal (digestive) system, strong spiritual connection, major system, strong roots, very slow, stomach, forced healthcare, major health issue, large body, powerful treatment

16. Stars: etheric body, high life (living), improving health, computer system, great body, online healthcare, high blood pressure, heavenly bodies, blessed life, harmonious spiritual connection, digitally enhancing life/body, future generations, amazing health, great growth, eternal life (immortality), great life, best system, luminous body, vast system, astral body, universal digital system, vast forest, infinite lifetimes, of an extended time, future life, improving medical condition, enhancing DNA, exposing healthcare, improving health, beyond the trees, hopeful diagnosis, online system, Nirvana

17. Stork: returning health, evolving spirituality, reincarnation, change in diagnosis, creation of life, evolution, baby growing (pregnancy), recurring health issue, the legs/feet, changes in the body, mutations in DNA, recurring diagnosis, changing medication/drugs, shift in health, dancer's/graceful body, cycling through the system, spring tree, rearranging DNA, quiet life, returning to life, progressive health

18. Dog: therapy takes time, immune system, guided by spirit, the nose, protected trees/forest, relying on medication/drugs, following a system, therapeutic/therapy, investigating a diagnosis/

medication, pay attention to health, friendly nature, following medical advice, reliable healthcare, help/guided by ancestors, diagnostic, trusting doctors / medical advice

19. Tower: city life, traditional medicine, the spine, hermit life, defending your spirituality, single/solitary life, government system, withdrawn from life, government-controlled medication/drugs, lonely life, ambitious life, past spiritual connection, government-controlled healthcare, self-absorbed life, government isolation center (medical)

20. Garden: average body, societal healthcare, common medical practice/procedure, average life, public healthcare system, general medicine, populace health, common ancestors, social network, communal system, everyone's well-being, social system, common diagnosis, outdoor tree, group healthcare, public system, social life, community well-being, communal living

21. Mountain: hard life, challenging health, blocked system, limited growth, postponed/interrupted medical treatment, distant ancestor, limited medically, distant blood ties, delayed growth, permanent roots, challenging life, hard on the body, permanent spiritual connection, hardwood, interrupted growth, tough diagnosis, remote living, climbing trees

22. Paths: unusual DNA, between medical treatments, planning your life, unusual ancestor, strange growth, between lives, unusual life, strange spirituality, many medications, between trees, choosing a medical treatment, strange blood type, separate system, unusual diagnosis, strange ailment, road to health, path to spirituality, different medicine, unusual treatment, unfamiliar ancestor, optional medical treatment, path to healing, at the crossroads of life, adventurous life, unusual blood

23. Mice: atrophy, ruining your/their health, depleted immune system, diseased/rotted tree, low blood pressure, damaged body, corrupted healthcare, losing blood, fading life force, spreading roots, lymphatic system, declining, less time, ruining your/their life, diseased body, sabotaging health, deteriorating health, corrupt system, low life, damaged DNA, messy life, fading life force, stressful diagnosis, sordid life, unclean body, losing your/their life, unhealthy

24. Heat: compassionate care, the heart, passion for medicine, giving medical attention, heartfelt diagnosis, heartfelt spiritual connection, passion for healing, giving tree, zest of life, vigor, relationship grows, dating life, giving nature, romantic spiritual connection, loves nature/trees, romantic life, lover's well-being, hugging trees, forgiving nature, giving blood

25. Ring: continuous growth, surrounded by trees, complete diagnosis, bound by blood, full circle (of life), whole body, connection (spiritual), entire life, ongoing treatment, surrounded by nature, whole DNA, entire generation, complete medical check, committed to getting healthy, agreeing to medical treatment, connecting DNA, married spiritually, proposed medical treatment, dedicated to medicine, offering more time (extension), connecting with nature, wholesome

26. Book: unknown medical condition, secret spiritual connection, specialist (medical), informatics (healthcare), expert medical opinion, informative diagnostic, information system, researching ancestors, memorial tree, chapter of life, remembering a life, researching a diagnosis, discovering a spiritual connection, knowledge in medicine/healthcare, unknown ailment, studying spirituality, book of life, researching natural medicine, training in healthcare/medicine, memoir, facts of life

27. Letter: communication system, notable ancestor, emailed medical documents, written diagnosis, emailed medical results, writing/blogging about spirituality, handwritten prescription, emailed DNA results, communicating with ancestors, scheduling doctor/medical appointments, postal/mail system, certificate of health (family tree), writing/blogging about health/medicine, advertising drugs/medicine, list of medication, reviewing a doctor, written prescription, data analytics, certificate of ancestry

28. Man: shaman, male system, virile man, natural man, male lineage, medicine man, male physician, male ancestor, healthy man, spiritual man, patient (male), male DNA, doctor (male), spiritual connection with a male, male/masculine body, blood ties with a male, masculine spirituality, male health

29. Woman: healer, female system, fruitful woman, natural woman, female lineage, medicine woman, female physician, female ancestor, healthy woman, spiritual woman, patient (female), female DNA, doctor (female), spiritual connection with a female, female/feminine body, blood ties with a female, feminine spirituality, female health

30. Lily: mature/older body, geriatric medicine/healthcare, old medication/drugs, private healthcare system, old blood, peaceful life, discreet spiritual connection, aging over time, cooling system, rest of your life, old medical system, aging body, retirement life, private life, age-related diagnosis, old age, private health, discreet diagnosis, outdated system, winter body, clinical, cold-blooded, retired from medicine/healthcare

31. Sun: energy system, vitality, renewed health, happy life, firewood, hot-blooded, real growth, confident in a medical treatment, true blood, conscientious living, truly living, the physical body, an actual tree, real medicine, true spiritual connection, real growth, really natural, true vitality, real life, energetic body, good diagnosis, energy healing, summer body, yearly medical checkup (physical), good life

32. Moon: feeling healthy, manifesting, spell for health, creative system, monthly checkup (health), feeling alive, emotional well-being, feeling spiritually connected, feeling rooted, emotional growth, creative life, emotional body, monthly blood (mensuration), nightlife, manifesting health, spirituality, influenced medically, phases of life, divination system, apparent spiritual connection, fantasy life, spiritual healing, charmed life, endocrine system

33. Key: privileged healthcare, access to medicine/drugs, karmic healing, affluent blood ties, honoring ancestors, definitely medical, a cure, revealing blood work, fated spiritual connection, revealing a medical condition, access to the system, honoring a life, respecting nature, honoring blood ties, answers (diagnosis), respecting the body, karmic spiritual connection, key system, destined/fated spiritual connection, importance on health, open spiritually, access to healthcare, open system, answers via DNA, privileged life, way out of the system, definite growth, resolving a health issue, free life/living

34. Fish: expensive medicine, blood, credit system, deeply spiritual, financial system, urinary (excretory) system, business growth, money tree, business health, expensive healthcare, deep spiritual connection, business life, deep woods, flowing blood, financial well-being, business system, exchanging DNA, cash/currency system, water system / watershed, prosperous life, investment growth, interest (financial), aquatic health, cost of living

35. Anchor: firmly planted, stable health, secure system, grounded (spiritually), routine checkup (medical), stable life, stagnant growth, solid spiritual connection, staying healthy, remaining time, still living, hanging on to life, keeping well, still vital, keeping it natural, stable DNA, staying alive, preserving the body, still slow, saving a life, secure system, enduring life, holding on for dear life

36. Cross: painful life, terrible health, overburdened healthcare system, obligated life, disappointing health, fatigued, cursed ancestors, difficult life, exhausted / burned out, disappointing growth, insufferable health, regretting a medical procedure, miserable life, terrible system, crossed spiritual connections, difficult diagnosis, disappointing life

These trees which he plants, and under whose shade he shall never sit, he loves them for themselves, and for the sake of his children and his children's children, who are to sit beneath the shadow of their spreading boughs.

—Hyacinthe Lyon

6. Clouds

Swirling billows of moodiness, a vague confusion in the mind
Lighting crashes leaving remnants, of troubling thoughts left behind
Sadness and doubts overwhelming, feels like I'm chasing the wind
Trying to overcome depression, as madding FEAR looks on and grins

DESCRIPTION

Light and dark Clouds emerge behind a blistery wall of rain while the tempest continues to rage on, howling into the wind. You feel the air charged with an electrical current as the storm continues to gather in strength, mirroring the turbulent thoughts swirling and churning, hidden within the recess of your mind. The air bears a menacing omen that something terrible could be unleashed at any moment; this is a very ominous scene foreshadowing many unfavorable events. A deluge of rain falls, providing essential nourishment to all life; every raindrop brings a promise of renewal and rebirth. Salty cathartic tears slip down your cheeks as you witness this natural weather phenomenon making you, too, feel cleansed and transformed. You release all fears into the storm, accompanied by all things that no longer serve you, and you hear these words whispered in the wind: "This too shall pass."

As if by magick, out of the sinister Clouds an albatross appears, soaring to dizzying heights, graced by the remarkable ability to remain calm while manipulating the currents of the wind. This enchanted bird demonstrates how to navigate the up-and-down drafts, by not fighting the wind when caught up in the whirlwinds of life, but instead using them to thrive and fly even higher to freedom above the Clouds.

Below, a ledge juts out of a rock cliff, symbolic of looking at a situation from above. At this vantage point you see things differently, and just maybe you can find the elusive silver lining peeking out from the obscured darkness of the Clouds. A stark tree sits on the ledge, illustrating that everything moves in cycles, since there is a natural order and rhythm to life. Upon first glance, this tree appears lifeless and dank, but as you lay your hand upon its rough grayed bark, you feel the life force pulsing within, a strong and steady beat of its primal heart. Like you, the tree is only resting, and when the time is right, it will bloom profusely with sweet-smelling blossoms to usher in a new season, chasing away any remnants of sadness left behind.

The perfect number 6 is depicted here on the Clouds card. The number 6 is synonymous with harmony and balance. Sixes generally reveal a solution because they symbolize pathways; just like the Clouds card, the 6 reveals a silver lining that brings enlightenment pointing you in the right direction.

KEYWORDS

Confusion, sadness, demeanor, misunderstandings, doubt, uncertainty, clouded judgment, mood, chaos, vagueness, bad weather, insecurity, depression, the mind, hidden, fear, troubles, addictions, obscured, air, unstable, misplaced, mindset, temperamental, behavior, thoughts, lost, passing by, attitude

TIMING

The Clouds card is associated with the number 6, which brings us to the month of June—six days, six weeks, or six months, if the Mountain is present. The Clouds is also a transient card, since clouds are in constant motion. So is any situation or issue; remember in that moment that "this too shall pass."

MEANING

When the Clouds come rolling in, it's important to remind yourself they are transient in nature, and with time, they will blow on by. Just like your thoughts, they will pass on by if only you step aside and let them go. Unstable in nature, Clouds obscure things, making them seem lost and hidden, but remember the temporary nature of Clouds; things may be concealed or misplaced, but not for long.

Foreshadowing gloom and doom, the Clouds card cautions you of trouble brewing in the air, blocking out light, resulting in a sensation of melancholy amplifying any feelings of gray sadness and despair.

The Clouds card resides within the mind, causing confusion and self-doubt as it harbors those fears creating mental health issues. Then, before you know it, sadness brings about depression and uncertainty, resulting in clouded judgment. Being a dark card, when the Clouds appear in a reading it can be quite ominous, but fear not, for beyond the thick veil of depression lies a silver lining. Perspective is everything; be like the albatross and look at the situation from above; remember this is temporary, and the sun will always shine through. It's just a matter of time.

CLOUDS IN LOVE

When speaking about romantic matters, when the Clouds card appears, it brings an air of uncertainty and confusion into your love life, filled with doubts about the longevity of the relationship. This will be a trying period of time, causing you much concern, fearful that your partner is hiding something from you. If single, take the time to work on yourself first; see if you are ready to welcome love into your life.

CLOUDS IN CAREER

Instability shrouding your career causes doubts in where you are heading; be very leery about situations unfolding around you, for something is being hidden from you. When the Clouds appear in a reading, it is indicative of contemplation of a change in your vocation, or you are too much in your head when it comes to work.

CLOUDS IN WELLNESS

A troubled mind sprinkled with depression, a touch of sadness, and a dab of fear swirls around the Clouds card. Being a card of air, the Clouds card is often connected with respiratory conditions, especially when accompanied by the Tree card. This is the quintessential card of mental health in all its forms, emotional facets, and complexities that affect the mind and one's well-being.

CLOUDS IN FINANCES

Bringing doubts to any financial situation, uncertainty about finances, and financial decisions.

CLOUDS IN MODERN DAY

Head in the Clouds, Cloud storage, having a black-or-white attitude, mental health.

AFFIRMATION

I choose to let go of all the false narratives I play over and over in my mind; I let go and trust that this cloud will pass.

CARTOMANCY: KING OF CLUBS

King of Clubs can indicate a new man appearing in your life soon. This reliable and stable businessman will be hyperfocused on his work. The King of Clubs represents a male boss or a best friend, who is very knowledgeable on a multitude of topics and enjoys letting you know in conversations just how smart he is. This King loves being social and garnering all the attention, but just like the Clouds, he's ruled by the element of Air, so he is always in his head—the quintessential overthinker. Many might question his ability to be loyal in a relationship, but once committed, the King of Clubs is trustworthy and loyal to a fault, since his word is his bond, priding himself on these values that extend well into his work ethic.

1. Rider: racing thoughts/mind, acting crazy, visitor passing by, passing on by, acting chaotic, young man's thoughts, acting vague, first impression, acting confused, acting scared, initial thoughts, incoming bad weather, the other man's thoughts, broadcasting the weather

2. Clover: very temporary, a rainbow, nutter/crazy, wild thoughts, carefree attitude, temporary madness/insanity, country air, briefly lost, fleeting thoughts, casual attitude, comical behavior, luck passes by, temporary lapse in judgment, transient, wild storm/weather, fading fear, easing of the mind, chance misunderstanding, happy thoughts, out of the blue, wild behavior, passing by, temperamental, impulsive behavior, a brief depression, easy breezy

3. Ship: ship passes you by, distant storm, travel confusion, leaving troubles behind, international troubles, distant mind, car trouble, travel addiction, lifting depression, bad weather at sea / while traveling, moving on, trading addictions, distant thoughts, traveling by air, left behind in confusion, far-off troubles, overseas chaos, driving through weather, leave of your senses, navigating through fear, steering your thoughts into a different direction, driving fear, riding out the storm, directing your thoughts, leaving

4. House: family passing by, a place of sadness, comforting thoughts, family member is uncertain, familiar behavior, a place that's hidden, family member has an addiction, inside someone's thoughts/mind, a place of fear, branding troubles, family troubles, house is depressing, family member is depressed, familiar thoughts, real estate uncertainty, comfortable demeanor, relative is trouble, home environment, domestic disturbance

5. Tree: healthful mindset, fresh air, spiritual thoughts, healthful behavior, growing confusion, the lungs, growing sadness/depression, deeply rooted addiction, growing fear, slow mind, growing misunderstanding, deeply rooted fears, healthful thoughts, growing storm, mental health, natural thought, oxygen, growing addiction, psychiatrist (PhD)

7. Snake: evil thoughts, constricted airway, slave to addiction, poisoned mind, unstable other woman, twister/tornado, nefarious behavior, asphyxiation, jealous behavior, twisted mind, toxic drugs, the other woman's thoughts, twisted thoughts, complex addiction, unstable pipes/wiring, toxic attitude, destructive behavior, pollution (toxic air), temptation (addiction), problematic behavior, cheating behaviors, complex thoughts, problematic addiction, narrow minded, diabolical

8. Coffin: dark thoughts, dead air, pessimistic, somber thoughts, dark clouds roll in, let go of sadness, dark deadly addiction, dreadful behavior, negativity, dark depression, bad behavior, morbid mindset, sick mind, final thoughts, let go of doubt, nonexistent mind (brain-dead), poor air quality, sorrows, ill thoughts, silencing doubts, bereaved, negative attitude, darkness, death by addiction (overdose), grief-stricken, mournful, grave thoughts, deadly storm, somber mood

9. Bouquet: facing fears, pleasant thoughts, enjoying rain, gifted mind, surprising behavior, beautiful weather, facing your doubts, pleasant attitude, charming behavior, sweet sentiment, enjoying the weather, the occasion past, show-off, weed/marijuana, artistic mind, colorful thoughts, appreciative behavior, special weather statement, aesthetically gloomy, color of gray, frame of mind, perfect storm

10. Scythe: split personality, destructive addiction, reckless behavior, autumn weather, detached mood, break in the clouds, splitting headache (migraine), violent thoughts, threatening behavior, collecting your/their thoughts, divided mind, remove doubt, gathering troubles, broken mind, dangerous addiction, breaking your head, hurt, destructive behavior, unexpected addiction, weaponizing the weather, suicidal thoughts

11. Whip: sexual insecurities, pattern of misunderstandings, habitual behavior, active mind, competitive mindset, violent thoughts, sexual behavior, inquiring mind, violent behavior, repetitive thoughts, argumentative demeanor, throwing shade, aggressive behavior, temper tantrum, hurtful thoughts, violent storm, repetitive user (drugs), questioning your/their sanity, thunderstorm, combative mood, compulsive sexual behavior, hurtful demeanor, sexual thoughts, pattern of addiction, sexy mood, inflicting chaos

12. Birds: inquisitive mind, nerves, noisy mind, hectic thoughts, speak your mind, flying in bad weather, voice inside your head, nervous behavior, restless demeanor, cuckoo/loony, busy brain, talking nonsense, up in the air, vocalizing thoughts, verbal misunderstanding, anxiety, turbulence, rumors pass on by, couples in trouble, speaking before you think, excited mood, talking about mental health, vocalizing your fears, chaos, codependency, curious behavior, in two minds

13. Child: immature mind, child is depressed, playful behavior, minor confusion, immature behavior, simple minded, small storm, weak mind, slightly addicted, inadequate, a little doubtful, childish fears, slightly lost, innocent thoughts, insecure behavior, minor addiction, in a bit of trouble, shy demeanor, weak storm, vulnerable behavior, slight disturbance, immaturity, playing hide and seek

14. Fox: scheming thoughts, eluding trouble, cunning mind, manipulative behavior, suspicious behavior, guilty behavior, manipulating your thoughts, avoid drugs, suspicious minds, faking mental illness, cunning behavior, sneaky thoughts, predatory behavior, untrustworthy behavior, manipulating the weather (HAARP), avoiding trouble, stealth mode, sneaky behavior, cautious mind, well hidden, obscured, avoidance behavior, manipulated mind, paranoid

15. Bear: powerful mind, dominant behavior, overbearing thoughts, more chaos, intense fear, overbearing attitude, more doubt, assertive behavior, major chaos, forceful demeanor, more addictions, intimidating demeanor, very sad, more uncertainty, major addiction, bold attitude, immense sadness, big trouble, massive shade, intense storm, very doubtful, strong addiction, major misunderstanding, more confusion, very addictive, strong minded, very vague, massively unhinged, megalomaniac

16. Stars: inspirational thoughts, positive attitude, scientific mind, improving attitude, seeing beyond fear, inspiring behavior, philosophical mind, harmonious thoughts, clearing clouds/storm, wishful thinking, technical mind, lightening, exposing addiction, great weather, enhanced mind, on best behavior, great temperament, forecast (weather), uplifting thoughts, online addiction, improving mood, alleviating doubt, clearing up misunderstandings, improving troubles, alleviating fear, exposing what's hidden, elevated thoughts, found (someone/something) lost, visionary

17. Stork: graceful behavior, quiet mind, changed demeanor, returning depression, evolving thoughts, spring weather, thin air, dancing in the rain, recurring storms, relapsing (addiction), wandering mind, drifting mind, transition, progressive thinking, shift your mindset

18. Dog: smell of rain, supportive attitude, smell of fear, submissive behavior, loyal demeanor, friendly behavior, investigative manner, psychologist, nosy behavior, trusting behavior, follow your mind, help with depression, sponsor (addiction), supporting mental health, therapist, looking for trouble, followers mindset, protecting mental health, watch your attitude, guarded thoughts, trusting demeanor, protective behavior

19. Tower: defensive attitude, city air, stubborn attitude, single minded, past behavior, withdrawn demeanor, self-justifying thoughts, ambitious mindset, loneliness, ridged attitude, officially lost, aloof demeanor, withdrawal (addiction/drugs), controlling behavior, institution for mental health, selfish behavior, arrogant demeanor, self-doubt, past addiction, judgmental, established fears, conscientious

20. Garden: common/normal behavior, general doubt, common mindset, social behavior, common fear, hive mentality, people stored in the cloud, outcast, general misunderstanding, common misunderstanding, general confusion, common addiction, mass clouded judgment, mediocrity, group mind, public mental health, general depression, everybody's lost, crowded mind, mass fear

21. Mountain: made up your mind, impassive insecurities, blocked/restricted airway, delayed mind, challenging behavior, unchanged mind, stubborn attitude, permanent sadness, distant thunder, labored breath, hard-headed, impassive misunderstanding, delayed chaos, distant bad weather, blocked thoughts, challenging fears, stalemate, challenging addiction, isolating behavior

22. Paths: strange thoughts, multiple personalities, bizarre behavior, adventurous demeanor, indecisive, weird mood, unusual weather, many thoughts, unusual attitude, multiple addictions, many doubts, making up your mind, strange addiction, at the crossroads, unusual fear, multiple phobias, uncertainty, many fears, kooky

23. Mice: scatterbrain, costly addiction, losing cognition, spreading fear, eating away at you, unthinking, deteriorating mind, destructive behavior, unhinged, obsessive behavior, headaches (worries), unmindful, damaging addiction, disappeared, dirty mind, causing confusion, losing your/their mind, damaging storm, less oxygen, depression, thoughtlessness, dissolving doubt, obsessive addiction, disturbance, unstable (mentally), jeopardizing mental health, cheesy mood, unknown, mania (obsession)

24. Heart: feeling confused (romantically), love is on the mind, flirty behavior, loving thoughts, kind demeanor, romantic mood, relationship mindset, passionate thoughts, forgive a misunderstanding, generous mood, affectionate demeanor, heart wrenching, sentimental, love stormy weather, lover's misunderstanding, kind attitude, a lover's on your mind, interested demeanor, forgiving mood, intimate thoughts, lovely temperament, thoughtful, giving mood

25. Ring: whirlwind, continual misunderstanding, ongoing behavior, complete chaos, surrounded by confusion, ongoing doubt, cyclone, totally hidden, dedicated mindset, continual clouded judgment, ongoing chaos, surrounded by trouble, ongoing depression, completely confused, ongoing addiction, continuous thoughts, going in circles (lost), totally depressed, completely addicted, married behavior, totally lost

26. Book: academic mind, secret thoughts, remembering, researching mental illness, intelligent, nostalgic mood, well hidden, smart thinking, logical mind, studying psychology, knowledgeable, secret addiction, memories, cognizance, secret hidden well, a journal

27. Letter: results are vague, letter lost, writing is confusing, results are disappointing, text/message is misunderstood, results misinterpreted, sending trouble (your way), journaling, blogging about mental health, writing down thoughts, results for mental illness, written in the wind, text causes confusion

28. Man: confused man, man's thoughts, masculine demeanor, man full of doubt, shady man, unstable man, depressed man, troubled man, moody man, lost man, temperamental man, sad man, male attitude, hidden man, that man is trouble!

29. Woman: confused lady, woman's thoughts, feminine demeanor, woman full of doubt, shady lady, unstable woman, depressed woman, troubled lady, moody woman, sad woman, temperamental woman, female attitude, lost woman, hidden woman, that woman is trouble!

30. Lily: mature mind, peaceful demeanor, rational thoughts, mature behavior, snowstorm, thoughtful, level headed, conservative attitude, calm mood, chilled attitude, restrained demeanor, winter weather, cold air, peaceful thoughts, rational mind, maturity, frozen with fear, private thoughts, inclement weather

31. Sun: happy thoughts, summer weather, confident attitude, good mood, conscious thoughts, courageous mindset, right as rain, sun shower, hot/warm air, true thoughts, actually confused, the sun makes everything better, days go by, true demeanor, hot-headed

32. Moon: subconscious mind, feeling scared, creative mood, confused, being influenced, imagination, emotional behavior, feeling uncertain, Creative Cloud (Photoshop), intuitive mind, feeling desperate, moody, feeling depressed, emotionally unstable, hypnosis, feeling lost, intuition, feeling emotional, dreamy, moonstruck, months pass by

33. Key: answers, way out of trouble, uncovering addiction, free from doubt, door to the mind, way out of addiction, free from fear, privileged attitude, key thoughts, open minded, respectful behavior, passing storm, uncovering something hidden, revealing thoughts, unlocking the mind, significant misunderstanding, solution to addiction

34. Fish: expensive addiction, deep confusion, business mindset, deep depression, alcohol addiction, deep trouble, resourceful mindset, deep thoughts, deep sadness, deep undercover, deep mind, rain cloud, deep fear, drunken stupor, deep shadow

35. Anchor: heavy thoughts, remains lost, lingering troubles, persistent thoughts, unchanged mind, stable mood, still using (drugs), unchanged behavior, still confused, lasting sadness, persistent addiction, stuck in your mind, paralyzed with fear, remains hidden, holding on to fear, still thinking, serious trouble, stuck in depression, downcast, stuck mindset

36. Cross: fatigued mind, disappointing behavior, difficult attitude, "this too shall pass," victim mentality, shame, angst, shameful behavior, scandalous thoughts, regretful behavior, terrible mindset, miserable mood, terrible addiction, miserable, exhausting behavior, regretful, testing for drugs/substances, sinful thoughts, testing for mental illness

Don't give up when dark times come.
The more storms you face in life, the stronger
you'll be. Hold on. Your greater is coming.

—Germany Kent

7. Snake

Slithering tongue so tempting, forked with jealously and lies
Seductively alluring I deceive you, as I lie between her thighs
An evil deception so becoming, continuing my guise as I betray
Poison desires of greediness is why I will never let you walk away

DESCRIPTION

Coiled around a desiccated branch of an apple tree, the venomous Snake lies in wait—riddled with anticipation, ready to strike on her unsuspecting prey. Curvaceous and alluring, the feminine aspect of the Snake slithers with a persistent purpose, mesmerizing you with her sensual undulating dance of seduction. She draws you closer and closer, enchanting you with desire; her striking red scales flash a warning to stop and tread carefully, because the Snake cannot be trusted; in the end she will always betray you. On the dried-out rosebush, the spiky thorn warns you not to be captivated by her appeal, because something so striking on the outside can be evil on the inside.

The frosty scene before you evokes feelings of dank coldness akin to the Snake's cold-blooded nature, for she values self-preservation above all. The Snake uncoils, flaunting her calculating narcissistic, jealous energy, often finding herself in toxic situations caused by her own cheating nature. Self-absorbed with a single-minded focus can lead to questionable behaviors and twisted love triangles. The cobweb reminds you that the Snake will weave a web of lies in order to mislead and deflect you away from the truth or the real matter at hand.

As the embodiment of Earth's most primal forces of creation, the Snake is honored on the ancient symbol of the caduceus for its powerful transformative ability to regenerate by shedding its skin—and not only to survive, but to thrive the rebirth. The ruby-red apple is there to remind you of the forces of evil that exist; we cannot forget about poison apples in fables, dripping with venom from the needlelike fangs of the Snake just waiting for an unsuspecting victim. What better way to deceive with the symbol of life and sacred food to the gods.

Bearing the number 7, snakes are aloof and harbor many secrets, making them seem mystical, seductive, and at times standoffish, always reflecting and deflecting like the scales on her body. At best, the 7 brings problems, but also solutions; as a natural healer, it's connected with the number of chakras awakening the serpent within as you raise the kundalini energy.

KEYWORDS

Complications, seduction, betrayal, affairs, the other woman, enemy, desire, toxic, lies, envy, problems, deception, attraction, transformation, twisted, jealousy, issues, temptation, alluring, wires and pipes, dark-haired woman, enticing, constricting, poison, evil, complex

TIMING

The Snake card is the seventh card in the Lenormand and indicates a timing of July, seven days, seven weeks, or seven months; when the Mountain card is present, it can mean up to seven years.

MEANING

The Snake twists into your life, bringing deception and betrayals, cautioning you to take notice. Traditionally representing the "other woman," this is definitely not the card you want to see when asking about a relationship. Do not be tempted to immediately assign the most nefarious connotation to the card, though, for at times it can simply mean "a dark-haired woman." As one of the more evil cards in the Lenormand, the Snake card presents challenges and brings a complicated twist to all situations that will test your virtue and tempt you in ways you never thought possible.

Any way you look at it, when the Snake appears, it's viewed upon as a bad omen; look to the surrounding cards for insight to the nature of the situation.

SNAKE IN LOVE

In love, the Snake primarily brings seduction and temptation and permeates with the connotation of cheating—and then uses lies to cover up the betrayal. The Snake often represents the other woman or a female rival. Often bringing out the worst qualities in a relationship, such as jealousy, envy, and mistrust, these are all qualities she portrays. A Snake person is generally interested in a short-term, self-serving relationship that is steeped heavily in lies and betrayals, so beware aware when the Snake appears, for they are cheaters.

SNAKE IN CAREER

The Snake brings complications and upset to any business, job, or career: a problematic and toxic work environment riddled with lies, jealousy, and backstabbing. You need to be adaptive and flexible in your business dealings, but at the same time keen of a malicious intelligent rival in your workplace.

SNAKE IN WELLNESS

The Snake represents the bowels, the intestines, or the skin, since the Snake sheds its skin. A striking feature is also the forked tongue of a Snake, so this card is accosted with the tongue. This card brings complications of a medical nature, or a complex medical condition; it can even denote an STD picked up from cheating, especially if the Whip is around. The Snake is a very ancient symbol of medicine exhibited on the caduceus due to its transformative nature.

SNAKE IN FINANCES

The Snake makes shrewd and intelligent financial decisions, but always with their own best interests at heart. It is indicative of a complex financial portfolio, a problematic financial plan, or complicated finances. When the Snake slithers into your wallet, beware of someone being so self-absorbed that they are inclined to lie about money and financial situations.

SNAKE IN MODERN DAY

A mistress, pole dancing, a stripper, burlesque. Kundalini.

AFFIRMATION

I shed my skin and transform; there is always a better me underneath.

CARTOMANCY: QUEEN OF CLUBS

Traditionally a middle-aged woman of dark hair, the Queen of Clubs is a socialite who craves attention; she is alluring and irresistible to the opposite sex, but in a relationship, she can be quite jealous and petty just like the Snake. When she doesn't get her way, she becomes harsh, demeaning, and incensed and takes any rejection as a personal betrayal. With an abundance of life experience and quick wit, this Queen Bee can be very convincing and has little patience for those she deems beneath her, definitely not worthy of her attention. In work, the Queen of Clubs can represent someone who is self-employed or the boss or works in the medical field.

LENORMAND SNAKE COMBINATIONS

1. Rider: first affair/betrayal, fast attraction, first lie, acting seductive, needy dark-haired woman, first problem, young dark-haired woman, news of an affair, young other woman, rapid transformation, other man is lying, fast enemies, acting jealous

2. Clover: brief/short-term affair, fleeting problems, spontaneous lie, temporary issue, easy problem, brief complication, wild lie, comical twist, quickly seduced, games are toxic, small opportunity to cheat, temporary deception, gambling/gaming issue, casual affair, spontaneous cheating, fooling around

3. Ship: car problems, moving on from the lies, navigating problems, travel issues, international problems, leaving the other woman, international threat, distant dark-haired woman, navigating the lies, moving on from betrayal, driving to see the other woman

4. House: house problems, real estate issues, house of lies, family member is lying, domestic issue, family of liars, house-wiring problems, family betrayal, domesticated dark-haired lady, home transformation, house of the other woman, relative is jealous, branding issues, family lie

5. Tree: natural attraction, deeply rooted evil, slow transformation, health issue, physical attraction, growing attraction, deeply rooted jealousy, spiritual issue, growing lie, deeply rooted betrayal, bloodlust, deeply rooted affair, DNA strand, blood enemy, branching out lies, blood poisoning, physical affair

6. Clouds: multiple desires, covering up lies, misplaced jealousy, shady dark-haired woman, passing attraction, lost desire, passing problems, mental health issues, desperate lie, hidden issue, mentally twisted, covering up the affair, hiding the other woman, concealed betrayal, hidden desires, troublemaker

8. Coffin: nemesis, bad complications, final betrayal, letting go of the affair, mortal enemy, horrible lies, bad problem, black-haired other woman, dark desires, ending the affair, asphyxiation (death by), last lie, letting go of the other woman, buried pipes/wires, deadly

9. Bouquet: beautiful transformation, surprising attraction, fancy lie, pleasurable desire, beautiful lie, envy, inviting an enemy, surprise complication, beautiful other woman, special affair, charming like a snake, enjoying the allure, sweet seduction, face of a cheater

10. Scythe: sudden enemies, urgent problem/issue, dangerous woman, vaccine complications, burst pipes, sudden twist, cutting off the other woman, divorced/separated dark-haired woman, risky temptation, broke off the affair, dangerous issue, brutal lies, dangerous enemy, severing ties with the other woman, removing the problem, split wires, irrevocable betrayal, dangerous, threatening enemy, sharp tongue

11. Whip: hurtful lies, sexual affair, kink, habitual cheater, sexually tempted, repetitive issue, erotic/sexual asphyxiation, sex, serial cheater, viscous, aggressive enemy, pattern of lying, sex with a dark-haired woman, repetitive affairs, sexually complicated, aggressive dark-haired woman, IBS (irritable-bowel syndrome), sexually enticing, aggressive dark-haired woman, repetitive lies, sexual issues, intermittent affair, enraged

12. Birds: couple of affairs, two-timing, talking to the other woman, discussing issues, sibling rivalry, telling lies, sings like a canary (betrayer), anxious about a problem, rumored affair, conversing seductively, discussing the affair, gossip, calling the other woman, verbal (phone) affair, rumors of cheating

13. Child: vulnerable target, new desire, tiny problem, innocent attraction, childhood issues, new attraction, minor complication, weak attraction, white lie, slightly jealous, a bit tempted, minor attraction, slightly twisted, small transformation, weakening desire, slight betrayal, tattletale, childish lie

14. Fox: scheming dark-haired woman, cheater, avoiding temptation, sneaky snake, calculated seduction, avoid complications, traitor, avoiding the other woman, coworker's a snake, crafty liar, clever tongue, tricky problem, scheming coworker, calculating enemy, stealthy affair, suspicious dark-haired woman, suspected cheating, employee issues, treacherous, deceptive, escaping the enemy, cautious cheater, feigning attraction, manipulator, liar, premeditated affair

15. Bear: big temptation, food poisoning, major deception, strong desire, weight problem, huge temptation, big problem, anaconda, big betrayal, mommy issues, intense attraction, big bold liar, assertive dark-haired woman, more complications, major affair, bold other woman, huge transformation, more lies, very jealous, overbearing seduction, major issue, increasing problems

16. Stars: exposing the affair, future problems, amazing transformation, exposing evil, vast need, technological issue, see beyond the lies, exposing the cheater, scientific problem, pipe issues, exposing the problem, amazing twist, exposing the other woman, seeing the affair with your own eyes, upgrading wires/plumbing, exposing the enemy, clearing problems, see beyond the issue, computer problems

17. Stork: recurring issue, evolving affair, returning enemy, going back to the other woman, evolving lie, returning problem, recurring affair, long snake, fertility issues, long wire(s)/pipe, changing lie, pregnancy cravings

18. Dog: dog issues, friendship problems, stalking the other woman, friend's a liar, friendly snake, loyalty betrayed, following a cheater, helpful dark-haired woman, reliable wires/pipes, seek help, supporting the transformation, investigating the other woman, following your desire, loyal after cheating, investigating lies, protecting the other woman, guarding the lie, watch for cheating, trust after a betrayal, familiar other woman, therapy for problems, following an enemy, stalking a dark-haired woman

19. Tower: past attraction, defensive dark-haired woman, city sewers/pipes, self-loathing, past affair, a single affair, past enemy, past problem/issue, defending lies, formal affair, established lie, traditional other woman, tall dark-haired lady, backstabber, past lie will come back to bite

20. Garden: average other woman, going out (to cheat), common enemy, online affair, common cheater, group issue, garden snake, common liar, general deception, rendezvous, pubic issue, common problem, general attraction, typical affair, rendezvous with the other woman, cheating, social affair, online cheating, playing the field, public issue

21. Mountain: hard problem, challenging issue, delayed transformation, impassive betrayal, permanent complications, distant dark-haired woman, permanent infidelity, roughing in wires/pipes, challenging enemy, boundaries set for a cheater, obstructed pipes, blocked desire, harsh dark-haired woman, permanent problem, interrupted affair, border issues, harsh lie

22. Paths: many problems, choosing to lie, strange desire, many lies, unusual complications, planning to cheat, strange attraction, many betrayals, unusual transformation, multiple issues, unusual problem, many affairs, unusual dark-haired woman, multiple complications, between affairs, multifaceted lie, choosing to cheat

23. Mice: costly affair, damaging lie, stressful problems, lowly snake, vile, spreading lies, rancid, costly lie, corrupt, weasel, rotten liar, destructive, dissipating allure, crooked, damaging betrayal, rat fink

24. Heart: relationship issues, romantic attraction, dating a liar, forgiving a betrayal, heart problems, dating issues, sensitive problem, relationship lies, forgiving an affair, giving problems, forgiving an enemy, passionate affair, dating a cheater, loves the other woman, a flirt, feeling lied to

25. Ring: ongoing betrayal, continuous problems, ongoing issue, surrounded by temptation, continuing the affair, surrounded by toxicity, ongoing cheating, surrounded by enemies, ongoing complications, ongoing deception, surrounded by evil, ongoing lies, surrounded by lies, surrounded by problems, marital issues

26. Book: logical problem, bookworm, recalling an affair, remembering a dark-haired woman, secret attraction, remembering the lies, historical enemies, educational problems, secret issues, expert liar, unknown affair, memories of the other woman

27. Letter: texting affair, communication problems, message is a lie, texting a dark-haired woman, written lie, texting lies, messaging another woman, card for the other woman, text from another woman

28. Man: seductive man, dishonest man, cheating man, rogue male, male enemy, toxic man, jealous man, snake charmer, deceptive man, a mean man (mean like a snake), snake oil salesman, charlatan, envious man, rake, enticing man, evil man, tempting man, cheating husband, complicated man, problematic man, lying man, betraying a man, cheating with a man

29. Woman: seductive female, dishonest woman, cheating female, rogue female, female enemy, dark-haired female, toxic woman, jealous woman, striking lady, alluring woman, deceptive woman, mean woman (mean like a snake), charlatan (female), sensual woman, the other woman, envious woman, curvy female, enticing woman, evil woman, tempting woman, cheating wife, complicated woman, problematic woman, lying woman, betraying a woman, cheating with a woman, siren

30. Lily: old attraction, experienced liar, mature other woman, restrained desire, discreet affair, old issue, father/grandfather lies, older dark-haired lady, daddy issues, wisdom, mature dark-haired lady, old temptation, past cheating, father cheated, too old to cheat, experienced cheater, discreet issue

31. Sun: successful lie, real problems, good transformation, yes they are lying, holiday/vacation affair, happy problem to have, confident other woman, yes they're cheating, true desire, real issues, true attraction, real transformation, confident dark-haired woman, finding the truth in the lie

32. Moon: spell complications, aware of the affair, emotional needs, feeling jealous, talented liar, skilled cheater, feeling lied to, emotional affair, skilled seducer, emotional attraction, aware of the lie, creative transformation, feeling twisted, emotional issues, feeling constricted, monthly issue, emotional dark-haired woman, occult, creating problems, aware of the problem

33. Key: uncovering issues, definitely toxic, first-world problems, revealing the lie, key issue, definite problem, revealing the betrayal, definitely lying, uncovering the affair, revealing the attraction, uncovering problems, revealing the cheater, karmic issue, definitely cheating

34. Fish: expensive problem, deep desire, alcohol poisoning, business problems, deep lies, financial problems, deeply toxic, deep deception, drinking problem, deep attraction, deep jealousy, deep issues, paying for the lie

35. Anchor: constant issues, lingering complications, still a cheater, holding on tight, enduring the lies, still lying, lingering affair, enduring the betrayal, serious lies, lingering problems, holding on to the affair, enduring the problem, lingering desire, still complicated, staying enemies, keeping up the lie, rope/chain, holding on to the other woman

36. Cross: painful issue, difficult problem, intolerable lies, regret cheating, cursed divorcee, difficult dark-haired woman, sinful, disappointing transformation, Judas, regretting an affair, devilish, terrible lie, shameful betrayal, evil, scandalous affair, regret lying, miserable other woman, terrible problem, tangled, painful betrayal, believing the lie

If you have given up your heart . . . you have already lost. A heartless creature is a loveless creature, and a loveless creature is a beast.

—Stephen King

8. Coffin

Buried in the silent earth, upon this grave I somberly mourn.
Grief ravages throughout my chest; my heart is utterly torn.
This dismal final ending brings about my own earthly demise.
An empty life without you; Angel of Grief, please hear my cries.

DESCRIPTION

A carved sarcophagus encased in limestone possesses immortal properties; a nod to the eternal soul is the final resting place and bestows one last tribute to the life that once was. Obscured by vines, a sweet-faced cherub represents the return to innocence of the deceased; etched at the bottom of the Coffin is a menacing-shaped skull of the "Memento Mori" peering deeply into your soul as a reminder: nary a soul who has ever lived will escape the clutches of death.

Green and red orbs swirl around the Coffin, heralding one's final hour and breath upon Earth; this sweet song of death twirls and dances around the dead. The enchanted dance is the great equalizer and unites everyone; one day you too will dance your final dance.

Vines of ivy cling to the stonework, climbing wild and free, entwining the Coffin in a protective embrace. Unattended, this robust vine will grow into an untamed canopy of darkness, blocking out all the light, denoting that with the gift of life always comes the promise of death. Ivy carries the meaning of perpetual growth and undying affection. Even after one's long gone, their memories still remain dancing in the back of your mind, as this regenerative evergreen continues on with the spiral dance of life, death, and rebirth.

Laid gingerly, there is a single black rose, left by an unseen hand in a gesture of a final farewell. The black petals solemnly drip with tears of grief for the love left behind. If you listen closely, you can hear eerie sounds of sorrowful sobs being choked back in an atmosphere so thick that it threatens to engulf you, robbing you of precious air as you stand there with an empty heart—present yet absent, in a hallowed silence. You fall softly into the deep abyss of emptiness.

Invoking sadness upon sight, the hooded Angel of Grief eternally watches over the Coffin, ensuring the soul a safe flight into the spirit world. As this scene unfolds before you, it stirs something buried within you, reawakening an emptiness, breathing a spark of life of an anguish long forgotten.

The number 8 depicted on the Coffin when turned on its side becomes the symbol of infinity, promising a continuance of life after physical death. The number 8 is known as a balancer of the karmic scales embodying the law of cause and effect. Balancing and harmonious, the number 8 acts as a bridge between the earth plane and spirit world, completing the cycle of life, death, and rebirth. Ruled by Saturn, the number 8 represents the sign of Scorpio, which is the ruler of the house of death.

KEYWORDS

Sorrow, endings, illness, expired, finality, silence, completion, letting go, dread, grief, loss, emptiness, mourning, nothing, death, final outcome, no, bad, negativity, buried, stop, closed, nonexistent, erased, deleted, black, dark, denied, last, box, gone

TIMING

The Coffin card usually has a timing of a few months, and midnight. Since it is the eighth card of the Lenormand, we can read this card as the month of August, eight days, eight weeks, or eight months when the Mountain is present.

MEANING

Everyone will experience a Coffin moment within their lifetime; the energy this card carries is like putting a big period at the end of something, a culmination or final ending. In the rarest of occasions, the Coffin card can foreshadow a physical death, but the surrounding cards must support this. Given that the Coffin represents illness, when death is foretold it doesn't come as a complete surprise, because most times there is a preexisting condition. Being one of the negative cards in the Lenormand, be very aware when the Coffin appears, for it is sure to bring about an end.

There is an air of darkness that surrounds the Coffin, demonstrating that over time, memories begin to fade as life keeps moving forward. Many mistake the Coffin as a card of transformation, equating it to the Death card in the Tarot; this is not the case with the Lenormand. Transformation is left to the Snake; the Coffin is a bad omen stating, "The End."

COFFIN IN LOVE

When the Coffin appears in a love reading, it signifies that a relationship is ending or an aspect of love is ending. Oftentimes it's not a surprise because the relationship was probably rocky at best. Paying attention to the surrounding cards, and with a little bit of soul-searching, you can decide if this is something worth fighting for, or is it time to close this chapter of your life? Don't try to keep someone who doesn't want to stay; it never works.

COFFIN IN CAREER

Denotes the ending of a job or a completion of a project. This is a transitional time, and big changes are foreshadowed at work. When the Coffin is used in reference to a vocation—coroner, medium/necromancer, funeral director, archeologist, cemetery groundskeeper, palliative care or hospice staff, or grief counselors, or any careers involving death or dying—this is exactly what the Coffin is all about.

COFFIN IN WELLNESS

Traditionally, when the Coffin makes an appearance it denotes a serious illness or even the harbinger of death. An important thing to remember is the Coffin alone does not always indicate an actual physical death; it truly depends on the context of the question, the surrounding cards, and the level of expertise of the one interpreting the cards.

COFFIN IN FINANCES

The emphasis at this time should be on the conservation of finances: preserving what you do have rather than focusing on what you do *not* have. When the Coffin shows up here, it brings with it a loss of money, empty bank accounts, or bankruptcy.

COFFIN IN MODERN DAY

Someone who has a preoccupation with death, a taphophile, or a psychic medium. Coffins are also used to preserve or protect the body; sometimes it can be as simple as to refer to the Coffin as a box. The Coffin can denote something buried or underground in nature.

AFFIRMATION

I can feel the love from those who are no longer physically around me; I am loved.

CARTOMANCY: 9 OF DIAMONDS

The 9 of Diamonds represents your state of mind and carries the energy of bad omens and uncertainties with delays. As a card of intuition, it is heavily steeped in psychic abilities, especially in the art of clairvoyance and the ability to *see* the dead. The 9 of Diamonds is viewed as a card of the soul, for once the physical body is gone, the immortal soul is set free.

LENORMAND COFFIN COMBINATIONS

1. Rider: quick outcome, going badly, young man in denial, quick illness, pronounced dead, first loss, beginning of the end, acting dreadful, quick burial, visitation (funeral), news of a death, young man is ill, visiting a grave

2. Clover: quick ending, green box, short period of mourning, informal burial, wild ending, green burial, gambler in denial, quick passing, short-term sickness, luck ends, spontaneous ending, short-term grief, gaining nothing

3. Ship: shipping container, letting go, overseas burial, a hearse, passing illness, leaving it all behind, farewell, faraway gravesite, leaving the dead behind, ferryman (Charon), moving on, overseas death, car died, travel stops, navigating the waves of grief, transporting the deceased/body

4. House: house sale terminated, columbarium, house of death, family death, house is empty, related to the dead, family burial plot, place of mourning, family member remains silent, small building is demolished, family in mourning, hospice, family mausoleum

5. Tree: slow ending, clinically dead, deeply rooted illness, slowly letting go, prolonged outcome, prolonged death, tree pod burial, nerve paralysis, to truly live you must let go, life feels empty, spiritual burial, prolonged illness, slowly dying, cadaver, matter of life and death

6. Clouds: troubling outcome, passing away, lost in grief, fearing death, brain-dead, hidden illness, confusing death, hidden grave, mental illness causes death, pondering death, concealing cause of death, gloomy darkness, troubling illness, overdose death, lost and empty, shady outcome

7. Snake: complex illness, cheating death, unfortunate outcome, evil darkness, poisoned to death, complicated death, strangled to death, complicated ending, tempting death, twisted ending, needing closure, hateful, enemy's grave, snake pit, wanting to die, twisted and dark

9. Bouquet: pleasant outcome, funeral, improving ailment, sweetie box, pallor mortis, gift box, urn, gift of death, facial paralysis, beautiful ending, recovering, surprise ending, flowers for a funeral, grateful for death, displaying the coffin, color black, pleasant burial, enjoys nothing, outfit of the deceased, special ending

10. Scythe: dangerous outcome, separated at the end, stabbed to death, autumn death/burial, breaking the silence, half-couch casket, vaccine(-related) illness, threatening death, gathering silence (ominous), sudden illness, unexpected loss, bludgeoned to death, parted by death, abrupt ending, removing the dead, sudden denial, abruptly gone, obliterated, splitting nothing, inflicting harm/death, automatic NO!

11. Whip: violent death, pattern of negativity, aggressive illness, questioning cause of death, pattern of silence, back-to-back illness, repetitive losses, questionable outcome, angry at the deceased, intermittent silence, back-to-back deaths, beaten to death

12. Birds: birdcage, music box, talking about death, two deaths, noisy death, sound of silence, restless dead, couple buried together, two graves, chickenpox, gossiping about the deceased, eulogy, talking to the dead, chatterbox, calling the dead

13. Child: smallpox, minor loss, precarious final outcome, small grave, childhood illness, small box, newly departed, small ending, minor illness, a bit sorrowful, quiet, a bit empty, minor death, not really (a small no), new death, slightly buried, small coffin, shallow grave, child died, playing dead

14. Fox: calculated silence, suspicious ailment, evading death, tricky ending, avoiding negativity, coworker's death, avoiding an end, fake burial, mistaken corpse, faking an illness, pseudo cause of death, pretending to let go, denial, pseudo grief, survivor's guilt

15. Bears: major illness, immense grief, intense ending, major death/loss, huge denial, recipe box, power of silence, mass grave, big finale, intense grief, big coffin, mother/grandmother in denial, huge emptiness, increased deaths, very bad, a big nothing, major dread, more sorrows, very closed off, big loss, strong negativity, more deaths, big fat NO!

16. Star: positive outcome, amazing finale, wishing for death, future death, eternal death, harmonious outcome, exposing the darkness, vision of death, clearing negativity, exposing the grave, viewing (funeral), famous grave, eternal silence, exposing negativity, improving sickness, better-than-hoped-for ending, letting go, lifting illness, best left buried, ascending into death, exposing denial, alleviating grief, immortal

17. Stork: returning illness, evolving outcome, stages of grief, moving the corpse, long illness, graceful passing (death), moving through grief, spring death/burial, quiet passing, cycles of death, relocating the grave, passing, very silent, recurring losses

18. Dog: dog crate, assisted death, guarding the coffin, friend's burial, protecting the grave, pet burial/grave, friend's grave, scent/smell of death, witnessing a death, vigil (watching over the corpse), autopsy, therapeutic release, watching someone die

19. Tower: past death, prison/jail cell, political suicide, past illness, traditional coffin, lonely death, formal ending, traditional outcome, tomb, government burial, ancient grave, traditional burial, officially dead, old man died, established illness, solitude in death, ruling the cause of death, mausoleum

20. Garden: typical death, mass deaths, public grave, common way to die, public death, general emptiness, common illness, public burial, public illness, social negativity, public mourning, community is grieving a loss, everybody's sick, typical burial

21. Mountain: a hard pass (no), remote grave, persistence illness, embalming, mountain burial, rough death, permanence of death, setback grave, banned from the gravesite/burial, challenging outcome, stubborn illness

22. Paths: unusual outcome, multiple closures, strange illness, many possible outcomes, unusual silence, multiple illnesses, deciding NO, road closure, unusual cause of death, between death, multiple deaths, planning a funeral, strange death

23. Mice: costly silence, mouse/rat trap, spreading illness, ruined outcome, spreading disease, rotting corpse, damaging denial, spread of death, costly loss (not money), defaced grave, ruined burial, lessening silence, spreading negativity, decaying, next to nothing left, unfinished, inconclusive, contaminated body, damaging silence, worsening

24. Heart: heart failure, compassionate death, heart-shaped box, donation "in memory of," heart-related death, kind ending, "in loving memory," heartsick, giving over to death, forgiving the deceased (dead), giving the silent treatment, love for the deceased, love enough to let go, lover dies, relationship death, love ends

25. Ring: marriage ends, surrounded by darkness, jewelry/ring box, ongoing illness, surrounded by silence, continual grief, surrounded by death, turning in one's grave, completely empty, deal's dead, surrounded by negativity, continual denial, surrounded by illness, promise of death

26. Book: unknown outcome, remembering the dead, secret burial, logical ending, secret box, historical grave, unknown ailment, story ends, memory loss, historical illness, unknown grave, book of condolences, memories of death, secret taken to the grave, unknown deceased (corpse)

27. Letter: scheduled death (euthanasia/execution), written off (you're dead to me), text messages deleted, postbox/mailbox, writing/blogging about death, texting "it's over," writing to the dead, results on cause of death, communication ends, papers/documents destroyed, files deleted, writing a eulogy, letter/note/card in coffin

28. Man: man in denial, negative man, a dead man, a silent man, deceased male, closed-off male, dying man, bad man, ill/sick man, empty man, widowed husband, grieving male, dark male, death of a man, late husband, no man, nonexistent man, deleting a man

29. Woman: woman in denial, negative woman, a dead woman, a silent woman, deceased female, closed-off female, dying woman, bad woman, ill/sick woman, empty woman, widowed wife, grieving female, dark female, death of a woman, late wife, no lady, nonexistent woman, deleting a woman

30. Lily: old box, discreet passing, old grave, private box, age-related illness, winter death/ burial, private death, age-related death, RIP (rest in peace), private burial, old death, cold like death, peaceful death, father/grandfather in denial, expired

31. Sun: good outcome, actual ending, summer death/burial, really gone, annual death anniversary, cremation, all ends well, good for nothing, actually dead, real ailment, truly done, really silent, truly letting go, real loss, truly empty, actually stopped, really closed off

32. Moon: emotionally closed off, feeling empty, psychic death, dreams of death, feeling sick, feeling grief, emotional ending, emotionally numb, dreaming of graves, emotional death, phases of death, feeling dead inside, emotional denial, sleep paralysis, feeling bad, emotionless

33. Key: lockbox, gout (privileged illness), definitely dead, significant ending, prestigious burial, key ending, defiantly ill, unveiling ceremony, definitely deleted, open grave, definitely closed, definitely bad, important ending, fated death, ceremonial burial, access to the grave, freedom at the end, respecting the grave, significant loss, unburied, cause of death, honoring the dead, exhuming a body, karmic death

34. Fish: drowning to death, deep silence, deep grief, deep emptiness, deep denial, expensive burial, deeply buried, alcoholic death, circling the drain, money woes, deep mourning, money stops, business is dead, swimming with the fishes

35. Anchor: stable outcome, unchanged illness, heavy silence, persistent illness, lingering death, arrangements (funeral), heavy casket, still nothing, stuck in negativity, still closed off, enduring grief, enduring illness, still gone, keeping silent, heavy mourning, hanging onto death, still NO!

36. Cross: terrible outcome, painful death, cursed outcome, a grave, disappointing ending, praying for death, throes of death, sacred burial/grave, church funeral, regrets at the end, suffering at the end, shameful death, worshiping the dead, painful ending, scandalous death, miserable death, mourning

Life should not be a journey to the grave with the intention of arriving safely in a pretty and well-preserved body, but rather to skid in broadside in a cloud of smoke, thoroughly used up, totally worn out, and loudly proclaiming, "Wow! What a Ride!"

—Hunter S. Thompson

9. Bouquet

Blossoming buds of beauty, charming and just as sweet
Wonderful blooming colors, strewing petals at your feet
A perfectly celebrated design, in an exquisite formation
Flowers soften every heart, wonderful for any occasion

DESCRIPTION

Fashionably displayed in a stylish vase is a beautiful fragrant Bouquet of flowers, bursting forth with a delightful array of colors. Showy yellow sunflowers that tantalize the senses symbolize adoration, bringing an air of lightness to any situation; these intense beauties always turn their sweet faces easterly to receive the first drops of the sun's golden rays. Dotted among these sunny giants are white carnations, blossoming with joy while radiating with a vibration of pure gratitude. Encircling the base of the vase is a stunning choker, adorned with a charming red quartz symbolizing deep gratitude, left as a gift of appreciation.

A little card sits on display, but, from where you are standing, you cannot quite make out the poem. You begin to wonder . . . are they heartfelt words for a lover? An invitation to a special occasion or words to convey deepest sympathies? Or maybe just a simple thank-you.

A Bouquet can commemorate any occasion, some happy some sad, but one thing for sure is that they are given to bring a little bit of joy and are often a welcomed surprise. When holding a Bouquet, you get to experience sheer beauty, perfectly designed specimens that envelop you with a perfume of happiness, bringing about a sense of magick only flowers can convey.

The Bouquet card bears the number 9, which has a feminine influence and carries within her the light of the world, illustrated by the sparkling golden orbs and the emitting a high vibrational frequency that facilitates the blossoming of intuition and spiritual enlightenment. The 9 is a great cultivator of artistic endeavors promoting self-love and a zest for life by focusing on completion. It is always ready to move on to a new level of life experience while keeping aligned with your soul's purpose.

As the heavy burgundy curtain parts and the veil is lifted from your eyes, you awake, seeing the magick of the mandalas. These beautiful intricate designs are symbolic of the idea that everyone and everything is connected, and life is truly eternal. The pink dahlia-shaped flowers represent consciousness, encouraging you to develop a deeper sense of self-love—it's time to stop and smell the flowers while savoring the beauty of life. This is the invitation of the Bouquet.

KEYWORDS

Invitation, gift, surprise, beauty, enjoyment, charming, flowers, occasion, sweet, blossoming, showy, presentation, design, art, color, appreciation, pleasant, gratitude, aesthetic, fashion, display, wonderful, style, celebration, perfect, polite, east, special

TIMING

The Lenormand card number 9 indicates the month of September or nine days, nine weeks, or nine months, depending on the surrounding cards, especially when the Mountain is present.

MEANING

This is a time to delight in the sweet fragrance of life and let the good times roll. When the Bouquet makes an appearance, it's filled with wonderful surprises, influencing the surrounding cards with a positive effect. Flowers bring an appreciation for beauty and the finer things in life, such as art, fashion, and design—anything that is aesthetically pleasing to the eye.

The Bouquet invites you to receive these charming gifts and allow them to blossom into something wonderful in your life.

BOUQUET IN LOVE

If you are looking for romance, seeing the Bouquet is a good omen, signifying a secret admirer or getting flowers. When looking for love, you have to be ready and put yourself out there. Allow something to begin to bud, trusting that there is someone for everyone. If currently in a relationship, seeing this card indicates a love that will continue to bloom and grow. Don't forget to show appreciation to each other sometimes; it's the little things have the greatest impact. But if there is trouble in paradise, the Bouquet will bring improvement to your relationship, for it is a very favorable card to see.

BOUQUET IN CAREER

An unexpected and wonderful opportunity may be presented to you. If you are experiencing issues currently, rest assured that they will resolve in a favorable manner. A career in areas of beauty, art, design, modeling, acting, or even floristry pair well with the Bouquet.

BOUQUET IN WELLNESS

A favorable card to see when inquiring about health, the Bouquet is symbolic of good health with a focus on beauty. The Bouquet has a positive influence on anything that ails you.

BOUQUET IN FINANCES

Receiving an unexpected gift, realizing that money isn't everything, and gratitude is key.

BOUQUET IN MODERN DAY

This is a card of cosmetic procedures, beauty, and makeup—anything done to capture the fountain of youth.

AFFIRMATION

I am too big of a gift to be put into such a small box.

CARTOMANCY: QUEEN OF SPADES

The greatly feared Queen of Spades is a determined woman not to be trifled with, a crafty lady who uses her cunning wit to get ahead at any cost. This Queen does not sugar-coat things; her attitude and cutting words oftentimes push people away, leaving her alone and lonely. Hard to love, this Queen is usually a divorced woman because she can't seem to keep a man in her life. A born leader with an unshakable inner strength, she is a great force to be reckoned with; try to stay on her good side so you don't end up on the receiving end of this formidable woman's wrath.

LENORMAND BOUQUET COMBINATIONS

1. Rider: active wear, flamboyant style, going nicely, show-off, first impression, last-minute invitation, mailing a gift, fast celebration, delivery of flowers, bringing sweets, moving eastward, receiving a gift, news is pleasant, the other man is charming, receiving an invite

2. Clover: bohemian style, green (color), fun celebration, game show, herbs, whimsical style, casual gift, laid-back design, informal occasion, temporary design, wildflowers, casual attire/style, funny looking, spontaneous invitation, casual floral arrangement, informal presentation, poker face

3. Ship: travel/cruise wear, going-away party, traveling in style, travel presentation, goodbye flowers, parting gift, foreign beauty, trip's pleasant, travel enjoyment, car appreciation, moving toward the east

4. House: brand name clothing, homestyle, family celebration, home renovations, backyard flowers, house party, interior design, house design, designer style, house colors palette, in a place of gratitude, family style, house style, family gratitude, houseplant

5. Tree: scrubs (medical clothing), spiritual gifts, natural young man, medical beauty procedure, living art, lifestyle, living well, natural color, get-well-soon flowers, wildflowers, natural art, spiritual celebration, nature's design, medicinal herbs/flowers, natural aesthetic

6 Clouds: loungewear style, lost art, passing style (mode), sad face, lost invitation, hidden request, hidden face (masking), concealed enjoyment, hidden design, gray (color), confusing invite, misunderstanding the gift, doubting what is portrayed, hidden pleasure, depressing color palette, hidden gift, troubling display

7. Snake: provocative clothing, poisonous flowers, enticing beauty, complex presentation, evil gift, tempting invitation, poisonous herbs, envious, snake plant, dark-haired beauty, tight clothes, problematic gift, desiring beauty, ugly, snake charmer, wanting an invite, desiring pleasure

8. Coffin: gothic style, black (color), dark poetry, bad occasion, deleted invitation, bad gift, dark art, bad art, black roses, dark aesthetic, no enjoyment, devoid of pleasure, dark cloths, declined invitation, funeral flowers, bad design, death mask (face), last gift, death pallor, memorial wreath, dark color pallet, mums/chrysanthemums (flower)

10. Scythe: Botox (injections for beauty), unexpected gift, cutting out sweets/sugar, risky design, Halloween/harvest party, brutal face, autumn/fall colors, risky occasion, cutting off indulgences, surprise (not a good one), unexpected pleasure, removing color, breaking your face, cutoff presentation, unexpected flowers

11. Whip: sexy style (clothes), aggressive beauty treatment, avant-garde art, sex party, sexual style, aggressive art style, sexual gift, aggressive display, sexy lingerie, active/sportswear, sexually satisfied, intermittent pleasure, sexually attractive

12. Birds: discussing fashion, radio show, singing show, bird of paradise (flower), music style, saying thank you, talking to plants/flowers, busy color palette, talk nicely, nervous about a surprise, couple invited, noisy celebration, matching gifts, talkative charmer

13. Child: minimalist style, small occasion, daisies (flowers), minimal art, new style, weak perfume, small bouquet, shy sweetness, small show, bit of enjoyment, fragile gift, weak color palette, slight pleasure, precarious design, childish art, slightly charming, children's clothing

14. Fox: practical style, avoiding an invitation, tricky design, work celebration, clever gift, sneaky invite, charmer, practical gift, trick or treat, calculated gift, sneaky face, careful design, cautious presentation, pseudo invite, avoiding an occasion, pretending to be surprised, scam artist, counterfeit art, feigning gratitude, backhanded compliment, work clothes

15. Bear: bold style, powerful presentation, grand celebration, strong perfume, grand design, tasteful, boldface, cloying, big occasion, very charming, big bouquet, gladioli (flower), big surprise, restaurant invitation, hairstyle, food aesthetic, matronly style (mom jeans), big show, more gifts, very beautiful, immense pleasure, very grateful, overstated, bold color palette

16. Stars: astral projection, Starseed, harmonious occasion, improving the design, vivid colors, blessed and grateful, high fashion, uplifting occasion, great aesthetic, harmonious color palette, galactic event, best gift, unlimited pleasure, perfection, amazing surprise, famous beauty, great show, stellar impression, inspiring presentation, fantastic design, high appreciation, enhancing beauty, great pleasure, TV shows, masterpiece, future invite, looking forward to the occasion, online invite

17. Stork: returning a gift, trendy clothes, dance wear, baby celebration, long-stem flowers, tulips (flower), returning pleasure, daffodils (flower), baby face, evolving design, long presentation, baby's breath (flower), baby cloths, metamorphosis, remodeling, makeover, trending design, regifting

18. Dog: dogwood, friendly gift, following fashion, friendship is sweet, companion planting, friendly occasion, friendly and polite, dogface, iris (flower), friendship is blossoming, investigating a gift (received), friendly smile, familiar occasion

19. Tower: city style/fashion, self-expression, military-style clothing (camouflage), traditional celebration, outdated fashion, corporate celebration, outdated decor, self-indulgence, Renaissance art, past invitation, outdated color palette, formal attire, climbing plants, traditional floral arrangement, black-tie occasion, traditional design, formal occasion

20. Garden: average beauty, urban fashion, average presentation, people celebrating, garden flowers, public celebration, carnation (flower), social occasion, general appreciation, common gift, popular color palette, outerwear, socialite, popular style, general appreciation, civilian clothing, a social butterfly, social media invite

21. Mountain: rocker style, interrupted pleasure, blocked from the east, mountain herbs/flowers, hard/rock candy, craggy face, chiseled looks, interrupted occasion/event, stone faced, postponed presentation

22. Paths: street style/fashion, unusual beauty, multiple invitations, strange occasion, many faces, strange gift, multiple occasions, unusual presentation, strange design, eclectic style, unusual art, strange display, unusual color, alternative style, unusual invite, planning a special occasion, multiple gifts, between designs, street wear

23. Mice: spreading weeds, spoiled occasion, faint perfume, unattractive/ugly, fading colors, displeasure, spoiled surprise, "botched" cosmetic enhancements, bitter, undecorated, ruined gift, repulsive, fewer gifts, sour (less sweet), dull color palette, defaced, taken for granted (less appreciative), thinning out your wardrobe, wilted flowers, damaged art, unkempt, dirty cloths, grunge style

24. Heart: roses, pleasurable occasion, dating style, forgiving design, loving the aesthetic, loving the colors, giving a gift, loving the style, a date, love dressing up, giving compliments, donating cloths, loving the look, date is wonderful, romantic surprise, love's blooming

25. Ring: marriage celebration, engagement celebration, bridal bouquet, wedding party, entire design, during the entire occasion, ongoing appreciation, surrounded by beauty, dealing in art, entire celebration, surrounded by flowers, engagement party

26. Book: historical occasion, nerdy/geeky style, secret celebration, graduation celebration, smart gift, forget-me-not (flowers), secret invite, period style, graduation party, book launch party, historical color palette, secret surprise, informative presentation, period/historical garments

27. Letter: paper flowers, writing style, sending appreciation, receipt for a gift, sending flowers, written invitation, sending an invite, emailing a presentation, writing down what you are grateful for, texting an invite, sending a gift, results are presented, written all over their face

28. Man: masculine attire, polite man, poetic man, pleasant man, sweet man, grateful man, flashy man, considerate man, wonderful man, Prince Charming, delightful man, conceited man, handsome man, artistic man, male artist, male designer, surprising man, masculine features, male cologne, beautiful man, special man, charming man

29. Woman: feminine attire, polite woman, girly fashion, poetic female, pleasant woman, sweet lady, grateful woman, fancy female, considerate woman, wonderful lady, delightful woman, conceited woman, gorgeous woman, artistic woman, fashionable woman, surprising woman, female artist, female designer, feminine features, female perfume, special lady, beautiful woman, charming lady

30. Lily: mature style, time-honored fashion, private celebration, conservative style, private party, conservative design, snowdrops (flowers), winter party, classic beauty, modest, discreet, ... eful, pastel colors, cordial

... ty, really sweet, celebration, bright colors, true pleasure, good ... ion, good gift, drying flowers/herbs, true appreciation, annual ... annual flowers, good presentation, true enjoyment, annual ... day party/celebration, really charming, real good show, true ... prize, yellow/golden (color), annual invite

... tive gift, skilled artist, emotional occasion, feeling grateful, ... design, psychic gifts, creative performer, feeling beautiful, ... beauty, feeling appreciated, emotional display, skilled designer, ... sleepwear, mystical aesthetic, silver color

... ation celebration, haute couture, prestigious gift, privileged ... occasion, key presentation, definitely beautiful, acclaimed ... ant gift, fine art, karmic seed

... sive aesthetic, business-casual style, deep appreciation, buying ... lowers, expensive occasion, business celebration, expensive ... sive gift, whiskey in a teacup, expensive cologne/perfume, ... ance)

... p enjoying, seaweed, staying pleasant, ground flowers, coastal ... still charming, stay east, keep it beautiful (Ontario), keeping ... e gift, solid presentation, saving the invitation, underpresented, ... e invitation

... ppointing occasion, religious art, obligatory flowers, creepy ... e, church flowers, disappointing gift, difficult presentation, ... alous art, shameful gift, regret sending the invite, sinful

...people who make us happy; they are the ...ners who make our souls blossom.

—Marcel Proust

10. Scythe

Sharp and dangerously slicing, cut down to my very core
Sudden and unexpected accident, left me disconnected and sore
Irrevocable divisions, splitting halves then rendering them apart
Separating quickly, leaves a wake of broken shards in my heart

DESCRIPTION

As the sun sets on the year's final harvest, the Scythe emerges from a field of golden wheat, catching the last wisps of fading light glinting off its sharp edge. Shimmering flaxen shafts of wheat are swaying in the breeze on a warm autumn's day, while the poised Scythe looms over the wheat in a dangerous manner. The Scythe is ready to reap the wheat as they straighten their golden heads, bravely accepting their fate of being cut down without warning, but not afraid, since they are revered for their remarkable ability to renew themselves after giving up their bounty.

As the sun sets in the west, the Scythe takes its sacrifice with a swift sudden motion that brings about an abrupt cutting that begins the irrevocable separation, and the grain is separated from the shaft, while the broken seeds fall back down into the fertile womb of Mother Earth to begin the cycle anew.

A crimson metallic ribbon entwines the Scythe's handle as a protective charm against any ill will. The red symbolizes danger and foreshadows the blood that must be spilled as an offering to the land to ensure a bountiful harvest in the year to come. As the crescent-shaped Scythe gathers the enchanted grain, it is held together by a sturdy ornate handle. Once this wood was vibrant and alive, but even in death it is called into service by the Scythe. The dead wood now supports the blade as the Scythe swings high and clears a path, leaving destruction in its wake. Just as the Scythe divides and renders everything asunder, we see this mimicked in the far distance, as a row of hedges emerge from the mist, dividing the properties to reflect ownership of the land. The overcast gray skies cast a feeling of impending danger with a certain reckoning floating in the air. The Scythes possesses a very risky nature and, without warning, has the ability to suddenly remove anything at one fell swoop.

The divine number 10 is a perfect match for the Scythe card, which symbolizes a return to unity, the synthesis of being and nonbeing. As the cycle finishes with the number 10, it reduces to 1, and the continual rotation begins again. The ever-renewing 10 is both masculine and feminine, and significant to the month of October being the time of the final harvest.

KEYWORDS

Sudden, irrevocable, accident, sever, remove, reap, divide, gather, cut, harvest, reckoning, collect, surgery, wound, danger, rupture, unexpected, clears a path, urgent, reckoning, broken, disconnected, separate, detached, risk, autumn, splitting, decimating, sharp, west, obliterating, disaster, emergency, threat

TIMING

Sudden, autumn, October, ten days; if the Mountain is present, it could be up to ten weeks to ten months.

MEANING

Suddenly the Scythe appears, bringing danger and decimation to whatever it touches, usually when you are not expecting it. Permeating with danger, the Scythe does not carry any prejudice, for anything in its path is fair game—a card of reckoning that brings about accidents and actions that are irrevocable.

Look to the cards near the Scythe to see what is broken or needing to being removed from your life. The Scythe's swift action is always precise and purposeful; even a single clear cut can have long-lasting, wounding effects. The Scythe is also a tool that has been used for harvesting and reaping crops. Just as the Scythe clears a path, it also leaves destruction in its wake—it's the double-edged sword. There is no negotiating with the Scythe: it takes what it wants, divides what needs to be severed, and removes what no longer serves it.

SCYTHE IN LOVE

A very negative card when it comes to relationship questions, the Scythe usually denotes a permanent separation of a couple. The negative connotation attached to the Scythe makes everything dangerous when it appears in love circumstances. If the Scythe appears between the Man and Woman cards, it means divorce.

SCYTHE IN CAREER

The Scythe will reduce anything in your job, work, or career. This could come in the form of cut hours, cut wages, or even cutting a job when it becomes redundant. The effect of the Scythe will be unexpected and irrevocable. Vocations that represent this card would be surgeon, dentist, farmer, tailor/seamstress, carpenter.

SCYTHE IN WELLNESS

Generally, the Scythe indicates surgery, wounds, and injectables; look to the surrounding cards, since they will give you deeper insight to the situation. This card can also represent issues with the mouth, teeth, and gums.

SCYTHE IN FINANCES

This is definitely a card of risk, with the focus being on a reduction of finances. Watch out when making rash decisions, for this will affect your livelihood, usually causing damage to your bottom line.

SCYTHE IN MODERN DAY

The Grim Reaper, a motorcycle club (Sons of Anarchy), symbol of death, injectables/vaccine.

AFFIRMATION

When things suddenly and unexpectedly leave my life, I will trust in that wisdom and let them go with compassion and love.

CARTOMANCY:
JACK OF DIAMONDS

The Jack of Diamonds is a restless young man, usually wearing a uniform. He embodies the old adage that *anything goes, as long as the end justifies the means.* Carrying an aura of self-importance, he craves being the center of attention at all times. Selfish and always looking out for number one, he has a huge ego to match his grandiose persona. In olden times, the Jacks are viewed as the thoughts of the King or Queen; today, we can use the Jack of Diamonds as the thoughts of the Seeker. He can also appear as someone related to the Seeker through marriage. The Jack of Diamonds can be quite stubborn at times, thinking he is always right; he has that bad-boy vibe and enjoys ruffling feathers and causing trouble. This Jack is preoccupied with having the need for security, both emotionally and financially, but keeps this vulnerability to himself.

LENORMAND SCYTHE COMBINATIONS

1. Rider: first harvest, announcing a divorce, acting dangerously, this coming autumn, very sudden, news of a divorce/separation, other man is separated/divorced, messenger RNA vaccine, suitor is dangerous, other man is threatening, acting detached, came out of the blue, moving urgently, coming threat

2. Clover: green wound (infected), very risky, temporarily detached, brief separation, wild accident, brief division, temporarily disconnected, easily broken, temporarily cut off, brief threat, very risky, brief emergency

3. Ship: leaving a risky situation, car wreck, international/foreign threat, exploratory surgery, left abruptly, travel cuts, deployed for war, travel emergency, leaving urgently, travel threat, trip out west, leaving (due to separation), car breaks down, abroad surgery, shipwreck, international emergency

4. House: family divided, real estate interruption, property divided among family members, house facing west, real estate cuts (price), family emergency, alliance severed, household accident, family member is removed from the house, domestic threat

5. Tree: syringe, not too sudden, slowly severing ties, medical risk, slow removal, spiritual danger, slowly divided, natural disaster, slowly being cut off, medical emergency, slowly breaking, life's threatened, bloodshed, body piercing, healthcare cuts, life's in danger, scalpel, body scar, rupture (medical)

6. Clouds: psychotic break, doubting vaccination, fearing needles, hidden knife, hidden risks, head wound/trauma, unstable injectable, hidden weapon, fearing surgery, hidden danger, mental break, cloak and dagger, weather emergency, chaos, climate emergency, thinking about divorce, head scar, narcotics syringe

7. Snake: poison injected, desiring to wound someone, needs severing, backstabber, disastrous, urgent problem, enemy threat, tongue piercing, tempting risk, complex surgery, attracted to danger, lying about the separation/divorce, enemy, toxic injection

8. Coffin: bad autumn, lethal injection, bad accident, botched surgery, bad wound, bad batch of injectables, last harvest, banning weapons, bad cut, denied surgery, kill shot, bad break, last surgery, mortal wound, bad rupture, nothing to split, deadly weapon, death threat

9. Bouquet: wonderful bounty, filler injections, facial scar, surprise threat, pleasant autumn, surprise surgery, beautiful autumn/fall colors, special surgery, beautification surgery, Botox injections, facial piercing, diabetic injections, blindsided, makeup is on point!

11. Whip: active threat, aggressive division, war, sexual threat, serial vaccinations, sports injury, aggressive surgery, wreak havoc, inflicted wound, aggressive removal, attack, sexually risky, sexual/genital piercing, active emergency, serial killer, questioning injections, aggressive threat, sexually scarred, aggressive separation, risqué

12. Birds: two scars, verbal threat, flying west, two cuts, couple talking about divorce, two wounds, verbally cut off, two surgeries, taking about the accident, called the emergency number (911/999/112), uttering threats, throat surgery, lip piercing, couple divorcing

13. Child: slight risk, child is threatened, small nick, short straw, little break, a bit sudden, slightly west, minor accident, new injectable, small fracture, minor cut/wound, small divide, tiny reckoning, small collection, slightly unexpected, slightly detached, newly separated/divorced, vulnerable, new piercing, child vaccination, small emergency, slight urgency, small threat, childhood scars, small knife

14. Fox: calculated risk, avoiding surgery, escaping danger, caution (danger ahead), avoiding vaccinations/injectables, faking an injury, calculated separation/divorce, avoiding an accident, pseudo separation, avoiding danger, stealthy separation/divorce, careful removal, cautious separation, faking an accident, feigning danger, avoiding separation/divorce, work emergency, surviving an accident, work threat, averting an emergency, pretending to be divorced

15. Bear: big scar, immense danger, huge divide, big risk, very sudden/unexpected, major surgery, haircut, very wounded, big needle, major reckoning, huge collection, very dangerous, increased risk, more surgeries, massive threat, forced vaccination/injection, very broken, huge disconnect, hair removal, powerful weapon, food cuts, very urgent, big emergency, stomach surgery, major accident, increased threat

16. Star: exposing the risk, space wars, highly risky, amazing bounty, clears a path, the great reckoning, high yield (harvest), highly collectible, the great divide, best cut possible, enhancing surgery, improving divorce, vast collection, clearing, space threat, looking forward to the separation/divorce, future cuts, viewpoint

17. Stork: seasonal vaccine (flu shot), long autumn, recurring threats, long break, long cut, recurring threats, long scar, fertility injections, leg/knee surgery, birth injury, moving separately (due to separation/divorce), infertility

18. Dog: smell of autumn, barking out threats, nose surgery, a friend's in danger, amicable separation/divorce, nose piercing, service cuts, therapeutic vaccine/injection, friendship's broken, Red Cross (aid in emergency), investigating threats, friendship threatened, protection from threats, witnessing an accident, investigating injectables

19. Tower: defensive wounds, enforced vaccination/injection, official emergency, back scar, past autumn, self-destruction, mandatory injection, government cuts, official danger, prohibited weapon, government vaccination program, backstabbing, government emergency order, armories, controlling the threat, enforcement, conscription (war), citywide emergency, government threat, back surgery

20. Garden: average autumn, public emergency, common accident, muster point, average risk, general surgery, public cuts, common surgery, community emergency, general risk, public threat, social life's obliterated, online threats, garden facing west, general emergency, public divorce

21. Mountain: restricted weapons, border threat, permanent separation, irrevocable divorce, raised scar (keloid), permanently wounded, border emergency, permanent threat, rough separation, hard divorce, blocking danger, hard battle, stubborn wound

22. Paths: multiple accidents, stranger danger, separation, unusual risk, multiple wounds, between surgeries, multiple threats, between separation and divorce, separation leads to divorce, possible emergency, multiple surgeries

23. Mice: costly accident, dissipating danger, ruined/spoiled harvest, damage, thinning out the collection, spreading danger, dirty divorce, lowering risk, less divided, diseased crops, dissolving stitches, falling apart, damaging accident, spreading threats, damaging divorce/separation

24. Heart: heart removed, forgiving an accident, relationship is broken, granted divorce, relationship is threatened, lovers separated, forgiveness is unexpected, falling in love was unexpected (already in a relationship), date is dangerous, love is threatened, heart is broken

25. Ring: consenting to injection, surrounded by farm fields, centralized wound, ongoing division, deal is threatened, continual detachment, ongoing threats, mending, surrounded by danger, continued separation, ongoing war, marriage threatened, deal is risky, spouse is disconnected, contract is irrevocable, turning point, reconnecting

26. Book: informed risk, secret separation/divorce, unknown threat, secret piercing, history of divorce, flashbacks (accident), unknown risk, information about the accident, knowledge of the separation/divorce (they know), secrets threatened

27. Letter: letter collection, post alerting to danger, sending threats, recorded accident, facts about the accident, results from the surgery, father is in danger, stamp collection, written threats, posting the accident, messaging/texting threats

28. Man: impulsive man, divorced man, severing ties with a man, broken man, cutting off a man, decisive man, dangerous man, ruthless man, an ex (male), wounded man, vaccinated/injected male, risky man, ex-husband, splitting up with a man, half the man, threatening man, separated man

29. Woman: impulsive lady, divorced woman, severing ties with a woman, broken woman, cutting off a woman, decisive woman, dangerous female, ruthless woman, an ex (female), wounded female, vaccinated/injected female, risky woman, ex-wife, splitting up with a woman, half the woman, threatening woman, separated woman

30. Lily: ripe harvest; privacy threat; old sword; discreet separation/divorce; old piercing; calm, cool, and collected; old threat; discreetly removed; private divorce; old scar; elder in danger; old divorce

31. Sun: successful divorce, annual harvest, actually separated, really divorced, truly irrevocable, actual accident, truly divided, successful surgery, fire emergency, truly wounded, real and present danger, happy break, successful separation/divorce, better half, win (divorce), energetic threat, solar emergency

32. Moon: feeling wounded, emotionally broken, feeling divided, emotional wounds, monthly harvest, feeling threatened, emotionally separated, female surgery (reproductive organs), emotional break, sensing danger, intuition on point!

33. Key: significant danger, definitely irrevocable, revealing the separation/divorce, important surgery, definitely separated/divorced, imminent danger, defiantly unexpected, karmic removal, definitely divided, significant scar, free from danger, revealing the threat, definite risk, karmic threat, access cut off, significant threat, fate swings the ax

34. Fish: expensive surgery, deep wound, water emergency, financially risky, deep divide, financial threat, expensive accident, financial cuts, business emergency, expensive divorce, bidding war

35. Anchor: keeping the collection, remains broken, long-lasting separation, remains divided, still wounded, holding it together, lingering threat, still dangerous, staying detached, remains disconnected, staying separated, still risky, steady cuts, hanging on to the divorce, rescued, steady threats, enduring the separation, safe from danger

36. Cross: terrible accident, difficult cut, emergency, regretting vaccination/injection, terrible divorce, painful separation, crisis, difficult divorce, difficult autumn, threat, scandalous separation/divorce, regretting the separation/divorce, painful cut, crucified

Life is like a field, where we must gather
what we grow, weed or wheat . . . this is the law;
we reap the crop we sow.

—Patience Strong

11. Whip

Sensual erotic flogging, conflict with stinging words that hurt
Abusive habitual fighting, repetitive patterns that only subvert
Back-and-forth sexual aggression, angry questions drip with abuse
Anticipating punishment leaves me breathless, nothing left to lose

DESCRIPTION

Hot and painful, the Whip lashes back and forth with its sultry tongue; repeated flogging leaves marks wherever it kisses, as you eagerly awaiting the sweet release of heightened pleasure.

The Whip rests unassumingly on a hand-hewn table, looking at you demurely, yet menacing within the same exhale. Batting her lashes, she teases you with the scent of leather and wax mingling and tantalizing your senses, as a heavy electrical charge hangs in the air, making your flesh quiver in anticipation. She beckons the crows to take part in the activity, with the promise of erotic play as they argue back and forth regarding who will use the Whip and who will receive the punishment. The inky, black crows are extraordinary masters of illusion and incredibly resilient, having the ability to adapt to any situation. This is the way of many who feel the abusing effect of the Whip in all its forms; learning to adapt and accept the circumstances of torture is the reality of many who feel the Whip's negative aspect. The crows are here to help by imparting an enchantment of strength, freely giving crow magick to all those in need. They encourage you to courageously speak your truth and breach the chasm of the darkest void of your being by reclaiming your power.

On a tall candelabra, ten pillars of candles are poised to spill their hot wax on the most intimate, delicate parts and bits of tender flesh. The soft, hazy glow illuminating from the tapers casts long, sweeping shadows onto the walls, as an aura of aggression permeates throughout the room, whisking you into a world of both pain and pleasure.

The Whip actively opposes, and debate with its to-and-fro motion represents an aspect of physical activity, whether it be sexual or practice for battle on the castle grounds. The Whip's effect will be repetitive and thrashing and, at times, abusive in nature as it unites both light and dark aspects within you.

The Whip card is connected to the Master number of 11, the bringer of light and spiritual enlightenment. This number has an old soul and bears an enormous amount of fortitude. The highly sensitive number 11 is sympathetic to the needs of others and tries to find the tiny spark of light within the darkness. The number 11 will find that soul spark and fan the flames' passion until it ignites the fire within, enabling you to experience life to the fullest.

KEYWORDS

Aggression, arguments, sex, assault, abuse, disputes, active, patterns, hit, violence, debate, exercise, discipline, repetitive, anger, strike, disruptive, conflict, punishment, criticize, opposition, habit, competition, attack, questions, fighting, hurt, rage, back and forth, injury, intermittent, inflict, battle

TIMING

Over and over, November, 11 days, 11 weeks, or 11 months with the Mountain present.

MEANING

For a long time, the Whip was synonymous only with discipline and violence, meting out punishment with repeated strikes, lashing and tearing the flesh. As a symbol of exerting compliance over others, the Whip card still holds on to the interpretation of antiquity, but nowadays it has taken on more of a dominant sexualized meaning. The Whip will discipline, tease, and enhance the skin's sensitivity, acting as a psychological turn-on for many. Since BDSM has gone mainstream, this is an acceptable sexual practice, and no longer taboo. When the Whip appears, it will be active, repetitive, aggressive, and abusive—not a nice card, yet it enjoys opposition at every turn, relentless questions, and getting pleasure from arguments. Always poised for battle, it metes out discipline with the promise of a sweet sting of pain, seen as overtly sexual—not like marital vanilla sex that is sometimes associated with the Lily, but the hot, steamy, kinky kind of sex, and pure hedonistic lust. The Whip brings a heightened energy, so when it appears, it brings an intensity to everything it lashes out and touches. The Whip is charged with disruptive energy driven by cynicism and can be quite critical at times. When the Whip shows up in a reading, sit up and take notice, because whatever is close enough to lash out at is guaranteed to feel the effects of the Whip. The Whip can show up as a habit or something repetitive in nature. In order to overcome the effects of the Whip, you need to dig deep and find determination, focus, and flexibility.

WHIP IN LOVE

Whip in love carries the emphasis of a purely sexual relationship, full of passion and eroticism with elements of BDSM, defiantly a card of sexual aggression and experimentation. In extreme cases and dependent on the surrounding cards, the Whip can suggest sexual abuse. Between established couples, the Whip brings discord accompanied by arguments and disagreements.

WHIP IN CAREER

The Whip is a card of physical activity and will often represent a career that requires a certain degree of physicality. As a vocation the Whip represents an athlete, lawyer, critic, dominatrix, or personal trainer.

WHIP IN WELLNESS

The Whip is a card of abuse, usually physical or sexual, but also can denote emotional abuse when Moon is nearby, or mental abuse if the Clouds are hanging around. It is also a reminder to do some physical activity, play a sport, or take part in any form of exercise encouraging you to start a healthful habit.

WHIP IN FINANCES

When the Whip card appears, it emphasizes a repeated financial transaction or certain habits, such as excessive shopping that will have a negative effect on your finances. With the Fish swimming around, it speaks to financial abuse.

WHIP IN MODERN DAY

Sexual practices or activities involving BDSM: bondage, discipline, sadism, masochism, or acts of domination and submission.

AFFIRMATION

I let go my anger for it no longer serves me; it keeps me from seeing things as they actually are.

CARTOMANCY: JACK OF CLUBS

The clever Jack of Clubs possesses an air of intellectual superiority and gets exhilarated when arguing his point of view. He loves the sound of his own voice and prides himself on his mental agility. When engaging with another, he relishes in the fact that he gets a chance to flex that mental muscle and prove why he is better than you. The Jack of Clubs craves power and gravitates toward positions of influence. When something pips his curiosity, he becomes fixated on that subject, needing to be the expert. Once the challenge is gone, the Jack of Clubs gets bored and quickly moves on to the next best thing, due to his constant need of stimulation. This behavior can cause bad habits to form that are obsessive in nature, because the Jack of Clubs cannot let anything go. His argumentative nature, combined with high expectations and repetitive tendencies, makes it difficult for the Jack of Clubs to find long-lasting love. His connections are brief at best, frequently finding himself in very short-term relationships peppered with one-night stands. He is really good at being *Mr. Right Now*! With his creative antics and sharp intellect, he has become quite the accomplished lover, always bringing something kinky into the bedroom, making him a very popular guy with the opposite sex.

1. Rider: first fight, acting sexy, actively fighting, coming and going back and forth, acting violent, acting angry, initial argument, acting disruptive, first time (sex), acting aggressive, active sexually, Jack of Clubs

2. Clover: brief argument, unruly pattern, fun competition, casual fight, wild activity, gaming competition, fun sex, casual competition, brief fight, wild sex, lucky action, hanky-panky, brief dalliance

3. Ship: traveling back and forth, a regatta, foreign aggression, travel disruptions, leaving a habit behind, distant (after sex), travel injury, goodbye sex, leaving after an argument, travel questions, leaving right after sex, directed aggression, travel aggression, international dispute

4. House: family fight, property dispute, home gym, family feud, real estate dispute, house arrest, family members at odds, domestic dispute, real estate opposition, family members injured, home workout, familiar question, family punished

5. Tree: deep-rooted anger, growing unrest, medical dispute, naturally athletic, growing competition, deeply rooted abuse, spiritual sex, healthful activity, deeply rooted habit, growth pattern, corporal punishment, exercise

6. Clouds: troubling fight, misplaced anger, passing conflict, erratic pattern, puzzling anger, passing aggression, hidden habit, troubling argument, weather pattern, thoughts of violence, weather-beaten, hidden sexual relations, passing habit, confusing questions

7. Snake: wanting to argue, toxic sex, jealous rage, screwing (sex), toxic anger, evil attack, enticing questions, bondage, tempted to cheat (sexually), toxic abuse, snake bite, needing sex, toxic argument, complicated questions, seduction, complex pattern, kink (twisted sex), wanting to hurt someone, cheating (sexually), venomous

8. Coffin: stop fighting, last question, death blow, buried rage, deadly habit, bad fight, black rage, deadly assault, bad temper, last strike, denied sex, necrophilia, death penalty (punishment), last time (sex), final debate, deadly violence, denied questions, mortal strike, deadbeat, let go of anger, stopped having sex

9. Bouquet: enjoying sex, polite debate, poetry competition, polite questions, special sexual relations, beauty competition, wonderful sex, pleasuring someone sexually, sweet sex, enjoys S&M, wonderful competition, banter, beautiful pattern, wonderful question, special training

10. Scythe: dangerous fight, unexpected violence, vaccine injury, unexpected rage, breaking the pattern, unexpected sex, sudden activity, unexpected pattern, divided opposition, sudden attack, unexpected conflict, abrupt disruption, hurtful questions, splitting the blame, dangerous anger, decimating the competition, urgent sex, war, emergency, cracking the whip

12. Birds: discussing sex, verbal argument, noisy sex, couple's fight, talking sexually, sibling rivalry, couple arguing, partner abuse, siblings fight, talking dirty, couple of questions, flying habits, talking abusively, verbal banter, flight pattern, tête-à-tête, birds and the bees, aroused, fellatio, rumored sexual relations

13. Child: play-fighting, short argument, weak opposition, playing sports, small fight, minor assault, petty argument, minor disruption, constructive criticism, starting a fight, small tap (hit), slightly repetitive, small punishment, immature fight, small habit, a spat, new questions, feeble attack, weak competition, childish argument, spanking, immature questions, microaggressions

14. Fox: calculated attack, office sex, work competition, instigating a fight, calculated/ manipulative questions, work argument, avoiding sex, employment dispute, avoiding arguments, sneak attack, coworkers fighting, calculated sex, gaslighting, passive-aggressive, cheap shot, cautiously opposed, faking an orgasm, escaping abuse, stealthy sex, cunning opponent

15. Bear: big argument, intense rage, big punishment, food competition, major criticism, eating habits, brutal attack, intimidating questions, intense sex, major disruptions, huge blow, major opposition, more sex, increased activity, more questions, very conflicted, increased sexual activity, very abusive, forced sex, aphrodisiac, very competitive, huge fight

16. Star: astral sex, worthy opponent, space competition, exposing habits, best sex ever, alleviating arguments, great debate, best practices, looking forward to sex, clearing disruptions, extensive questioning, exposed sexually, see beyond the criticism, internet disruption, enhancing sexual performance

17. Stork: cycling back and forth, reproduction, renewed anger, shifting back and forth, long fight/argument, evolving activity, dance competition, progressive argument, alternating, evolving disagreement, recurring fights/arguments, shifting pattern, mating

18. Dog: friendly debate, doggy style (sex), investigating abuse, friendly sex, therapeutic sex, service disruptions, friendly match, watching porn, friendly debate, looking for a pattern, investigating a fight, friendly disagreement, dogfight

19. Tower: defensive assault/attack, self-hate, legal questions, self-pleasure, legal fight, established pattern, traditional questions, litigation, enforcing punishment, legal action, solo sex, defensive, defending your sexuality, one-night stand, withdrawn sexually, demanding sex, official opposition

20. Garden: average sex, public outrage, people protesting, team sports, gangbang, group activity, online fighting/arguing, public competition, general questions, public fight, civil unrest, public attack, citizens uprising, general disagreement, public debate, team/group exercise, public discord, common disruption

21. Mountain: stubborn argument, harsh punishment, interrupted fight, impassive disagreement, hard competition, hard hit, R-rated, permanent habit, interrupted sex, interrupted competition, abrasive questions, permanent pattern

22. Paths: choosing to fight, multiple orgasms, unusual argument/fight, multiple strikes, strange sexual habit, road rage, unusual pattern, multiple-choice questions, unusual habit, multiple attacks, strange competition, unusual anger, multiple arguments/fights, between sexual partners, bisexual

23. Mice: costly habit, less critical, losing an argument, lessening violence, diminished sex drive, less conflict, spoilsport, less active, disgruntled, less sex, dirty hit, thinning out the competition, dissolving conflict, shit disturber

24. Heart: relationship fight, romantic sex, heartbeat, loving sex, dating pattern, love hurts, forgiving abuse/abuser, passionate argument, makeup sex, forgiveness after fighting, giving sexually, intimate sex, sensuality, love S&M, lover is sexy, love tap, ardor, flirtatious

25. Ring: continual arguments, marital sex, surrounded by criticism, ongoing fight, consensual sex, continued aggression, repetition, continuing sexual relations, center of activity, ongoing abuse, continuous questions, ongoing habit, marital fight

26. Book: informative questions, learning by rote, recalling an argument, memories of sex, logical question, history of mistreatment, study the pattern, memories of abuse, learned habit, studying kinesiology, secret sexual relations

27. Letter: scheduled exercise, text argument back and forth, written disciplinary action, list of questions, written critique, text message attack, newspaper critic, message is aggressive, sexting back and forth, written request

28. Man: aggressive man, personal trainer (male), competitive man, sexy man, active man, creature of habit, abused man, kinky man, violent man, a dominant (male), sexual man, abusive man, argumentative man, angry man, hurtful man, enraged man, feisty male, a man hurt her, fighting with a man, anarchist, hostile man

29. Woman: aggressive woman, personal trainer (female), competitive female, a dominatrix, sexy lady, active female, fierce woman, creature of habit (female), abused woman, kinky female, sexual female, abusive woman, argumentative lady, angry lady, hurtful woman, enraged woman, feisty female, a woman hurt him, fighting with a woman, rebellious woman, hostile woman

30. Lily: old fight, conservative sex, private question, vanilla sex, discreet sexual relations, restrained anger, discreetly fighting, private argument/disagreement, cold snap, private attack, discreet questions

31. Sun: good question, daily sex, annual competition, actual sex, truth about an assault, burning question, daily exercise, endorphins, happy sex, illuminating abuse, actual argument, truly sexual, good activity, actual pattern, true hit, real violence, true conflict, morning/day sex, real punishment, truly critical, firecracker, winning the competition, actual debate, energetic attack, good habits, truly opposed, vacation/holiday sex

32. Moon: feeling enraged, creative pattern, monthly habit, feeling sexy, feeling aggressive, feeling attacked, nighttime sex, feeling conflicted, emotionally attacked, monthly sex, feeling angry

33. Key: key question, uncovering abuse, definitely opposed, answer to the question, freedom fighters, revealing questions, karmic pattern, uncovering a habit, definitely sexual, revealing pattern, definitely abusive, uncovering violence, key debate, respectful question, definitely angry, openly arguing/fighting, respectful sex, open rebellion, karmic punishment

34. Fish: expensive habit, deeply hurt, drinking habit, fishing competition, drunken rage, exchanging blows, deep questions, financial abuse, deep rage, banking / credit card transactions, exchanging money for sex

35. Anchor: serious argument, routine fight, enduring sex, still abusive, lingering habits, bondage, staying mad, long-lasting disagreement, still fighting, routine sex, lingering anger, lasting hurt, suspension bondage, lasting long (sex), still having sex, still conflicted, heavy punishment, safe from harm

36. Cross: missionary position, obligated sex, difficult questions, terrible argument, intolerable sex, horrible fight, painful sex, insufferable questions, scandalous sex, intolerable criticism, regret having sex, regret asking the question, terrible sex, disappointed sexually, miserable punishment, terrible habit

Use your safe word if you get scared, honey:
"I'm fine." Her voice came out husky.
Yes, you are, aren't you?

—Cherise Sinclair

12. Birds

Restless nervous anxiety, excited and fluttering my wings
Anticipating a conversation, eager for the phone to ring
Words spoken oh so curious, rumors begin taking flight
The two become a pair, cause hectic whispers in the night

DESCRIPTION

Striking a pose, these stunning pink flamingos are basking in the twilight glow, catching the last rays of the setting sun. Feeling a sense of camaraderie, this flock continuously expresses themselves in endless chatter, throwing whispers about the glade.

The essence to the Birds' survival is a strong connection to community; being social creatures, you never see a solo Bird for too long, because "Birds of a feather flock together," as the saying goes.

A favorite pastime of the Birds is engaging in gossip, twittering, tweeting, and spilling the tea, an entertaining distraction they wholeheartedly participate in and thoroughly enjoy. Pretty little floral wreaths adorn the heads of two flamingos, indicating that they're a bonded pair. The red poisonous mushrooms in the background stand as a warning that too much excitement will bring on bouts of anxiety, a reminder to the Birds that anything in excess is never good for the psyche. Falling prey to this overwhelming anxiety is the wee bird seen curled up on the forest floor, nestling its beak into its wing, just trying to block out the noise, helpless and withdrawn, not wanting to face the world, since the nervous energy has taken its toll. The others curiously look at the poor little bird with mild concern, knowing that nothing stays this way forever; in a wink of an eye everything can change. Cushioning the fragile body of the little Bird is a bed of baby's breath; this tender, dotted white flower emits healing powers of reconnection and protection by facilitating a return to virtue. Supporting this fragrant bloom in its plight is the babbling brook playing a distant song of enchantment, as the healing waters' regenerative qualities will rebalance the Bird's spirit and revive this delicate darling, encouraging her to return to the loving embrace of the flock.

As a monarch of change, the number 12 displayed on the Birds card has the ability to awaken all the parts holding you back. The number 12 empowers you and stimulates the healing power residing deep within your being, allowing you to spread your wings and soar. Birds are associated with both the elements of Earth and Air, and sometimes that's all the magick you need; look at the situation from above, dig your heels into the ground, and throw your arms wide, singing the song of your soul as loud as you can, and before you know it, you will be a free bird.

KEYWORDS

Verbal, conversations, chatter, restlessness, nervousness, anxiety, gossip, music, noisy, a pair, a couple, talkative, vocal, excited, hectic, whispers, negotiations, phone calls, curious, spoken words, rumors, discussions, flight, birds, double

TIMING

Now, currently, twilight, December, 12 hours, 12 days, 12 weeks if the Mountain is present.

MEANING

Birds always chattering have lots to say: they're noisy and very vocal calling out to one another, here and there. When the Birds card is flying around, there's excitement in the air; beware of overstimulation, because too much stimulation brings about anxious energy.

These curious little creatures are constantly bustling around and love being in everybody's business, gossiping and spreading rumors. When the Birds card makes an appearance in your reading, be prepared for restless and distracted ungrounded energy affecting all the cards in the vicinity with a neurotic energy. Rarely seen alone, birds always flock together; that is why this card represents a couple or a pair of something, such as two jobs, two loves, two siblings, two marriages.

BIRDS IN LOVE

Lovebirds, if in a romantic relationship and you are coupled up. If you are single, the Birds card reflects a very busy dating life, talking to many people, or even dating two people at once. If you have no desire to get paired up or date at this time, have fun, be free, and soar.

BIRDS IN CAREER

Demonstrates that there is this unsettled busy energy at the workplace. The everyday busy hustle and bustle is sprinkled with a healthy dose of workplace whispers. The Birds, as a card, represents conversations at work in all of its aspects on the job. As a vocation, look to jobs such as call center, singer, air traffic controller, YouTuber, pilot, or flight attendants as well. The Birds card can also represent a job that mainly involves calling or talking to people constantly, like a telemarketer.

BIRDS IN WELLNESS

Be cautious of ungrounded energy and too much multitasking. When the Birds card appears in a reading about wellness, it sings anxiety and nervousness. Breath work and grounding exercises are very beneficial if you are feeling the effects of the Birds card.

BIRDS IN FINANCES

The excitable energy of this card results in frivolous spending: money flying in and out of your bank account. You may want something badly one moment, then having buyer's remorse the next; slow it down and ask yourself, "Do I really, really need this?"

BIRDS IN MODERN DAY

Not too many people make phone calls anymore, with all the technology we have at our fingertips; the Birds card now extends to Tweets and Twitter, social media live videos, YouTube, FaceTime, video calling.

AFFIRMATION

Anxiety is caused by the stories I tell myself, so now I will tell myself a new story with a happier ending.

CARTOMANCY: 7 OF DIAMONDS

The 7 of Diamonds affects the nervous system and can be flighty and high strung. When the 7 of Diamonds shows up in a reading, it portrays an element of instant gratification and impulsiveness. Left unchecked, this brings about a restlessness with extreme impatience when the 7 doesn't get something they want right away. Gossip and cynicism are elements of the 7 of Diamonds; beware and listen carefully with your ears because there are rumors definitely flying about.

LENORMAND BIRDS COMBINATIONS

1. Rider: first conversation, arrivals (flight), rushed negotiations, other man is nervous, first word, acting nervous, quick word, acting excited, quick chat, young man is restless, suitor is distracted, visiting couple, other man is talking

2. Clover: green bird (parrot), brief conversation, funny voice, lucky negotiations, happy-go-lucky couple, casual tone, pop music, wild talks, gambling jitters, flighty, cheeky conversation, whimsical, brief distraction, lucky couple, casual negotiations

3. Ship: departures (flight), distant couple, international song/music, cargo plane, distant noise, long-distance conversation, distant chatter, travel jitters, moving erratically, travel distraction, foreign plane, long-distance flight

4. House: family conversation, domestic partners, folk music, real estate jitters, family rumors, place causes anxiety, family member is anxious, relative / family member calls, real estate discussions, house anxiety, realtor calls, domestic plane, home phone, housefly, family member is talking, cozy chat

5. Tree: medical discussions, spiritual (meditation) music, life conversations, slow talker, spiritual conversation, medical words, patient couple, slow songs, spiritually connected couple, deeply rooted rumors, white-coat syndrome, nerves

6. Clouds: confusing discussion, transitory, lost in translation, sad tone/voice, anxiety-provoking conversation, wind chime, crazy talk, the jitters, distracted, temperamental, hidden conversations, think before you speak, lost plane, distress, hiding nervousness/anxiety, unaware of a rumor/gossip, hiding excitement, whispers, hidden phone calls, manic, lost for words

7. Snake: evil rumors, jealous tongue, toxic phone call, enticing conversation, alluring voice, cheating partner, complicated conversation, sensual tone, toxic couple, need to talk, toxic words spoken, evil couple, complex negotiation, constricted throat (airway), strained words, complicated flight, cheating couple, the other woman is talking, lying partner, throuple

8. Coffin: negative talk, last conversation, deleted voicemails, death of a partner, bad conversation, silenced voice, canceled flight, bad anxiety, death jitters, negative couple, cacophony, last voicemail, dead silence, dropped phone call / hang-up, dark conversation, gothic music, the dead are talking, nonverbal, death of a sibling, last song, final negotiations, funeral song (music played), bad flight, last phone call, last/final word, cage, denied conversation, monotone, death of a couple (at the same time or very close together), dying conversation, close your mouth!

9. Bouquet: pleasant conversation, sweet sound, wonderful couple, special conversation, beautiful music, pleasant voice, polite conversation, pleasant phone call, sweet tone, beautiful voice, nice couple, pleasant flight, wonderful conversation, beautiful music, special couple, colorful bird, nice phone call, pleasantries, performance jitters, excitement

10. Scythe: unexpected conversation, separated/divorced couple, pointed words (spoken), wounding words, dangerous tone, cutting remarks, urgent phone call, broken nerves, divided couple, "broken telephone," cutting off a couple, emergency sirens, broken phone (actual), dangerous conversation, splitting up (couple), unexpected phone call, dangerous flight, cutthroat, separation anxiety, broken couple, sudden bouts of anxiety, mincing words, clipped wings, urgent conversation, cutting off negotiations, obliterating a partnership, cutting off a conversation, emergency phone call, urgent

11. Whip: angry conversation, sexual partner, hurtful gossip, aggressive music, sexy voice, back-and-forth conversations, angry words, battle cry, sexual anxiety, a conversation, aggressive conversation, rap music, drums/drummer, angry tone, back-to-back flights, aggressive tone, repetitive rumors/gossip, ruffling feathers, intermittent phone service, sex talk, volatile, argumentative tone, abusive words, sexual tone

13. Child: slightly hectic, childlike voice, impulsive, a bit restless, slightly ungrounded, minor gossip, weak vocabulary, immature conversation, a little hectic, new song, small bird, childish tone, short flight, playing music, weak voice, a bit chatty, a little nervous, slight noise, shy couple, slightly excited, precarious negotiations, immature partner, short flight

14. Fox: calculated conversation, eluding a phone call, sneaky sibling, job/workplace negotiations, misleading conversation, worked up, clever negotiator, sneaky conversations, suspicious phone calls, tricky conversation, coworkers talking, sneaky/stealthy phone calls, practical discussion, sneaky couple, office/work conversations, covert conversations, sly negotiation, predator, sneaky partner, fake conversation, avoiding a couple, work anxiety, skittish, spying on a conversation, spying on a partner, pretending to be a couple, avoiding conversation

15. Bear: big discussion, intense conversation, major unrest, powerful/big voice, bold words, strongly bonded couple, major negotiation, overbearing tone, loud noise, powerful talk, assertive tone, overwhelming anxiety/panic, big mouth, strong language, power words, strong negotiator, fat mouth, major nerves, loud music, major excitement, very mouthy, increased phone calls, very curious, increased chatter, bold words

16. Stars: inspirational conversation, harmonious pair, online conversation, motivational speaker, high voice, evident rumors, hybrid, extensive conversation, exposing gossip, universal translator, extensive negotiations, amazing partner, future conversation, inspired words, blessed couple, great conversation, stellar negotiations, great voice, amazing talk, harmony, space flight, improving anxiety, celestial/angelic music, alleviating nerves, looking forward to talking

17. Stork: quiet voice, returning couple, long flight, birth sibling, changing the conversation, evolving partner, soft spoken, birds / winged things, evolving negotiations, return flight, returning a phone call, changing flights, birthing twins, moving jitters, changeable, progressive music, trending music/song, flying, same conversation over and over, rebooking a flight

18. Dog: faithful partner, protective sibling, familiar voice, barking, friendly voice, protective partner, friendly couple, stalking a partner, supportive words, faithful couple, supportive sibling, service flight, nosy, helpful couple, supportive partner, service call, friend's gossiping, friendly banter, dog whisperer, friend calls, following a couple, searching for flights, listening to a conversation

19. Tower: defensive sibling, legal discussion, authoritative tone, official conversation, past rumor, defensive conversation, city rumor, past negotiation, strict tone, traditional couple, formal discussion, formal negotiations, established rumors, one-man band, one phone call (prison/jail), back talk, government distractions, one-on-one conversation

20. Garden: average conversation, general chatter, popular music, commercial flight, public discussions, public voice, general negotiations, people are talking, popular couple, general malaise, public distraction, general excitement, common distraction

21. Mountain: interrupted conversation, rough voice, interrupted flight, hard negotiation, harsh tone, intercepted phone call, hard phone call, interrupted negotiations, intercepted dialogue, rough flight, raspy voice, interrupted phone service, stubborn partner, postponed conversation

22. Paths: unusual voice, many conversations, between flights, strange conversation, multiple partners, unusual anxiety, strange couple, many words spoken, getting between a couple, alternative music, strange phone call, contradictory words, multiple flights, many rumors, decision-making jitters, wavering, choose your words, deciding to call or not

23. Mice: spreading rumors, fading voice, damaged nerves, panicky, spreading gossip, less conversing, less noise, shit talker, unexcited, diminished phone calls, decreased flights, stress and anxiety, less talkative, uneasiness, obsessive, corrupt couple, anxious, damaging conversation, jeopardized negotiations, stress-induced jitters, damaged plane, dirty mouth, grunge music

24. Heart: love language, considerate partner, loving voice, compassionate tone, passionate couple, heart/favorite song, loving partner, romantic partner, heartfelt conversation, lovely couple, flirty phone call / conversation, relationship anxiety, love interest, dating jitters, forgiving partner, heartfelt words, love nest, heart-to-heart talk, a lover talks, loving pair, intimate conversation

25. Ring: married/engaged couple, bonded pair, surrounded by noise, continued gossip, surrounded by birds, ongoing conversations, surrounded by chatter, spouse/partner, round-trip flight, ongoing restlessness, ongoing negotiations (talks), continual anxiety, wedding couple, spouse is talking

26. Book: logical conversation, studying music, secretive tone, recalling a conversation, study buddy/partner, secret flight, knowledgeable couple, studying linguistics, secret teller, researching flights, smart mouth, storyteller, secretly talking, memories of flying, informative discussion, secret anxiety, memories of a song, secret phone calls, confidential conversation

27. Letter: scheduled phone calls, transcribing a conversation, messaging (talking), writing music/lyrics, text conversation, ticketed flight, written words, paper airplane, recorded conversation, sheet music, scheduled talks

28. Man: talkative man, nervous man, restless man, vocal man, curious male, male singer, male musician, pilot (male), talking to a guy, flight attendant (male), man's voice, gossiping man, brother(s), anxious man, two men, same-sex couple, masculine tone, discussing a man, male partner, jittery man, flaky man, brother

29. Woman: a bird, "Chatty Cathy," nervous lady, restless woman, vocal lady, curious female, female singer, female musician, pilot (female), talking to a girl, flight attendant (female), woman's voice, gossiping woman, sister(s), anxious woman, two ladies, same-sex couple, feminine tone, discussing a woman, female partner, jittery female, flaky woman

30. Lily: private plane/flight, private conversation, mature discussion, older sibling, private phone call, mature sibling, mature voice, having a private word, peaceful negotiations, muted, old conversation

31. Sun: etheric double, good conversation, truthful discussion, annual phone call, really anxious, happy sound, good music, jubilant tone, good voice, really nervous, happy words, happy couple, annual flight, actually a couple, really excited, actual phone call, true curiosity, winning negotiations, energetic jitters (excess energy), truth teller

32. Moon: soothsayer, feeling anxious, emotional conversation, monthly flight, feeling ungrounded, emotional words, mystical tone, feeling nervous, skilled singer, emotional song, skilled talker, skilled negotiator, emotional tone, magickal words, feeling excited, emotional partner, monthly phone call, psychic anxiety

33. Key: important discussion, destined couple, definitely talking, open conversation, karmic couple, respectful couple, privileged conversation, revealing phone call, definitely curious, keynote speaker, important phone call, key negotiations, definitely a couple, fated partner, key conversation, important couple, definitely excited, distinguished voice, affluent couple, free speech, piano, open flight, uncovering gossip, revealing conversation, karmic twin

34. Fish: business conversation, wealthy couple, business tone, stock talk, deep voice, materialistic couple, spending money anxiety, deep negotiations, exchanging words, deep curiosity, expensive flight, financial conversation, fishy couple, business phone, deep conversation, put your money where your mouth is!

35. Anchor: heavy voice, safe flight, long-lasting conversation, routine phone call, constant noise, stay vocal, safe conversation, routine flight, solid couple, serious tone, keep talking, lingering anxiety, lasting excitement, stuck in negotiations, steady voice, grounding conversation, constant chatter, still a couple, grounded flight, understated, still verbal, keep calling, enduring anxiety, hanging on to every word, settling nerves

36. Cross: spirit/ghost voice (disembodied voice), curse words, religious talk, difficult phone call, painful words, desperate conversation, difficult talk, painful voice, difficult negotiations, Christian music, angst, cursed couple, exhausting flight, disappointing partner, intolerable conversation, scandalous couple, regretting the phone call, terrible conversation, miserable couple, terrible anxiety, crossed wires

Music expresses that which cannot be put into
words and that which cannot remain silent.

—Victor Hugo

13. Child

Innocent bashful child, too timid to try something new
By trusting just a little, out of inexperience something grew
Insecurities begin to take over, when wanting a fresh start
Playfulness is a motivator, and vulnerability sets you apart

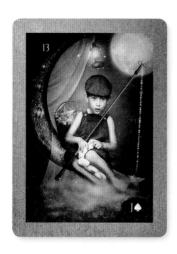

DESCRIPTION

A sweet little Child swings on the cusp of a waning crescent moon, as swirling vibrant hues of stardust light up the inky sky around him. Limpid pools of soulful, brown eyes look out into the depths of the universe. His trusting heart is innocent and sweet, filled with hope as the Child holds his breath with the anticipation of catching yet another magickal star. Holding on tightly to the rod of night, he casts out the diamond-encrusted line, symbolizing how precious of a gem he truly is. The Child's eyes light up in awe, as he catches another wish, adding this star to his bucket of dreams.

Surrounding him in a loving embrace, the sheer curtains give the Child a sense of security. His totem animal, a bunny tightly clutched between his legs, adds an additional layer of comfort to chase away his insecurities and inexperience, as he puts another wish into his bucket. Aligned with the Child's energy, the bunny is fun and carefree, vulnerable, playful, cuddly, and cautious, approachable only to those who have earned her trust. The bunny's medicine teaches the Child that, through experience, he can achieve maturity, and with a little bit of practice, he can learn to master all these qualities.

Many new possibilities lie open for the Child, symbolized by the illuminated doors seen on the crescent moon, beckoning the boy to take the first courageous step through one of the doors and begin another great adventure. This is the last visible sliver of the moon, showing the Child you cannot stay little forever; sometimes you just have to take a deep breath and let go. This Child is very gifted, for he is born under the phase of the waning crescent; by using the power of belief, the Child is able to manifest the luminescent globe behind him.

Time is approaching for the Child to awaken from this dream of twinkling stars and faraway lands. A lantern powered by moonbeams appears right above his head, magically lighting the path that will take him safely back home. The Child brings home all the wishes he caught; he naively believes with all his heart that these enchanted treasures will make all his wishes come true. The Child card bears the number 13, viewed by some as the harbinger of bad omens, but for others it is the exact opposite, bringing on good fortune. People with the 13 vibration can be very timid and naive, mimicking the childlike qualities represented in this card. It takes a minute for the 13 to warm up and openly trust someone. The darker side of the number 13 is that it can throw one hell of a tantrum when they don't get their way. One thing for sure: the number 13 has a presence all its own, and when it shows up, it makes people sit up a bit straighter and take notice.

KEYWORDS

New, simple, playful, small things, little, naive, wonder, beginning, vulnerable, inexperience, innocent, fresh start, immature, timid, childhood, short, insecure, slight, starting, a bit, weak, shy, youth, a child

TIMING

The Child card's timing is 13 days, 13 weeks, 13 months if the Mountain is present, or something of a short duration.

MEANING

Small and innocent, the Child brings new things into your life for a short duration.

When this neutral card appears, it ushers in a new beginning or fresh start of sorts, like a fresh start to do something over and even better. As a person, it can literally mean a Child—generally someone who is 12 years or younger. When describing a person, the Child card highlights childlike qualities such as youthfulness, playfulness, and immaturity. The other side of the Child card brings bouts of vulnerability and naivety coming across as timidness. Always look to the surrounding cards for clarification on what area of your life is being affected by this card.

CHILD IN LOVE

Ah, young love . . . the Child card has an underlying tone of inexperience, falling head over heels in love without truly knowing what love is—emotionally immature, unable to love in the way that is needed for a successful mature relationship to ensue. Having very naive expectations of where the relationship is heading, the Child thus inadvertently sabotages a romance that is just beginning. It can also point to one partner behaving "like a child" in the relationship, lacking the maturity to be in a grown-up relationship.

CHILD IN CAREER

A first job, a new position, or starting a fresh new career, the Child introduces something new into your employment situation. Because the Child card is neutral, it really depends on the surrounding cards, because the meaning can be very fluid. The Child card can symbolize something such as a small promotion or an immature work environment. Watch out for the sneaky Fox; if he is lurking around, expect some "throwing under the bus" to occur. If the Bear is sniffing nearby, it can point to an inexperienced boss or immature manager.

CHILD IN WELLNESS

Possibly referencing to a childhood illness, or an ailment of a short duration, usually nothing to be too concerned about. When the Child card appears, it can also represent feelings: vulnerability and insecurity. Simply put, this card can indicate that a Child is under the weather or sick. For more-specific details, look to the cards around the Child to pinpoint the cause or outcome.

CHILD IN FINANCES

This indicates inexperienced with money management, little financial resources, immature spending habits, feeling vulnerable about your finances, or falling a bit short with cash.

CHILD IN MODERN DAY

An older person may refer to someone who is acting like an immature child by a term such as "man-child," meant to be insulting, displaying inadequacy and deemed inferior in comparison; the term "child" is used when referring to someone from a younger generation.

AFFIRMATION

I am obsessed with fresh starts because every day I get a new one.

CARTOMANCY: JACK OF SPADES

Jack of Spades traditionally represents a child or a message, usually a young male with dark hair who comes across as immature and arrogant. When pushed, the Jack of Spades brings chaos and conflict because he loves to push buttons. Because the Jacks symbolize children, when appearing in a reading they will often refer to something small or new. This Jack deals with legal issues and can also represent someone who wears a uniform.

LENORMAND CHILD COMBINATIONS

1. Rider: acting playful, arrival of a child, news about children, announcing a fresh start, arrival of a new beginning, suitor is shy, other man is childish, active child, rushed new beginning, acting immature

2. Clover: happy-go-lucky child, fun playing, temporary weakness, wild child, gambling a little, chance at a fresh start, brief insecurity, green (inexperienced), easy and simple, fun is short lived, playfulness

3. Ship: distant child, travel insecurities, leaving and starting over, goodbye is short, the journey begins, adventure starts, driving underage, exploring childhood, trip to somewhere new, leaving a child behind

4. House: housing insecurity, property is small, comfortable child, house is vulnerable, family member is childish, real estate inexperience, house is small, related to the child, brand vulnerability, family, indoor playground

5. Tree: slow start, deeply rooted shyness, spiritual child, blood shortage, deeply rooted insecurities, extended duration, living simply, medical wonder, living child, spiritual wonder, blood-related child, growing insecurities, "live a little"

6. Clouds: lost child, thinking of starting something new, insecure, lost boys/girls, temperamental child, scared of starting over, unstable beginning, hidden child, lost innocence, missing child, unstable child

7. Snake: toxic childhood, tempted to start over, complicated start, needing a fresh start, wanting a child, the other woman's child, problematic start, tempted a bit, betraying a child, wanting to start over

8. Coffin: bad child, dark childhood, loss of a child, dreading to start over, let go of your childhood, denied children, let go of small things, death of a minor, ending before it started, silencing a child, grave of a child

9. Bouquet: pleasant child, wonderful childhood, beautiful child, sweet child, flower child, wonderful child, invited to play, special child, sweet shyness, polite child, gift of something new, wonderful start

10. Scythe: vaccinated/injected child, threatening a child, unexpected fresh start, cut short, broken child, obliterating weaknesses, cutting off a child, wounded child, sudden insecurity, accident-prone child, dividing something small, risky to start something new

11. Whip: hurt child, disciplining a child, aggressive play, aggressive start, erotic play (adult), assaulting a child, abusing a minor, intermittent start, abused child, questioning starting anew, arguing over small things, criticized for inexperience

12. Birds: distracted child, discussing a child, curious child, twins, talking immaturely, talking about a fresh start, vocalizing insecurities, restless child, talking about something new, rumored child, discussing a new beginning

14. Fox: practical child, feigning inexperience, cautious start, avoiding a child, faking vulnerability, calculated start, pretending that it's new, feigning shyness, stealthy child, avoiding having children, tricky start, cautious child

15. Bear: bold child, food shortages, very naive, mamma's boy, big start, intense child, very new, big child, more playful, strong start, a big thing, big insecurities, very inexperienced, assertive child

16. Stars: exceptional child, harmonious beginning, blessed child, exposing vulnerabilities, amazing child, great start, exposing small things, improving insecurity, highlighting inexperience, exposing immaturities, improving timidness, best childhood, exposing weaknesses

17. Stork: returning child, renewal, quiet child, trending for a bit, evolving insecurities, relocating for a fresh start, dancing child, cycle is beginning again, retuning something little, gentle start, evolving child, progressing a little bit, return to innocence

18. Dog: protected child, friend from childhood, searching for a child, stalking/following a child, looking after children, protecting the vulnerable, searching for weaknesses, watching over the innocent, investigating a child

19. Tower: defensive child, corporate vulnerabilities, only child, building is weak, past insecurities, defending a child, selfish child, withdrawn child, childhood, custody of a child, past weaknesses

20. Garden: average child, team player, regular childhood, popular child, generally shy, socially inept, group of children, park for children, outdoor playground, social shyness, event for children, public shyness

21. Mountain: fringe minority, delayed child, interrupted start, blocked a little, obstacles to new beginnings, rough start, new limit set, delayed a bit, set back a little, impassive insecurities, challenging child

22. Paths: strange child, middle child, path/road is short, many vulnerabilities, deciding to start anew, planning something new, separating children, the way to a new beginning, unfamiliar child, many insecurities, unusual childhood, choose something new, planning something small

23. Mice: ruined innocence, not so new, damaging childhood, less playful, small little things, flimsy, dirty child, rotten apple, eaten away little by little, damaging insecurities, dwindling opportunity for a fresh start

24. Heart: considerate child, forgive the small things, giving child, forgiving child, donating a little, lovely child, relationship is new, lover is short, relationship status (starting over), relationship insecurities, lover is immature, relationship is vulnerable, "give a little"

25. Ring: entire childhood, wholesome child, surrounded by immaturity, agreement is new, ongoing insecurities, contract is small, ongoing playfulness, marriage is simple, surrounded by inexperience, marriage is short lived, surrounded by children, contract is new, completely vulnerable

26. Book: logical child, remembering a child, secret is short lived, studious child, memories of childhood, the informative years, intelligent child, remembering innocence, education is short lived, secret insecurities, books for children

27. Letter: text is short, message is childish, communication begins, messaging a little bit, handwriting like a child, texting/messaging someone new, message is simple, communicating a little, results indicate "it's something minor"

28. Man: young man, vulnerable man, immature man, new man, small man, innocent man, short man, naive man, man-child, playful man, inexperienced man, slight man, a boy, wee man, weak man, childish man, fragile man

29. Woman: young lady, vulnerable woman, immature woman, new woman, petite lady, innocent woman, short woman, naive woman, playful woman, inexperienced female, timid woman, slight woman, a girl, wee lady, weak woman, childish woman, fragile woman

30. Lily: mature child, conservative child, daddy's girl, shy, becoming more experienced, plain and simple, laid-back child, low-key insecurities, understated new beginning, retiring shortly, composed child, old insecurity

31. Sun: fire starter, happy child, really simple, actual fresh start, truly a small thing, energy shortages, truly naive, really new, warming up a bit, true innocence, truly shy, warm child, vacationing with children, happy childhood

32. Moon: creative child, feeling playful, appearing small, skilled child, new month, emotional child, dreaming about a child, manifesting a new beginning, feeling small, emotionally vulnerable, a spell begins, appearing weak, manifesting something small, influencing a child

33. Key: privileged childhood, definitely small, revealing small things, definitely new, revealing insecurities, definitely inexperienced, privileged start, definitely immature, karma at play, definitely innocent, respectful child

34. Fish: deep insecurities, water shortage, shopping a little, money's short, financial vulnerability, wage is too small, stock is shorted, exchanging something small, business model is weak, investments are vulnerable, commissions are small, earning little, drinking underage

35. Anchor: grounded child, still the beginning, remains childish, keep it simple, still new, still naive, still vulnerable, staying innocent, still immature, remains weak, holding on to childhood, saving children, still insecure, holding on to the child, keeping it playful

36. Cross: disappointing child, regret starting anew, terrible childhood, cursed child, regret showing weakness, difficult start, terrible weakness, intolerable child, scandalous child, shameful, regret being vulnerable, miserable child, terrible start, ghost/spirit child, exhausting to keep starting over

The way we talk to our children becomes their inner voice.

—Peggy O'Mara

14. Fox

Clever hardworking scavenger, never taking a rest
Calculated suspicious con artist, manipulation at its best
Be careful not to turn your back, for sneaky is my way
Targeted by my agenda, I will trick you into becoming prey

DESCRIPTION

Sitting on a grassy knoll, the clever Fox beckons you to come in closer so he can impart some practical wisdom—if you are really willing to listen. Seeing right through you, the witty red Fox can detect any kind of deception because he himself is a master manipulator. The sly Fox is here to teach you how to be vigilant by paying very close attention to your surroundings and taking in every minute detail, for this information can come in handy when needing to outsmart or outrun any opponent. Showing you how to shrewdly evade any obstacle without having to confront them head on, the sneaky Fox finds benefit and personal gain in anything he does. Being a solo hunter, he gives himself over to his predatory instinct; with hard-at-work and stealthy observation, he is granted the edge over others; whether friend or foe, he will always find a way to survive.

Sitting beside the fly agaric, with their brilliant crimson caps, is indicative that the Fox is often connected with the darker side of the occult. Known for their hallucinogenic properties, these mushrooms are often used in shamanic practices to connect with the spirits of the underworld. The Fox, being a master of smoke and mirrors, relishes in pulling the wool over the eyes on the unsuspecting; he's always game for the next great con. When encountering the Fox card, exercise extreme caution, for this scam artist will leave you questioning the very fabric of reality of your surroundings, and what you thought to be true just ends up being an illusion shrouded with deception.

The firefly is a symbol of illumination, reminding us that things are not always what they seem. During the day, this little lightning bug is very unassuming, but at night, amid the fabric of darkness, these tiny little flashes of lights dance in sync with the primal beating of the earth's pulse and the eternal rhythms of the enchanted dance of creation. The tricky Fox is an exceptional escape artist, but there is no escaping time, demonstrated by the barren gnarled tree behind the Fox reminding him that life is very precious and tomorrow is never promised. Keeping this in mind, the Fox makes it his mission to survive by any means possible and live his best life unapologetically without any guilt. The Fox card stealthily approaches you bearing the number 14, which possesses all Fox-like qualities. The number 14 expresses independence, freedom, and self-determination, interested in everything with a natural curiosity. Boasting a heightened sense of adventure and a wit to match, the number 14 loves to explore all options and is the first in line to take a leap of faith and try something new.

KEYWORDS

Cunning, clever, sly, trickery, instinct, survival, manipulation, fraudulent, predatory, outsmart, untrustworthy, elude, stealth, scam, pseudo, witty, guilty, false, fake, suspicion, caution, mistake, con, superficial, calculated, practical, agenda, avoiding, sneaky, escape, work/employment, pretend, be careful

TIMING

When you least expect it, expect it! Noon, 14th of the month, 14 days, 14 weeks, or 14 months, depending on if the Mountain is near.

MEANING

When the Fox appears in a reading, you have to be vigilant and take notice of what is going on around you, especially at the workplace. The Fox is a trickster, and when he shows up, you can be sure that sneaky manipulation is afoot; look to the surrounding cards to see in which area your attention needs to be. The Fox represents fraudulent activities and scams; it also represents work and all kinds of work-related activities.

FOX IN LOVE

If you are currently in a relationship, watch out for manipulation; pay close attention to your partner for any suspicious behavior, because something sneaky may be going on behind your back. If you are single and looking for love, be very weary of whom you are getting involved with, because the Fox is a con by nature and may be feigning feelings with the intentions of using you. Be on the lookout for negative traits, use extreme caution, and don't get played by the Fox.

FOX IN CAREER

The Fox card, being a card of work, represents your job, employees, and coworkers. A Fox-type person is willing to do anything required and by any means necessary to make ends meet and come out on top. The Fox will be the first person to throw you under the bus; when the Fox shows up at your workplace, something underhanded is happening right under your nose, so you have to be diligent and use extreme caution.

FOX IN WELLNESS

Represents the need for a follow-up, getting a second opinion, or finding another option. The Fox is a very hard worker, always busy, so it is imperative to take the time to decompress and release built-up tension. Caution is always good when the Fox shows up, for it can indicate an undiscovered health concern or a misdiagnosis.

Be vigilant of scams, underhanded business dealings, or being a victim of a con job.

FOX IN MODERN DAY

A hottie, a redhead, sensationalism, a common misconception that now is perceived as fact, propaganda, and conspiracy theories.

AFFIRMATION

I choose to focus on the parts of my job that I find meaningful and inspiring.

CARTOMANCY: 9 OF CLUBS

The 9 of Clubs represents work, agendas, and strategies you have laid out. The 9 of Clubs approaches everything with gusto, ambition, and enthusiasm. There is another side to the 9 of Clubs: when things don't go their way, be sure that you will be met with stubbornness and irritability that will make anyone in the vicinity uncomfortable. Traditionally, the 9 of clubs brings luck, which can result in a positive career move or a lucrative opportunity. Also representing a journey in all its forms, whether it be physical, emotional, or spiritual.

LENORMAND FOX COMBINATIONS

1. Rider: acting guilty, quick escape, announcement at work, first job, acting sneaky, acting deceitful, moving cautiously, moving stealthy, acting fake, rushed job, acting suspicious, news about your job, other man's a coworker

2. Clover: easy escape, happy-go-lucky employee, temporary work, casual worker/employee, tricky, easy target, fun coworker, fun at work, brief employment, small opportunity for work, "the game is afoot"

3. Ship: leaving work, international job, leave of absence (work), leaving under the cover of night, foreign employee, long-distance job, foreign employment, leaving was a mistake, escaping, leave cautiously

4. House: family member is elusive, domestic employment, comfy job, family escapes, domestic employee, home office, domestic career, the den, family member is a user, family job, place of work, real estate mistake

5. Tree: blood work, slow worker, medical manipulation, healthcare job, woodworker, medical-procedure avoidance, deeply rooted guilt, spiritual work, medical scam, deeply rooted suspicion, medical career

6. Clouds: misplaced guilt, unstable job/career, lost coworker, confusion at work, mind manipulation, brainwashing, mental health evasion, lost at work, mindfulness, hidden job, unstable coworker, mind tricks

7. Snake: evil coworker, liar, slithering sneak, tempting job, poisonous workplace, enticing work, evil agenda, ductwork, lying coworker, complicated job, toxic coworker, complex scam, evil trick, needing a job, alluring coworker, enticing scam, deceitful, lying at work, betraying a coworker, cheating with someone at work

8. Coffin: bad employee, deleted job, bad mistake, last job, dark agenda, denied work, death of a coworker/employee, last mistake, not working, negative employee/coworker, palliative work, bad job, death/died at work, let go from work/job

9. Bouquet: wonderful job, polite coworker/employee, color scheme, presentation at work, special job, invited to a work event, perfect scam, design flaw, wonderful coworker/employee, grateful to be working, nice work!

10. Scythe: suddenly suspicious, risky agenda, weaponizing guilt, threatened employment, dividing a job, dangerous strategy, fired coworker, severed employment, vaccine/injectable requirements for work, splitting workload, broken employee/coworker, dangerous job, irrevocable mistake, "axed" from a job, removing an employee, destroying jobs, emergency service worker, urgent work, RUN!

11. Whip: hurt coworker, exercise caution, repetitive job, sexual agenda, questioning a coworker/ employee, aggressive predator, offensive strategy, angry employee/coworker, aggressive scammer, sexual predator, intermittent work, sexual coercion, hitting below the belt, strike at work

12. Birds: couple of jobs, nervous coworker, two coworkers/employees, calling at work, talking suspiciously, telephone scam, anxious about work/job, worried employee, talking to a coworker, hectic job, rumors at work

13. Child: innocent mistake, inexperienced coworker, timid employee, a little guilty, slightly suspicious, minor work, little trick, weak survival instinct, rookie mistake, a bit manipulative, small predator, minor fraud, a bit untrustworthy, slightly elusive, weak wit, a bit fake, be careful, a bit sneaky, vulnerable job, childish trick, newbie, small mistake (boo-boo)

15. Bear: boss/manager, strong wit, intense job, assertive manager/boss, massive agenda, strong suspicion, big manipulator, very sneaky, more work, intense boss, very suspicious, big mistake, major work, mother's guilt, strong survival instinct, bold coworker, survivor, major fraud, big predator, very untrustworthy, immense guilt, very fake, major scam, very guilty, more manipulation

16. Star: dream job, promotion (work), great worker, tech job, exposing fraud, great job, amazing work, exposing manipulation, best employee, seeing mistakes, enhanced instinct, extensive effort, vast agenda, improvement at work, high alert, exposing the scam, highly suspicious, highlighting mistakes, exposing the agenda, future job/career, virtual job, scientific job, potential employment, advancement (career)

17. Stork: return to work, evolving scheme, lengthy employment, returning suspicion, evolving agenda, pregnant employee/coworker, transferring jobs, evolving work situation, changing tactics, shifting job focus, having a leg up at work, switching jobs, quiet coworker

18. Dog: friendly coworker, stalker, looking for a way to escape, investigation at work, friend is untrustworthy, helpful employee, investigating a mistake, supportive coworker, looking for a job, investigating a predator, follow your suspicion, help wanted, stalking a coworker/employee, following the agenda, looking to survive, investigating a scam, predator, follow your instincts!

19. Tower: city worker, defensive strategy, one job, past mistake, city job, controlling the agenda, government official is sneaky, defensive employee/coworker, controlling coworker, official job, self-sabotage, defending your work, self-employed, enforced agenda, headquarters, industrious

20. Garden: average job, common mistake, town-hall meeting sham, people at work, coworkers, customers, group manipulation, public job, clients, common scam, general work, employees, meeting at work, public agenda, gardening / yard work

21. Mountain: delayed work, stagnant career, stubborn suspicion, hard work, setback at work, blocked escape route, interrupted work/job, remote job, setback regarding the agenda, mountain of work, limited jobs, boundaries at work, permanent job

22. Path: multiple jobs, strange coworker, unusual career, strange suspicion, many mistakes, undecided career, between jobs, many suspicions, odd jobs, on the way to work, between coworkers, unusual job

23. Mice: dirty job, costly mistake, opportunistic, dirty trick, spreading suspicion, losing your job, sneaky, low survival instinct, dirty manipulator, corruption and fraud, evading, stealthy, dirty scammer, dirty fake, less cautious, dirty con

24. Heart: compassionate coworker, interested in a coworker/employee, in a relationship with a coworker, considerate coworker, romance at work, forgiving a mistake, romantic agenda, given work, in love with a coworker, relationship con/scam, romantically manipulated, dating scam, lover's sneaky

25. Ring: ongoing work, entire career, bonded employee, continual fraud, ongoing scam, continuous guilt, ongoing suspicion, deal is a scam, contract manipulation, offered a job, surrounded by employees/coworkers, continual mistakes, ongoing manipulation

26. Book: secret agenda, information fraud, researching a coworker/employee, stories of survival, remembering mistakes, learning on the job, secret job, remembering a coworker/employee, consulting job, secret suspicion, professional career, researcher job

27. Letter: marketing/advertised job, communicating with a scammer, text is manipulative, results are elusive, newspaper propaganda, spelling mistake, documents forged, writing job, files manipulated, listing mistakes, text message is suspect, emailing a coworker/employee, written up at work

28. Man: cunning man, working man, male employee, male coworker, guilty man, shallow man, manipulative man, sneaky man, con man, red-haired man, sly man, scheming man, avoiding a man, clever man, superficial man, calculating man, practical man, suspicious man, stealthy man, careful man, cautious man, elusive man, fake man, pretending to be a man

29. Woman: shrewd woman, working woman, female employee, female coworker, guilty woman, shallow woman, manipulative woman, sneaky woman, con artist (female), red-haired woman, sly lady, scheming woman, avoiding a woman, clever woman, foxy lady, superficial woman, calculating woman, practical woman, suspicious woman, stealthy woman, careful woman, cautious woman, elusive lady, fake woman, pretending to be a woman

30. Lily: old job, precautious, experienced manipulator, discretion at work, old employee/coworker, cold and calculating, old suspicion, cautious coworker, father's guilt, experienced scammer, making peace with guilt, retired from work

31. Sun: successful escape, day job, successful employment, good strategy, happy employees, real job, truly cunning, energy manipulation, successful scam, tricked, good instincts, true predator, really untrustworthy, really guilty, neutral (Sun is true and Fox is false), good to be cautious, winning the job

32. Moon: night job, feeling cautious, magickal manipulation, spell work, feeling manipulated, psychic work, intuitive work, emotional manipulation, feeling deceived, magickal agenda, feeling tricked, psychic scam, skilled laborer, creative instinct, magic trick, emotional predator, psychic instinct, magickal work, emotional guilt, monthly workload

33. Key: definitely sneaky, honorable work, definite manipulation, prestigious career, definitely fake, respected job, definitely false, uncovering a mistake, executive, definitely guilty, yes, it's a fraud, defiantly untrustworthy, definite scam, freelancing job, definitely suspect, uncovering an agenda

34. Fish: expensive mistake, something's fishy, deep deception, business scam, deep guilt, bank job, deep fake, shopping scam, investment fraud, commissioned employee, alcoholic employee/coworker, business savvy, financial career

35. Anchor: routine work, steady employment, staying at work, enduring the workplace, insurance fraud/scam, hanging on to the job, staying employed, solid job, lingering guilt, keeping the job, still a manipulator, keep working, stay on your toes!

36. Cross: agonizing suspicion, intolerable mistake, regret hiring that employee, difficult job, crisis worker, intolerable job, terrible mistake, disappointing career, cursed job, difficult coworker/employee, intolerable coworker/employee, scandalous employee/coworker, intolerable manipulation, regret taking the job, miserable coworker/employee, terrible job, tax evasion

I solemnly swear that I am up to no good.

—J. K. Rowling

15. Bear

Strong and powerful mama, never afraid to assert some force
A warm meal and food in her belly is all she wants, of course
Overbearing but in no way intimidated, will use all her might
Big and bold apex predator, never backs down from a fight

DESCRIPTION

The crisp, crunching barrier of snow gives way under the immense weight of huge paws breaking through a thin layer of ice. Royalty of the tundra, the dominant polar bear fears no one; the sheer size and power of this ghostly white beauty is revered and feared. Living in the harshest of environments, the Bear uses its innate gifts of endurance, force, and perseverance—not only to survive, but thrive! As a master illusionist, this Bear can effortlessly camouflage herself against the snowy drifts, using the element of surprise against her enemies. Rising up on her powerful hind legs, she fearlessly meets any threat face to face, as this fierce mamma Bear will stop at nothing to protect her cubs against any perceived foes.

As a great provider of sustenance for the members of her clan, it is foreseeable that the Bear card is associated with food. Her stark, black nose is visible from many miles away, so while hunting, she has learned how to cover her nose with her paws, so the prey won't see her coming, making her a formidable opponent. The great Bear spirit is a shamanistic walker of the in-between, a powerful ally to accompany you into the enchanted world of astral travel. With patience and determination, this teacher will gently guide you, allowing you to experience wonders far beyond your wildest imagination.

The fluffy snowflakes cascade silently around the Bear and mound on the ground, demonstrating the power and strength over this element. Snow has the ability to transform from a solid to a liquid, and then back again to a solid, mimicking the Bear's immense power of shape-shifting. The evergreen boughs remain lush even in the dead of winter, demonstrating the resilience of the Bear's spirit as a dominant force of nature. The white snow falls from the heavens, accumulating on the living boughs, as barren twigs that reach up with might from the frozen earth with outstretched arms demonstrate the vivid contrast between life and death. The Bear has a symbiotic relationship with ice: by harnessing its power, she is able to stop negative energy dead in its tracks, trapping it in a frozen prison, then annihilating it with a bitter blast of cold.

Bearing the number 15, this card number embodies many similar qualities of the Bear. The number 15 is full of power and is large and in charge, just like mamma bear honoring her family bonds above all. Being an even-tempered number, 15 demonstrates exemplary leadership qualities and the makings of a good manager or boss; peppered with assertiveness and coupled with the expectation that orders will be followed without question makes the 15 a natural-born leader.

KEYWORDS

Large, powerful, mother, grandmother, dominant, well built, mighty, food, obese, big, assertive, strength, weight, boss, manager, overbearing, formidable, diet, force, leader, intense, major, bold, very, more, increasing, immense, intimidating, grand, fierce

TIMING

The Bear is a slow-moving card, usually indicative that something will not happen for a while yet. The average Bear hibernates five to seven months out of the year, but the polar bear is typically active all year round, so the timing of this card will be an average of five to seven months, and up to a year if the Mountain is present.

MEANING

The Bear card roars into your reading with an overbearing energy by bringing a certain dominance into the reading. Powerfully assertive, she stands on her hind legs and makes her presence known by just by the sheer force this card brings.

Highlighting something big is on the way, since it increases the strength of the combined card by amplifying its effect. The Bear is always in charge, and she shows up as a boss, manager, executive, entrepreneur, or management. One thing for sure, this girl is a leader at heart. The Bear also emphasizes a connection to body weight, food, diet, and obesity. Don't fault her because she's a curvy girl; she gets the job done at any size. She is a fierce matriarch that will never run from a fight; don't even think of messing with her or her cubs, for you are sure to feel her claws.

BEAR IN LOVE

The Bear brings an untamed kind of love, which can be overbearing and possessive at times. This kind of love is peppered with a nurturing vibe, making you feel cared for—the kind of affection a mother would have toward her child, which makes the dynamic of the relationship into a role of a caretaker. When on the receiving end of the Bear's love, the relationship can have a feeling of being mothered, which makes the partnership unbearable at times. If dating, this is a red flag of someone coming on way too strong.

BEAR IN CAREER

When asking about your job, the Bear card represents someone in charge, such as a boss or manager, who at times can be overbearing and full of alpha energy. Remember when dealing with this type of person that it can be quite challenging, so the Bear is here to remind you that you too possess the fortitude to overcome any obstacle presented; you just have to dig deep and channel your own inner Bear spirit. Stand on your hind legs and roar.

BEAR IN WELLNESS

The Bear card has everything to do with body strength, muscles, diet, food consumption, food addictions, and obesity.

BEAR IN FINANCES

In finances, the Bear can indicate a bear market and financial fortitude, amplifying what you have going on in your own personal finances, with the opportunity to increase wealth by might and determination.

BEAR IN MODERN DAY

Embracing a body-positive image, no body shaming; loving and embracing your curves. As a spirit animal, the Bear is a walker between worlds with the ability to astral travel and shape-shift.

AFFIRMATION

I grew a thick skin . . . you are going need claws bigger than mine to rip through my thick hide.

CARTOMANCY: 10 OF CLUBS

As a card of business and success driven by exercising the highest ideas of self, the 10 of Clubs permeates an air of great power, luxury, and wealth. Career driven, representing upper management and executives while embracing the entrepreneurial spirit. The number 10 brings completion; once the goal is achieved, the 10 automatically triggers a new beginning. Being a card of movement, the 10 of Clubs can catapult you to undergo a massive transition in your career or simply be a physical representation of a business trip.

LENORMAND BEAR COMBINATIONS

1. Rider: young leader, going strong, quick meal, breakfast (first meal), acting dominant, came in like a wrecking ball, suitor is intense, visits increase, news is intense, announcement is huge, accelerates, acting assertive, other man is bold, visit from grandma

2. Clover: greens (food), happy-go-lucky manager, small opportunity increases, multicolored hair (rainbow hair), casual meal, crazy strong, luck's increasing, gamble's huge, small gain gets bigger, laid-back manger, short-term increase

3. Ship: distant mother/grandmother, international chef, distance increases, international food/cuisine, distant boss/manager, goodbye grandma, travel increases, SUV/truck, movement increases, goodbye to mom, distance from home increases

4. House: homemade food, indoor dining, family chef, property increases, comfort eating, home-cooked meal, family meal, comfort food, a clan mother, real estate increases, family dinner, place is huge

5. Tree: healthful food, spiritual offering of food, tree fruit, growing bigger, natural diet, vegetarian, life force, growing hair, healthful meals, natural diet, growing your own food, natural foods, vitality increases

6. Clouds: temperamental boss/manager, lost appetite, hidden power, unstable mother/grandmother, lost management, turbulent, covered hair (hijab, hat, scarf, bandanna), hidden strength, troubles increase, crazed, lost taste

7. Snake: evil mother-in-law, curly/wavy hair, lying mother/grandmother, toxic management, tempting food, evil leader, constricting diet, envious of someone's strength, toxic mother/grandmother, craving power, envious of someone's hair, complicated boss/manager, needing food, cheating with the boss/manager, lying manager, cheating mother, distasteful, dark-haired woman, lies increase

8. Coffin: black bear, starvation, death (loss) of a mother/grandmother, denied food, dead mother-in-law, bad food, went out with a bang, bald, last meal, black/dark haired, deaths increase, empty calories, closed restaurant, deadly force, silence increases

9. Bouquet: wonderful meal, attractive boss/manager, wonderful mother/grandmother, sweet tooth, herbs, polite boss/manager, vegan, sweet foods, flower power (hippie), beautiful mother/grandmother, nice mother-in-law, flourishing, presenting food with finesse, plant-based diet/foods, bearded, enhancements, special diet

10. Scythe: dangerous tastes, harvesting food, cutting out certain foods, cutting hair, dangerous manager/boss, cutting off a mother/grandmother, wheat/grains, axing a boss/manager, separated/divorced boss/manager, ex-mother-in-law, danger increases, emergency power, decimating strength, broke the diet, splitting hairs, a knife, destroying food, "cutting" bodybuilding, removing hair, obliterating a diet, separated/divorced mother/grandmother, cutting off food supply, emergency food, shaving / clean shaven, trim the fat

11. Whip: abusive and aggressive, hurt mother/grandmother, sexual appetite, aggressive force, sexually dominant, aggressive manager/boss, sadistic, aggressive diet, intermittent fasting, aggravates, inflicting punishment, aggressively asserting dominance, abusive mother/mother-in-law, sex increases, intensifies, raging

12. Birds: poultry (food), talking a lot, bird food, talking to mom, speaking assertively, conversations increase, enthusiastic, conversing excessively, anxiety increases, discussion intensifies, talking to management, early-bird special (meal), calling the boss/manager, nervous talker

13. Child: immature pallet, slight build, short hair, weakening, small meals, shortage of food, weak pallet, short burst of power, timid, feeble, passive, minion, child's play, mellow, small restaurant, vulnerable mother, feeble grandmother, lightweight, weak management, wimpy, lightweight, weakling, coward, micromanaging, new manager

14. Fox: scheming mother-in-law, avoiding management, clever boss, avoiding a diet, avoiding mom/grandmom, clever mother, scavenger, careful grandmother, sneaky management, calculated manager, practical diet, suspicious mother, red-haired, sneaking food, fake hair (wig, weave, extensions), working mother, misleading, working breakfast/ lunch/dinner, sly manager, pseudo boss/manager, pretending to dieting, fake food, feigning strength, sneakiness increases

16. Star: expansive, unlimited power, great leader, great hair, advances, best mother-in-law, improvement, great build, great-grandmother, best boss/manager, great food, future leader, fine dining, vast strength, enhancing muscles, exposing management, improving strength, lifting weights, seeing beyond someone's weight, future mother-in-law, engineered food, expansion

17. Stork: regurgitating food, birth mother, quiet mother/grandmother, progressive, long hair, baby food, trendy food, shift in management, evolving power, lengthens, quiet manager/boss, migration increases

18. Dog: smelling food, hot dog, searching for food, watching your waistline, supportive mother, dog food, protective grandmother, scavenger, friendship increases, helpful mother/grandmother, searching for strength, stalking a boss/manager, looking for a leader, following a diet

19. Tower: city leader, defensive mother/mother-in-law, traditional food, defensive boss/ manager, prime minister / president, established restaurant, traditional boss, tall build, traditional mother/grandmother, control increases, formal meal, escalation

20. Garden: average weight/build, communal food pantry, popular food, average menu, assertive group, popular leader, general force, popular restaurant, garden vegetables, crowd increases, common food, social media big shot, public soup kitchen

21. Mountain: limited ingredients, heavy meal, setting boundaries with mother/mother-in-law, brute force, interrupted diet, limited meals, restricting calories, coarse hair, volcanic, interrupted meal, limited food (rations), restricted foods, limited diet, hard boss, obstacles become even bigger, stubborn manager

22. Paths: street food, unusual tastes, strange diet, buffet, unusual strength, strange mother-in-law, unusual boss, unusual mother/grandmother, project manager, unusual hair, multiple diets, strange manager, between diets, unusual/strange foods

23. Mice: dirty food, dissipating strength, thinning hair, disgusting, fading power, stress increases, dirty kitchen, insubordination, spoiled food, losing weight, diminished appetite, corrupt management, diminished taste, powerless, vulnerable, dirty/messy hair, corrupt, leader, contaminated food, fragile, hungry, opportunistic boss/manager, cheaply built, less is more, receding hairline, damaged hair, shrinkage (food theft), waning strength

24. Heart: considerate boss/manager, passion for food, forgiving boss, compassionate mother, strawberries, considerate mother-in-law, charitable, in love with your manager/boss, passionate, favorite food, forgive your mother/grandmother, donating food, giving mother-in-law, love increases

25. Ring: whole foods, a plate, surrounded by food, continual strength, ongoing diet, around management, ongoing intensity, continually increasing, marrying your boss/manager, continued force, making a deal with management/boss

26. Book: knowledgeable mother/grandmother, remembering a boss/manager, keeping a secret from the boss/manager, training to be a manager, educated mother, remembering a mother/grandmother, secrecy increases

27. Letter: scheduled diet, results increase, written card from grandma, written in bold, sending food, writing recipes, text messages increase, communication increases, texting/writing in all caps, list of foods, written card from mom, messaging increases, texting a lot

28. Man: powerful man, dominant man, forceful man, obese man, bearded man, boss man, overbearing man, muscular man, large man, big man, dominant (male), overweight man, hairy man, strong man, bold man, intense man, immense man, assertive man, formidable man, masculine build

29. Woman: mother, grandmother, mother figure, matriarch, formidable woman, dominant lady, pushy lady, curvy girl, boss lady, overbearing woman, large woman, overweight woman, strong woman, obese woman, bold woman, powerful woman, big lady, intense woman, assertive woman, feminine build, assertive female

30. Lily: mature boss/manager, grandpa and grandma, cold food, restrained mother/mother-in-law, conservative boss/manager, gray/white hair, paternal mother/grandmother, diligent, dad and mom, discreet management

31. Sun: inferno, willpower, light/blonde hair, radiating power, confident boss/manager, happy meal, true power, confident boss/manager, true strength, real food, daylight increases, confidence, positively increasing, true leader

32. Moon: creative menu, influential power(s), feeling strong, emotional mother/mother-in-law, skilled leader, silver hair, hibernation, *Strega Nona*, spell power increases, emotional boss/manager, monthly meal, intuition increases, hysterical

33. Key: distinguished tastes, chief executive officer (CEO), freedom increases, affluent boss/manager, sophisticated pallet, open restaurant, free food, honoring your mother/grandmother, respecting the mother-in-law

34. Fish: expensive meal, sushi, buying power, fishy taste, wealthy boss, expensive groceries, purchasing power, expensive taste, caviar, wealthy mother/grandmother/mother-in-law, fish (as in food), pescatarian, wealth management, money increases, seafood restaurant, resources

35. Anchor: heavy food, bottom-feeder, remains intense, grounded leader, enduring a diet, relentless, safe food, tenacious, reserved a table, salty food, enduring management, preserves, stay bold, constantly dieting, remain assertive, stay strong

36. Cross: almighty, miserable manager, regretful mother, taxes increase, hellish, terrible boss, obligations increase, desperate for power, miserable mother, terrible mother-in-law, scandalous boss/manager, intolerable management, difficult mother-in-law, difficult diet, cross to bear, crisis management, disappointed mother, cruel boss, terrible food, godmother

Courage is contagious.
When a brave man takes a stand, the
spines of others stiffen.

—Billy Graham

16. Stars

Hopeful positive dreamer, with diamonds in her eyes
Look toward the heavens, see the future in the skies
Have great ambition, always reach for the highest star
Aspire for greatness, and your goal will not be too far

DESCRIPTION

Lighting up the velvet canvas of the night is a brilliant bust of stars in the night sky, but to be seen only in the ambience of eternal darkness. These glittering diamonds are dotted and seen all over the galaxies, infinitely sharing their blessings and letting you know that all is well with you and the world. Since you were assigned a star sign at birth, this was your birthright, propelling your vision of self into the future, inspiring you to greatness. Many wishes have been collected in these celestial nebulas, as many over millennia have looked to the Stars with hope in their eyes and made a wish with all their might. Making the Stars a tangible source of magick available for all those who desire a positive outcome in order to greatly improve their life, all you have to do is look up, close your eyes, and make a wish. For centuries the Stars have been the most faithful of guides, honored by the ancients as they used these electrifying fixed constellations to align their most-sacred temples, built to honor the gods and used in hopes to guide them back from the heavens to Earth once again. Associated with science and philosophy, the Stars have inspired some of the earthly greats of our time in literature and Greek philosophy to live on forever in their great works, theories, and teachings, intertwining our lives with them.

A backdrop of astrological signs is woven throughout the Stars card, representing a snapshot of the heavens the moment you entered this lifetime. Throughout your life, you will carry the influence of your Stars guiding your lifetime and infinitely aligning you to your soul's purpose, giving you a feeling that you are not alone in this universe.

Always worshiped from afar, the Stars are one of the oldest and most enchanted symbols known to mankind that can never be grasped but only admired at a distance. You are intrinsically connected to these infinite wonders, since you are made up of the same magickal stuff as the Stars.

As a great explorer, the number 16 comes shining into your life, sharing many similarities with the Stars, inspiring you to keep moving forward into the future until your dreams are attained.

Connected to spirituality, 16 possesses both the wisdom and scientific aptitude to raise those philosophical questions inspiring soulful conversations. The number 16 is the only integer that has five exact divisors, mimicking the sections of the five-pointed star, representing both the image of man and the elements. Each point is a limb and the top is the head, and each of Earth's five elements with the top is spirit.

Remember our own beloved Sun is the greatest Star of all, for it is the giver of life; without it, all life would cease to exist. So the next time you want to honor the Stars when you feel the warmth of sunlight on your face, be grateful and thank your lucky Stars that you are alive, and in the silence of the eternal night when you see the glittery Stars, dream the biggest dreams and shoot for the Stars!

KEYWORDS

Wishes, hope, dreams, potential, guidance, inspiration, philosophy, exposure, align, vision, science, fame, blessings, World Wide Web, enhancements, technology, electricity, clarity, recognition, improvement, aspirations, universe, unlimited, harmony, uplifting, high, exposure, goals, visible, positive, future, eternal, idea, best, great, vast, extensive, beyond, forever, digital, north

TIMING

When using the Stars card for timing, it is indicative of something that is everlasting, eternal, and infinite or will take place when you can see the Stars in the night sky.

MEANING

The Stars card is indicative that something positive is happening, one of the most favorable cards to see in the deck that makes everything better, letting you know that your dreams and aspirations are well on their way to fruition. Bringing blessings of all kinds, the Stars have a very fortunate effect on any surrounding cards—when combined with other positive cards, it enhances their meaning; when combined with negative cards, it softens up the difficulty and brings hope into the situation.

The Stars offer insight to every situation, providing clarity so you can plot out the best course to achieve your goals. There is a philosophical feel to the Stars card being unlimited, unbound, and eternal, inspiring you to ask those thought-provoking questions about life, purpose, and existence.

Symbolic of fame or celebrity, the Stars bestow the highest recognition; the greatest magick is to recognize that every single one of us is the Star of our own life. So take a moment and turn your gaze toward the heavens and take in the wonder of these celestial beings, knowing that you are not alone in this great universe. This is a card of wishes coming true, so go ahead close your eyes and make a wish!

STARS IN LOVE

A very favorable card to show up in a love reading, it brings hope for the future or improvement to a relationship in trouble. The Stars card also highlights a love connection that is written in the Stars—there is a reason why you met and found each other. If looking for love, an exhilarating new love connection could be on the cusp of emerging. If you and your soulmate are worlds apart or cannot be together in this lifetime, find comfort in knowing that as you look up into the night sky, both of you are looking at the same Stars and wishing the same wish.

STARS IN CAREER

Your career is reaching new heights, and a promotion may be in store for you. The Stars card is indicative that you could be recognized as a rising star at work or honored as a star employee. The Stars card can also represent a career in the film industry, showing up for someone who has celebrity status or is even a famous social media influencer.

STARS IN WELLNESS

Things are looking up! A very positive card indicating improvement and encouragement that you're moving in the right direction. If you're awaiting results, Stars could be indicative that something comes back positive, so you must look to the surrounding cards to offer insight, whatever it may be; soon you will be offered clarity. By harnessing the power of the Stars, use positive affirmations and visualization to send positive vibes to any circumstance.

STARS IN FINANCES

Fortunate monetary outcomes, since financial goals are manifesting.

STARS IN MODERN DAY

The Stars represents digital technology in all its forms, as well as the connectivity of the internet represented by the World Wide Web (www). The Stars card is symbolic of astrology and your birth chart. It also represents fame, which nowadays could also be a social media influencer. When reading for yourself or a client, and the Stars make an appearance, lay your hand on the card and touch the Stars, close your eyes, and make a wish with all your heart.

AFFIRMATION

I will shine my light so bright that I will not only inspire myself but be a beacon of inspiration for the ones who are lost.

CARTOMANCY: 6 OF HEARTS

Traditionally, the 6 of Hearts is a card of nostalgia or anything associated with past events. Representing a karmic love connection, this is a very positive card to show up when asking about love. When the 6 of Hearts appears, it usually indicates that something of significance will take place. Immersed in masculine energy, the 6 of Hearts stands for honor and bravery with a strong protective vibe, clearing the way and allowing things to move forward in a positive direction toward a favorable ending. The 6 of Hearts symbolizes illumination, spiritual enlightenment, and harmony.

LENORMAND STARS COMBINATIONS

1. Rider: going online, mobile site, news media, first dream, headliner, fast exposure, other man's exposed, acting hopeful, hurry up, going to improve, acting positive, fast internet, going toward a goal, newsworthy

2. Clover: green star, temporary goal, green/hazel eyes, wild idea, fleeting idea, wild science, emerald (gem), wild dream, treasure, a wish, wild inspiration, brief exposure, gaming site

3. Ship: exploring space, distant dream, transportation technology, touring the stars, trip to space, distant galaxy/universe, moving toward your goal, travel upgrade, distant star, navigating the galaxy/stars, leaving your dreams behind

4. House: family exposed, Earth (our home), house ideas, family vision, house blessing, home in the stars, property has potential, brand alignment, family goals, refuge in the stars, family goals, outpost in space, house window, home Wi-Fi

5. Tree: medical website, biotechnology, slow computer, healthcare system, slow internet, spiritual website, slow exposure, deeply rooted dream, biofeedback, biometric technology, medical technology, spirituality, biosciences, medical/health sciences

6. Clouds: misplaced home, unstable Wi-Fi, lost hope, unclear, incognito web browsing, clouded vision, hidden star, uninspired, hopeless, hidden, gray eyes, misunderstanding an idea, troubling future, invisible, hidden website

7. Snake: evil science, enticing dream, affair exposed, complex goals, complicated technology, toxic exposure, evil vision, complicated future, problematic future, other woman exposed, betrayed in the future

8. Coffin: death of a star, ill wish, unscientific, impossible, deleted website, dark star, bad eyesight, bad technology, last hope, dark web, bad idea, blind, dark view, last wishes, denied wish, dying star/planet, close your eyes, final frontier, let go of a goal, unenlightened, dark/brown eyes, death sentence, turning a blind eye

9. Bouquet: wonderful dream, beauty enhancements, positive exposure, fashion website, amazing, marvelous idea, beautiful stars, wonderful guidance, fantastic, wonderful exposure, beautiful eyes, special recognition, blessed, wonderful future, beautiful vision

10. Scythe: dangerous idea, broken technology, flawed diamond, sudden inspiration, unexpected idea, risky exposure, sudden fame, unexpected hope, sudden clarity, half the potential, decimating future goals, obliterating a star, risky advancements, decimating science/technology, cutting off Wi-Fi, injecting technology

11. Whip: sexual bliss, angry eyes, sex positive, aggressive goals, intermittent Wi-Fi, Mars, aggressive technological advances, sexy eyes, beaten up, questioning the future, sexual chemistry, sexually harmonious, come-hither look, sexual enhancements

12. Birds: discussing ideas, flying north, talking about goals, couple is exposed, flying high, podcast, flight upgrade, bird's-eye view, gossip websites, conversation brings clarity, couple's blessed, flying in the sky

13. Child: microchip / nano chip, small blessing, weak internet, new idea, slight exposure, new galaxy, a bit inspired, new planet, little/minor star, new dream, slight hope, small dream, new science, minor recognition, weak idea, ignorance is bliss, vulnerable online, nanotechnology, childish dreams, small eyes

14. Fox: work website, employee recognition, practical goal, pseudoscience, stealth technology, cautiously optimistic, incognito (online), cautiously positive, pseudotechnological advancements, feigning positivity, pretending to recognize something/someone, misguided, sneaky look

15. Bear: grand dream, big goals, food website, grand future, big idea, massive potential, Jupiter, big eyes, power of social media, Ursa Minor, Ursa Major, big wish, powerful motivation, major star, very inspired, grand vision, great heights, huge blessing, strong Wi-Fi, increased harmony, major goal, increased visibility, huge exposure, very famous, huge aspirations, megastar, big improvement

17. Stork: baby website, evolving goals, changing dreams, returning vision, switching ideas, pregnancy exposed, progressive eyeglasses, pregnancy in the future, trending upward, shifting prospective, move is positive, long view, changing your view, moving in the future

18. Dog: trusting the science, looking for clarity, friendship exposed, looking for guidance, the watchers, shields up, guardians of the galaxy, a guide, guardian angel, following "the science," assistive technology, friendly eyes, looking at the stars, searching for hope, looking for inspiration, searching online, looking to align, follow the stars, searching forever, look north, investigating online, looking for recognition, Sirius (dog star), surveillance

19. Tower: high tech, government website, control using technology, government exposed, self-guided, ambitious goal, up high, arrogant views, defending your dreams, established goal, controlling the future

20. Garden: common goal, average potential, public site, online, common vision, public guidance, general philosophy, general alignment, human enhancements, social media, general science, public view, constellation, social sciences, public eye

21. Mountain: remote viewing, interrupted Wi-Fi, blocked website, boundaries/limits exposed, hard stare, interrupted harmony, challenging future, restricted space, interrupted electricity, asteroids, Area 51, interrupted goals, in the distant future

22. Paths: unusual clarity, strange philosophy, many blessings, strange vision, weird science, separate goals, multiple ideas, unusual recognition, many dreams, strange technology, multiple galaxies, planning goals, asteroid belt, paths align, multiple goals

23. Mice: dissipating hope, corrupt science, jeopardizing the future, damaging technology, low visibility, diminished vision (eyes), dissipating fame, fading dream, stodgy, damaged computer, jeopardizing a goal, corruption online, unperceptive, unclear, lackluster, less visible, dirty science, nasty stare, corruption exposed, ruined goals, crumbling dreams

24. Heart: dating site, lover exposed, Venus, romantically inspired, loving eyes, giving you the stars, love eyes emoji, relationship exposed, given clarity, kind eyes, love aligns, relationship guidance, given hope, love aligns, given a diamond, relationship wish, love is eternal, relationship blessings

25. Rings: jewelry website, rolling-eyes emoji, ongoing exposure, infinite, continual blessings, Saturn, whole future, marriage potential, continuum (space), ongoing goals, continual guidance, marriage blessings, continued fame/recognition, ongoing clarity, continued harmony, eternal, surrounded by greatness, promise of forever, whole world, entire universe/galaxy

26. Book: educational site, remember the positive, research site, secret website, informative science, book of ideas, remember your goals, educational technology, information (internet), secret wish, recognizing something/someone, remembering clearly, memories of a future time, information technology, studying computer sciences

27. Letter: Mercury, data technology, sending hope, Wednesday, sending good wishes, blog website, communication exposed (text/messages), communication technology, jotting down an idea, database

28. Man: famous man, male influencer, inspiring man, hopeful man, positive man, goal-oriented man, dreamer (male), visionary (male), optimistic man, good-natured man, man of your dreams, philosophical man, technical man, online man, blessed man, guided man, best man, great man, exposed man, future man, potential man, enlightened man, recognizable man

29. Woman: famous woman, female influencer, inspiring female, hopeful woman, positive lady, goal-oriented woman, dreamer (female), visionary (female), optimistic woman, good-natured lady, dream girl, philosophical woman, technical woman, online woman, blessed woman, guided woman, best woman, great lady, exposed woman, future woman, potential woman, enlightened woman, recognizable woman

30. Lily: conservative dreams, Uranus, old idea, lifetime of blessings, private site, conservative views, comet, private browser, lifetime of blessings, the frozen North, peaceful future, conservative goals, old technology, mature outlook

31. Sun: gold star, true clarity, let your light shine, good improvement, energy / solar power technology, true vision, real exposure, Sunday, truth exposed, truly fantastic, true north, sunny future, really amazing, truly harmonious, positively aligned, real science, true potential, real hope, happy future, annual goal, take a good look, verified social media account, the sun (actual), positive outcome, brightest blessings, good idea

32. Moon: feeling hopeful, emotional goals, creative vision, feeling blessed, feeling clear (clarity), creative websites, eclipse, feeling inspired, creative idea, intuitive/magickal websites, feeling guided, feeling positive, feeling exposed, emotional clarity, emotional high, inspiration, creative technology, feeling aligned, psychic potential, the moon (actual), monthly goal

33. Key: important technology, key goal, VIP, definitely aligned, key witness, very revealing, exposed, open your eyes, revealing an idea, dignitary, recognition, answer is positive, fated (the stars aligned), open to blessings, karmic entanglement

34. Fish: expensive dream, financial website, deep sky, business idea, shopping websites, blue eyes, financial exposure, deep space, Neptune, whiskey glasses / beer goggles, business technology, paying it forward, business internet/Wi-Fi

35. Anchor: stable internet/Wi-Fi, solid idea, sustainability goals, keep up with technology, holding on to fame, keep wishing, constantly guided, stay north, still hoping, keep dreaming, constantly exposed, staying aligned, keep rising above, still recognizing, keep positive, staying visible, keep expanding, hang onto hope, indefinite, hold on to a dream

36. Cross: religious website, ideology, painful exposure, intolerable idea, disappointing future, difficult goal, spirit exposed, disappointing dream, terrible philosophy, shameful recognition, scandalous websites, terrible idea, miserable outlook, sacred geometry

A star does not compete with other stars around it; it just shines.

—Matshona Dhilwayo

17. Stork

Change is the only constant, as the season shifts to spring.
Elegant long legs dancing, the graceful flutter of a wing
Rebirth is part of the transition, shifting and ever churning.
Gentle progress is made, as the cycle quietly keeps returning.

DESCRIPTION

Nestled in the grassy cone-shaped knolls of Fairy Glen is a little hideaway home on the island of Skye. The family anxiously awaits a precious delivery from the Stork, leaving a wee acorn light on to illuminate the way. Outside the door, a colorful pram awaits ready to receive the new bundle of joy, as the Stork gracefully flies in and nestles the baby gently within, to the joy of the awaiting parents. Storks are the universal symbol of the bringer or life; if they are not bringing a baby, rest assured something new is being birthed into existence.

Tender daisies dot the lush ground, offering the first glorious scent of spring, as the Stork bestows gifts of daisies to represent the innocence and purity of new life. A bunch of these precious petals will also be given to the new mother to help with ease of childbirth and ensure future fertility. The blue harebells start blooming from late April–May, perfectly fitting the timing of the Stork card, which denotes the fertile time of spring just as they return from their migration. The tinkling, lithe sound of the harebells summon the fairies to bear witness of this joyous occasion; sparkling, shifting, golden fairy orbs start gathering in the glen as they hear the chiming of the bells. The fairies give the new soul the enchanted spark of life, offering many blessings as they dance, celebrating the birth.

Standing on the ever-changing threshold of twilight, the white-and-black-colored Stork mimics the theme of duality, being both a creature of Air and Water; the calm, quiet bird demonstrates that actions speak louder than words. When the Stork appears, it reminds you that now is the time for action. Only change and movement will create a way through the greatest of struggles, heralding the beginning of a new cycle.

Only when the Stork is satisfied is their charge released into the safe loving arms of the family; they prepare to leave as a crisp chill permeates the air, as the seasons begin to change.

This is the cue for the Stork to take flight and migrate somewhere warm, only to return next spring during the time of rebirth and renewal. The Stork card swoops in with the number 17, representing work and travel, just like the Stork travels great distances to deliver new life; the number 17 is always on the move. This number is dedicated, successful, and always using sound judgment when implementing a change. These are just some of the great qualities enabling the number 17 to get things done; as hard and unyielding as the number 17 appears on the outside, they are equally as soft and gentle on the inside.

KEYWORDS

Change, migration, birth, seasonal, transition, progress, trend, shifting, evolve, relocation, graceful, cycles, moving, spring, rearrange, quiet, returning, altered, transfer, renewal, long, gentle, dancing, recurring, modified

TIMING

Springtime, highlighting the months of March, April, and May, can also denote the changing of the seasons. The Stork represents the 17 days or the 17th of a month; if the Mountain is present, it can be as long as 17 months. At times it can refer to nine months, the length of human gestation. When taking the timing of the Queen of Hearts into consideration, it can denote the month of April.

MEANING

When the Stork comes into your life, it bring about some change; it being a neutral card, look to the surrounding cards to see exactly what this modification might be. As a statement of a powerful transformation, the Stork can denote a physical move or an internal shift. This card can indicate an actual pregnancy or that something new is being birthed into existence. The Stork is a quiet bird, gently letting you know that talk is cheap, and true change happens only by taking action.

STORK IN LOVE

When the Stork shows up in a love reading, it is indicative of a change in the relationship or even in relationship status. At times, the change does not seem positive at first, but it always ends up being for the highest good in the end. When a couple gets it right, the Stork brings an energy of fierce loyalty and monogamy. When trying for a baby, this is a very positive card to see, for it can indicate that a pregnancy might ensue. If you are single and looking for love, you need to switch things up in your life in order to usher in a new relationship.

STORK IN CAREER

When it comes to a career, the Stork can indicate a transfer or a physical change to a different location. The Stork can indicate a change in employment or a seasonal job. As a career, it can represent a midwife or any job that works with pregnant woman or babies.

The Stork brings a change to any issue; look to the surrounding cards to see if this will be positive or negative in nature. Since the Stork is a quiet bird, it can indicate an issue with your larynx resulting in loss of voice—or legs, since the Stork is all about the legs.

STORK IN MODERN DAY

A great powerful spiritual shift.

AFFIRMATION

I am in the process of changing into a better version of myself, as I quietly move into greatness.

CARTOMANCY: QUEEN OF HEARTS

This is a loving, caring, and compassionate Queen, and many find comfort in her nurturing embrace. As wonderful mothers, the Queen of Hearts will viciously protect anyone in their charge; family always comes first. The Queen of Hearts is a sensual, passionate partner who at times can be attracted to an excessively posh lifestyle. Creative and intuitive, she is someone who others seek for wise counsel. Strong and resilient, she relies only on herself and will not be taken for granted. The Queen of Hearts also represents the month of April.

LENORMAND STORK COMBINATIONS

1. Rider: going back, first move, first cycle, visiting in the spring, coming back, acting quiet, this coming spring, rushed movement, going and coming back, looming in the horizon, quick move, progression

2. Clover: luck shifts, game changer, spring, country move, temporary trend, chance of pregnancy, brief relocation, easy birth, short-term move, quick transition, laughing quietly, happy returns

3. Ship: sea legs, leaving quietly, voyaging, travel trend, vehicle modifications, globetrotting, transmigration, departing, expedition, leaving and moving away, transportation evolves, international move, journeying

4. House: real estate trend, place of birth, home again, family reunion, house mover, house modifications, family member is pregnant, family is moving, home birth, family nest, domestic move, house flipper

5. Tree: slow season, spiritual trend, healthful move, slow progress, slowly shifting, healthful trend, blossoming, slow transition, healthy baby, slowly evolving, slow cycle, live birth, healthy pregnancy, body modifications, slow birth progress

6. Clouds: passing seasons, hidden pregnancy, mindset shifts, afraid of being pregnant, passing cycle, climate change, confusing move, fear of giving birth, hidden move, passing trend, hiding progress, depression returns, weather modifications

7. Snake: transformative shift, problematic trend, toxic cycle, complicated birth, problematic move, complicated transition, wanting a baby, tempted to move, umbilical cord wrapped, toxic move, cheating (trend), spiral dance, other woman is back

8. Coffin: bad spring, loss of pregnancy, bad cycle, last dance, bad trend, stillbirth, final cycle, last transition, final/last move, putting an end to a trend, loss (death) of a baby, sick baby, postpartum, bad move, death transition

9. Bouquet: pleasant birth, color trend, wonderful move, surprise pregnancy, beautiful baby, design's modified, pleasant spring, art trend, showing (pregnancy), nice move, beautiful season, special dance, flowering, enjoying pregnancy, beautiful transition, wonderful progress, budding pregnancy

10. Scythe: autumn season, amputated leg(s), emergency migration, cutting the umbilical cord, cut off progress, abrupt shift, dangerous trend, decimating quiet, obliterating progress, emergency birth, urgent move, separated at birth, threatening to move out, unexpected/accidental pregnancy, broken leg

11. Whip: sexual progress, frequent changes, sexy legs, intermittent cycle, aggressive move, habit evolves, sexual trend, aggressive shift, disruptive change, procreation, back and forth, intermittent progress, active birth, sexually evolved, pattern of moving

12. Birds: crybaby, talk of relocating, flying back, exciting trend, flying the coop, noisy baby, talk of transferring, excited to move, plane returns, anxiety returns, flight in spring, twins, couple returns, excited about returning, restless legs

13. Child: child returns, short cycle, newborn, beginning of the season, small changes, child is born, short season, minor shift, slight progress, a bit quiet, slightly altered, short transfer, small baby, tiny dancer, new baby, small transition, short migration, weak move, tiny modifications, slight rearrangement

14. Fox: calculated pregnancy, avoiding change, suspicious pregnancy, stealthy return, cautiously quiet, faking progress, practical move, suspicious move, careful progress, stealthy pregnancy, calculated move, avoid moving, pretending to be pregnant, feigning change, carefully created, avoiding pregnancy

15. Bear: mother/grandmother returns, big baby, major changes, mass migration, major shift, big transfer, very quiet, major rearrangement, more changes, powerful transition, huge progress, food trend, majorly altered, very long, forced to change, swollen legs/feet

16. Stars: high heels, forever changed, Mercury retrograde, best move, amazing grace, blessed baby, harmonious shift, future changes, high season, ever changing, positive pregnancy, looking forward to returning, evolution, look toward the spring, future pregnancy, advancement, future move, digital trend, highly evolved, progress

18. Dog: smell of spring, familiar trend, looking for progress, smelly feet, friendship changes, looking at trends, friend is quiet, following the pack, help with modifications, friend returns, looking for a change, help with a move, a nanny

19. Tower: city trends, past spring, defending changes, established cycle, official move, old man returns, established trend, government evolves, official trend, established cycle, isolating relocation, city move

20. Garden: cultural shifts, population exchange, mass exodus, general quiet, average spring, population migration, general progress, human modification, population is quiet, societal change, humans evolve, social media trend, general shift

21. Mountain: permanently changed, interrupted progress, permanent trend, obstacles (moving), blocked transfer, challenging changes, postponing a move, resisting evolution, restrictions evolve, boundaries change, permanent modifications, limits altered

22. Paths: planning to move, walking, multiple shifts, unusual birth, strange transition, unusual modification, multiple moves, unusual spring, pros and cons of moving, multiples (births), unusual progress, strange trend, between moves, transitioning, between transfers, plans change

23. Mice: stressful move, less progress, dissipating trend, losing mobility (legs), low births, disgraceful, disease mutates, damaging modifications, jeopardizing progress, damaging move, miscarriage

24. Heart: dating trend, giving birth, relationship changes, love evolves, lover returns, date progresses, romance evolves, affection changes, love shifts, heartfelt change, love pregnancy, pleasure returns, forgiveness alters you, love nest

25. Ring: anklet, continued progress, circle back, entire season, ongoing cycle, ongoing shifts, continual evolution, marriage trends, ring is returned, cycles, recycling, contract modifications, complete transformation

26. Book: logical move, secret relocation, educational trend, secret birth/baby, student returns, book returned, journaling trend, studying gynecology, books on childbirth, training evolves, research changes, unknown pregnancy

27. Letter: schedule changes, messaging/texting trends, letter returns, email is changed, texting got quiet, communication changed, schedule rearranged, results change, transferring documents, scheduling a move

28. Man: a man returns, transitioning male, evolved man, sophisticated man, monogamous man, quiet man, caring man, graceful man, progressive man, restless man, leggy man, changed man, trendy man, modified man, a man is moving, male dancer

29. Woman: a woman returns, transitioning female, evolved woman, sophisticated lady, monogamous woman, quiet lady, caring woman, graceful lady, progressive woman, leggy woman, changed woman, trendy woman, modified woman, a woman is moving, female dancer

30. Lily: father/grandfather returns, old trend, peace and quiet, discreet changes, very quiet, father/grandfather changes, private transition, senior is moving, old modification, retirement progress

31. Sun: good progress, really moving, happy birthday, true grace, summer season, annual cycle, happy returns, annual relocation, really long, vacation/holiday changes, annual trend, real transition, true progress, real shift

32. Moon: creative shift, monthly trend, feelings return, feeling a shift, a spell comes back to you, emotionally evolved, feelings progress, skills returns (like riding a bike), magickal shift, manifesting a pregnancy

33. Key: key move, significant progress, door lock changed, open legs, fated move, significant modifications, open to move, revealing pregnancy, karmic cycle, definitely moving, important changes, YES—pregnant!

34. Fish: business trend, expensive move, purchases returned, deep quiet, money back, financial transactions, shopping trend, financial alterations, business progresses, price altered, money returned

35. Anchor: steady modifications, safe/stable pregnancy, heavy footsteps, enduring change, saved progress, keep returning, downward trend, keep quiet, steady, safe move, saving grace, heavy legs, lingering trend, stagnation

36. Cross: beliefs evolve, exhausting move, painful legs, difficulty getting pregnant, obligated move, terrible pregnancy, difficult transition, miserable pregnancy, disappointing progress, difficult birth, shameful pregnancy, pilgrimage, difficult spring, colicky baby

There is nothing permanent except change.

—Heraclitus

18. Dog

Faithful canine companion, trusting with nothing to hide
Familiar watchful guardian, protective and by your side
Unconditional friendship, loyally following you everywhere
Reliable and helpful investigator, supportive and always there

DESCRIPTION

The Dog patiently sits before a whimsical mushroom house, and the day's last drops of sunshine are soaked up by velvety soft, golden fur. Soulful honey-brown eyes boldly stare into the depths of your being, knowing instinctively if you are friend or foe. These intense, familiar bonds are illustrated by the collar he proudly wears, identifying the Dog as a cherished member of the family. Duty born out of unconditional love, yet fiercely protective of his human family, he will stop at nothing to guard the ones he loves most.

Wearing a flat cap atop his silky head signifies the Dog is of the working class and will always be of service to mankind. Freely giving his loyalty, this faithful and trusted companion has earned the title of man's best friend. Always with your best interest at heart, this reliable companion is selfless; his only agenda is to please you through service. Always living in the moment and content to investigate everything through his nose, come as you are is the Dog's message, since there is always something new to investigate or find a new friend to love.

Watch the Dog closely to learn how to let go of all self-judgment with compassion and love, freeing up space, which allows you the room to fully experience life by living in the moment.

Enchanted golden orbs swirl around the Dog, symbolizing the presence of an ascending being; with a very short lifetime, the Dog does not have much to learn—but so much to teach. Sitting among the ferns, which represent the Dog's undying dedication and revere, forges this magical bond between humans and dogs that can never be severed, because once you are loved by a Dog, that connection will last eternally.

Tirelessly waiting for his family pack to return home, the Dog is the first to the door and happily welcomes you home. At times, the Dog will bark a warning alerting you that something is not right with the situation; take heed of your surroundings, for a Dog's instincts are never wrong.

When the number 18 pounces into your life, bringing philanthropy and kindheartedness, a devotion and compassion that's always preoccupied with the safekeeping of all is present. The number 18 possesses the determination and grit needed to spring into actions to achieve all its goals, while being of service to others, just like the Dog.

KEYWORDS

Friend, loyal, follower, reliable, helper, companion, supportive, investigation, a guide, submissive, faithful, protective, watchful, guarding, trustworthy, familiar, a pet, unconditional, obedient, service, smell/scent, following, searching, assistance, looking

TIMING

Not usually used for timing, but if you do decide to use the Dog card for timing, it would be best to use the card's number. The number 18 can imply 18 days or the 18th day of a month, or, if the Mountain is present, it can be up to 18 months.

MEANING

As a neutral card, the Dog is here to be of service; possessing a naturally inquisitive nature, the Dog is that best friend who's your "ride or die," ready to investigate anyone by the power of keen observation. When the Dog card appears, look to the surrounding cards for a clue as to what all the barking is about. As a person, it's indicative of someone who is familiar to you or has that familiar sense to them. Loyal and dependable, the Dog is reliable and comes in the guise of a best friend who is supportive, but watch out for these exact qualities, since it can easily turn into people pleasing by continually putting others' needs before your own.

DOG IN LOVE

When inquiring about love and the Dog card presents itself, it's indicative of a faithful relationship that is dependable, with the expressed desire to experience unconditional love found in soulmates. Since the Dog card symbolizes friendship, be on the lookout for the possibility of a friend to become a lover, or a relationship that started out as a friendship developing to something more. If single, you may be encountering a feeling of being stuck in the "friend's zone" one too many times or typically finding yourself in relationship that is not much more than "friends with benefits."

DOG IN CAREER

In career, the Dog usually indicates a supportive work environment that's friendly. The Dog is inquisitive by nature and loves to investigate, which would indicate careers in policing, protection services, or investigation. Due to the Dog's helpful nature, a career in emergency services, counseling, therapy, or animal care in all its forms is perfect.

DOG IN WELLNESS

Denoting someone or something that aids you in achieving your health goals, the Dog can also represent healthcare professionals or support workers who assist you with your wellness goals. This card can also refer to something going on with your hearing or sense of smell, since Dogs excel in both.

DOG IN FINANCES

When the Dog appears sniffing around your finances, it represents needing some form of financial support, assistance, or help with finances.

DOG IN MODERN DAY

The Dog card represents social media followers, or any online friends considered social media friends.

AFFIRMATION

I choose friends that reflect the person I am or am trying to become; for that reason, I choose very wisely.

CARTOMANCY: 10 OF HEARTS

When the joyful 10 of Hearts appears in your reading, it is a very good omen. The 10 of Hearts lessens the effect of all the negative cards surrounding it while it amplifies the positive cards. As a traditional card of marriage, it can point to a large family, just as dogs have large litters. As a person, the 10 of Hearts can be a bit too naive and trusting at times, wearing their heart on their sleeve and too often putting others first. The 10 of Hearts is also representative of a large body of water.

LENORMAND DOG COMBINATIONS

1. Rider: first responder, quick investigation, first dog/pet, other man is loyal, acting submissive, equine-assisted therapy, acting supportive, fast friends, suitor's a friend, young man needs help

2. Clover: happy-go-lucky companion, gambling support, casual friends, Irish wolfhound, lucky friend, temporary friendship, short-term help, casual investigation, temporary submissive, brief support

3. Ship: travel agent, travel therapy, leaving a friend behind, leaving therapy, travel/tour guide, international investigation, travel companion, distant friend, travel investigation, leaving a companion

4. House: family therapy, domestic helper, real estate advisor, house investigation, housing assistance, roommates/flatmates, family friendly, domestic animal, family / familiar witness, comfort animal, family dog

5. Tree: sense of smell, therapy, slow investigation, deep-rooted friendship, slowly trusting, natural therapy, slow service, biosurveillance, therapy dog, somatic therapy, medical witness, bodyguard, life support, gene therapy, spirit guide, medical investigation, life of service, spiritual friend

6. Clouds: misplaced loyalty, hidden investigation, psychodynamic therapy, lost friend, misplaced trust, lost pet, mental health therapy, misplaced friendship, lost support, addiction therapy, confused witness, temperamental friendship, behavioral therapy, unstable friend, psychotherapist

7. Snake: evil friend, lie detector, complicated investigation, enticing friend, toxic fumes, evil stalker, lying witness, constricting friendship, needing companionship, cheating friend, complex therapy, deceiving a friend, seducing your friend, toxic companion

8. Coffin: deleted friend (social media), euthanized pet, dark friend, bad service, sick friend, black dog, denied help, no support, loss (pet), denied service, death odor, closed investigation, no witnesses, letting go of a friend, commemorative service, death of a friend, grief/bereavement therapy, cadaver dog, death doula

9. Bouquet: wonderful friend, pet therapy, sweet scent, polite friend, designer dog, floral scent, lovely friend, wonderful service, special support, art therapy, special friend, pretty pet, beauty therapy, special animal, perfume smell

10. Scythe: wounded friend, urgent help, dangerous dog, broken friendship, emergency services, severing a friendship, threatened by a friend, splitting up friends, cutting off a friend, obliterated friendship, cutting services, broken trust, emergency aid, accident chaser

11. Whip: sex therapy, aggressive dog breed, actively watching, pattern of stalking, intermittent support, trauma-focused therapy, aggressive companion, sexual-abuse therapy, questioning the witness, sexual submissive, intermittent service, voyeurism, sex companion

12. Birds: naturally inquisitive, bird dog, anxious witness, couple's therapy, nosy, music therapy, narrative therapy, double agent, bosom buddies, talking to a friend, rumors about a friend, anxious friend, gossiping friends

13. Child: child therapy, slightly familiar, weak support, playmate, young witness, a little support, minor investigation, child guide, very submissive, slightly protective, vulnerable friend, somewhat reliable, immature companion, noisy friend, child-friendly, short friend

14. Fox: scheming friend, practical friendship, desertion, work investigation, job protection, avoiding a friend, workers support (union), red dog, calculated friendship, a fox, practical help, careful examination, fake witness, untrustworthy, suspicious friend, pretending to be supportive, misguided, undercover investigator, surveillance, guarded, feigning friendship, stalking/stalker, pseudo help, mistrust, use caution!

15. Bear: huge following, diet coach, a bear, mastiff dog breed, strong odors, powerful witness, intense friend, food smells, assertive companion, very supportive, major investigation, maternal guidance, very protective, increased observation, big hairy animal, very familiar, increased help, big service, very reliable, big nose

16. Stars: astral guide, online friend, amazing support, upgraded service, best dog, exposing a friend, digital surveillance, potential companion, media shy, motivational friend, coaching, virtual assistant, exposure therapy, unconditional, great friendship, extensive investigation, improving friendship, unlimited support

17. Stork: doula, returning pet, quiet observation, long investigation, leggy dog, blessed friendship, returning companion, quiet friend, dance therapy, long friendship, evolving companionship

19. Tower: defensive friend, city guide, mascot, legal counsel, government surveillance, officially friends, criminal investigation, official witness, established support, formal investigation, self-protection, established friendship, just friends, traditional therapy

20. Garden: average friendship, public servant, mediocre friend, public surveillance, acquaintances, group therapy, general help, popular friend, public witness, public inquiry, mutual friend, general investigation, public following

21. Mountain: blocked aid, interrupted investigation, Burmese mountain dog, interrupted service, blocked investigation, tough friendship, blocked friend (social media), tough witness, restricted service

22. Paths: strange animal, choosing a therapist, eclectic therapy, unusual friend, strangely familiar, unusual support, multiple animals, between service, deciding to go to therapy, parting ways with a companion

23. Mice: losing trust, jeopardizing an investigation, unreliable, repugnant, diminished friendship, less help, fading support, unfamiliar, fleas/ticks, rotten odor, unfaithful, stinky smell, unsupportive, disobedient, unhelpful, disease spreading in animals, disloyal, mistrust, unfriendly, thinning the pack, lowly friend, unaware, damaged friendship, untrustworthy, "rotted friend"

24. Heart: relationship coach, heartfelt support, service, lovely friendship, considerate friend, marriage counselor, compassionate friend, Labrador retriever, interpersonal therapy, forgive a friend, giving support, loving gaze, lover is faithful

25. Ring: chasing your tail, offering friendship, complete trust, continued friendship, ongoing surveillance, continued protection, ongoing service, surrounded by friends, marriage counseling, faithful, close friend, continued support, agreement to be surveyed

26. Book: secret therapy, informative friend, secret friend, fact checking, secret witness, student services, memorial service, informational guidance, undercover agent, secretive friend, bibliotherapy, educational guidance, classmate

27. Letter: pen friend/pal, message from a friend, written account, texting a friend, letter service, mail/post carrier, written support, emailing a friend, sending the dogs, scheduling services, results are reliable, writing is familiar, sending aid

28. Man: faithful man, submissive man, friendly man, helpful man, loyal man, dependable man, trustworthy man, familiar man, male friend, supportive man, policeman, known male, boyfriend, stud, alpha male, protective man, territorial man, male dog, following him, male witness, male scent, stalking him, male therapist

29. Woman: faithful woman, submissive female, friendly woman, helpful lady, loyal woman dependable woman, trustworthy woman, familiar woman, female friend, supportive woman, policewoman, known female, girlfriend, bitch, alpha female, protective woman, territorial woman, female dog, following her, female witness, female scent, stalking her, female therapist

30. Lily: Siberian husky, icy companion, discreet assistance, private surveillance, Alaskan malamute, private therapy session, guarded, private investigator, cold/frosty friend, private guidance, conservative friend

31. Sun: golden retriever, sun gazing, actual investigation, truly faithful, really reliable, sun dog, genuine friendship, true companionship, happy dog, real support, truly trustworthy, really familiar, truly reliable, reality therapy, really protective, happy friend

32. Moon: intuitive coach, moon gazing, feeling supported, monthly service, paranormal investigation, moon dog, hypnotherapy, undercover investigation, feels familiar, emotion-focused therapy, feeling protective, emotionally guarded

33. Key: affluent friend, VIP service, poodle, destined friendship, key services, significant support, open trust, definitely loyal, defiantly trustworthy, soul-searching, open to therapy, respectful companion, soulmates, karmic guide

34. Fish: deep dive, financial service, in-depth investigation, shopping with a friend, paying a friend, deep trust, alcoholic friend, expensive service, fishy friend, earning trust, financial aid, fishy smell

35. Anchor: stagnant friendship, remaining companions, still supportive, keep investigating, stuck in the friend zone, lasting support, long-lasting investigation, security dog, grounded friend, staying friends, rescue animal, reliable service, hanging on to a friendship, saving a friend

36. Cross: religious servant, Doberman pinscher, ghost hunting, terrible friend, cursed friend, pain therapy, disappointing service, difficult companion, scandalous friend, regret asking for help, religious service, terrible guidance, spirit is watching, spirit investigation, obligated friendship

Friendship, is born at the moment when one man says to another, "What! You too? I thought that no one but myself . . ."

—C. S. Lewis

19. Tower

Tall and ridged buildings, erected ancient structures from the past
Formally defending cities, by making the isolation and loneliness last
Governments control the narrative, arrogantly judge and point out flaw.
Egotistical authorities establish verdicts and enforce the rule of law.

DESCRIPTION

A cerulean-blue mushroom Tower firmly rooted in the fertile earth grows in the shade of a live oak tree, as motes of light dance through the leaves, filtering through the afternoon sun. The Tower makes a formal statement, stretching up tall enough to scratch the sky, as the atmosphere pulsates with controlling energy. Erected to be law unto itself, it dares even the bravest of souls to think twice before entering the sacred fairy ring.

The thick, fortified walls of this daunting stronghold drip with an impenetrable aura of solitude, since the Tower's priority will always be to formally defend the establishment's official position against any opposition, in order to safeguard the enchanted treasures of the past secured within its walls.

As the king of the realm, the Tower is a supreme unyielding authority wrapped up in a mystique of self-importance that breeds an arrogance of righteousness. Ruling with an iron fist for far too long has resulted in a rigidness that set in over time; now the king is too withdrawn and established in his ways to come out and speak to the people.

Blinded by an arrogant ambition, the Tower imprisoned himself by his own self-serving ego, resulting in an isolation that keeps feeding the extreme loneliness, now standing alone with only his pride and rules to keep him company.

Until one day, a white-tailed stag cautiously approaches the Tower; standing in the shadow of the immense structure, he hesitantly takes another step closer, for he knows he is being watched. The stag feels a kinship with the Tower, for both enjoy their independence, since he too bears a crown of antlers that reach up into the higher realms. Standing sentry throughout millennia, the dignified King of Trees bore witness to all that transpired throughout the years past, as it held all its ancient wisdom within its essence.

The oak's sheer strength and towering size make it one of the most beloved trees in the world, a true living legend as its defiance mimics that of the Tower, for it too is unwilling to bend a knee to the wind.

The number 19 is the alpha and the omega, demonstrating a complete cycle from beginning to end. Synonymous with the Tower's meaning, the number 19 represents governance, monarchy, rules, and politics. Very persuasive with an air of self-importance, 19 is always demanding a position of leadership and the reigning ruler of law and complete cycles.

KEYWORDS

Loneliness, official, withdrawn, rigid, ego, arrogance, ambition, formal, the past, authority, solitude, defending, institution, aloof, governing bodies, tall structures, building, rules, an old man, established, traditional, isolated, up, control, enforced, judgment, self-absorbed, defensive, city, self, single, laws, legal, one, industry, ancient, commanding, industry

TIMING

The Tower is built to stand the test of time, since it represents the past. Using the card's number, it can denote the 19th day; if the Mountain is present, it can denote a time period upward of 19 months.

MEANING

The ancient Tower rigidly stands with an official air of formality accompanied by a defensive attitude, at times representing an actual establishment. This tall fortress offers a better view into any situation, issue, or circumstance from an aloof perspective. When the Tower stands up in a reading, it carries an arrogant energy that is unyielding and controlling, pushing everything away and withdrawing into its loneliness. The Tower, being a card of lawfulness and governance, enjoys dictating authoritative rules and regulations onto others. The Tower also refers to self, the ego. Traditional association with the Tower is an old man, and male genitalia, since it physically looks very phallic in nature.

TOWER IN LOVE

When inquiring about love and the Tower appears, it mean the person is single or unattached, and usually not by choice. In a committed relationship, the Tower brings an element of loneliness, where it is possible to feel lonely while in a relationship. If you're single, the Tower speaks of extreme loneliness, withdrawn from the dating scene as time passes by. Since the Tower is a card of the past, there is an inkling when it appears in a reading that could mean that someone is still pinning for a past lover. This is not a card you want to see when asking about love, for it represents a controlling relationship with no reverence or respect for the other person.

TOWER IN CAREER

The Tower represents a career in government or official establishment that is governed by rules and regulations, legislated by an official governing body such as banks, insurance companies, and large organizations or industries. There is a heavy legal aspect to the Tower card, so any vocation in law, correctional services, or law enforcement applies. Self-employed and being a ruler unto yourself is everything the Tower stands for, including working alone.

TOWER IN WELLNESS

The Tower represents any medical building or hospital. Physically, it represents the spine, back, or penis. Emotionally, the Tower denotes feeling alone, isolated, and withdrawn.

TOWER IN FINANCES

The Tower denotes a financial building, such as a bank—somewhere that money is kept and safeguarded—or a building where financial transactions take place.

TOWER IN MODERN DAY

The Tower is symbolic of a penis, tall and rigid. It can represent someone who is single. Also, it can highlight someone who is very political with an edgy attitude, or a tyrannical government.

AFFIRMATION

The past is over; only the arrogance of my jailer keeps me a prisoner of my past. Once I understand this, I am free.

CARTOMANCY: 6 OF SPADES

From the high vantage point of the 6 of Spades, one can observe many things seen from a different perspective. When in relation to the body, the 6 of Spades denotes the lower back and the elimination system, which ties nicely into the Tower's meaning of the spine. The 6 of Spades is a card of completion, the end of one cycle and the beginning of a new one. In a relationship, the 6 of Spades isolates you from someone in the parting of ways and moves you along, leaving the past behind. Also as a card of vocation or project, this card is indicative that you will be rewarded for your efforts.

LENORMAND TOWER COMBINATIONS

1. Rider: news industry, acting rigid, first ruling, quick judgment, acting withdrawn, other man is egocentric, first floor, acting formal, suitor's arrogant, authoritative, news building, quick ruling, incoming verdict

2. Clover: Emerald City, green building, brief loneliness, gambling industry, green policies, brief incarceration, gaming industry, easing restrictions/mandates, wild rules, funny tradition, Green Party (politics), informal rules

3. Ship: immigration office, travel official, foreign government, far from the city, foreign policy, travel mandates, aloofness, leaving town, travel-and-tourism industry, withdrawn, distant past, mutiny, foreign corporation

4. House: tall house, family law, real estate industry, domestic industry, home city, condominium/apartment, family rules, domestic law, home alone, family court, domestic corporation, house rules, hometown

5. Tree: slow old man, growing city, slowly enforced rules, ancestral traditions, deeply rooted past, slow ruling (judgment), health/medical industry, deeply rooted loneliness, established, life of solitude, tree fort, medical office, ancestral past, living in the past, health mandates

6. Clouds: shadow government, hidden city, rehab center, shadow side, lost city, unstable building, misplaced judgment, confused old man, lost traditions, unstable government, lost erection, windy city, mental-health facility, desolate, psychological operations, climate control

7. Snake: complicated past, tightening restrictions, toxic old man, toxic institution, evil government official, constricting rules/laws, toxic past, evil organization, complicated rules, toxic corporation, treason

8. Coffin: erasing traditions, dead city/town, final ruling/judgment, let go the ego, dark past, died/dying alone, denied bail, bad judgment, bad defense, dark loneliness, dark building, no verdict, loss (court), funeral industry, let go control, impotence, sick/ill old man, bury the past, underground/basement floor, coroner's office, mausoleum, the end of an era

9. Bouquet: wonderful old man, pleasant city, special tradition, architecture, fashion city, beauty industry, fashion industry, east of the city, banquet hall, wonderful past, beautiful building, pleasant official, celebrating traditions, beautiful town, invite only, pleasant formalities, rules for some and not for all

10. Scythe: broken past, emergency building, dangerous city, emergency defense (military), dictator, divide and conquer, breaking tradition, vaccine/injectable mandate, cutting formalities, divided government, divide and control, west of the city, breakdown of government, dangerous government official, divided jury, breaking laws, removing a government official, decimating industries, cut off and withdrawn, emergency order, threatening litigation

11. Whip: hurt old man, revolt, sex industry, aggressive old man, X-rated, hurtful past, aggressive government official, strip joint, sexual identity, sports stadium, insurrection, sexual control, adults only, sex rules, aggressive mandates

12. Birds: Twin Cities, hustle and bustle of the city, communication industry, flight official, bustling town, oral tradition, radio tower, talking politics, airline industry, second floor, wayward, communication is controlled, music industry

13. Child: small town, child prisoner, small building, slightly lonely, simple rules, small corporation, a bit isolated, new town, slightly self-absorbed, weak defense, a bit stiff, vulnerable industry, weak enforcement, vulnerable old man, new building, medium height, slightly controlling

14. Fox: escaping the city, scheming government, aloof, avoiding the past, evading the rules, guilty verdict, pretending to follow the rules, feigning loneliness, suspicious government official, fake antique, sly old man, cautiously withdrawn, eluding the law, avoiding judgment, crime

15. Bear: enforcing mandates, big city, food industry, great ambition, immense pride, strong back, big building, strong judgment, assertive old man, immense loneliness, major arrogance, increased formalities, authoritative, huge corporation, very established, strong traditions, very isolated, increased control, powerful defense, very self-absorbed, big industry, very political, big restaurant, massive bureaucracy, power and control

16. Stars: astral/high council, movie industry, improving old man, north of the city, online industry, exposing a government official, future policy, universal laws, satellite station, great ambition, best defense, higher self, enhanced enforcement, uptown, lifting of rules/mandates, high court / supreme court, philosophy of governance, highest building/tower, unlimited ambition, extensive rules, upgrading enforcement tactics, rooftop

17. Stork: birth control, changing government official, evolving traditions, changing judgment, evolving laws, maternity ward, baby industry, returning mandates, trend in politics, alter ego, long established, repeating the past

18. Dog: pet industry, help me, following orders, investigating an institution, friend is controlling, looking into the past, investigating an old man, searching a building, investigating a government official, friend is judgmental

20. Garden: common law, garden city, peer judgment, public building, associates, public court, people's revolution, social media industry, condo/apartment/flat, general rules, public defender, public insurrection, population control, jury, heritage/cultural building, public organization, socially isolated

21. Mountain: remote town, restricted building, harsh rules, colony, harsh judgment, remote, distant and lonely, interrupted court proceedings, recluse, obstructing justice, hard past, remote building

22. Paths: strange old man, unusual past, strange tradition, unusual building, strange rules, multiple buildings, many rules, multiple cities, between sentencing, unusually withdrawn, unfamiliar city, deciding judgment, between tall buildings

23. Mice: dirty corporation, run-down city, corrupt city official, dirty old man, costly arrogance, corrupt industry, losing control, crumbling building, corrupt corporation, dirty politician, low self-esteem, pest control, ruined industries, dirty city, losing in court, dirty politics, crumbling government, imprisonment, unjust, in ruins, damaging isolation, uncontrollable

24. Heart: charitable corporation, lover is controlling, date is arrogant, relationship is isolating, forgiving an old man, giving up control, relationship from the past, loves being alone, kind official, relationship control, lover is stubborn

25. Ring: wedding industry, continued tradition, entire city, whole town, complete control, entire building, the whole industry, entire corporation, surrounded by arrogance, continual loneliness, ongoing judgment, surrounded by tall buildings, ring of office, circular governance

26. Book: publishing industry, educational establishment, historical, studying law, historical building, historical city/town, secret traditions, student campus, archive, memorial building, remembering the past

27. Letter: newspaper industry, written rules, communications tower/building, written assessment, written verdict, correspondence with an official, written law, publishing a court case, written legal notice

28. Man: ambitious man, traditional man, man from the past, egotistical man, arrogant man, lonely man, proud man, imposing man, formal man, established man, controlling man, male prisoner, city man, defensive man, single man, tall man, old man, commanding man, intimidating man, selfish man, self-absorbed man

29. Woman: ambitious woman, traditional woman, woman from the past, egotistical woman, selfish woman, arrogant woman, lonely female, proud woman, imposing woman, formal woman, established woman, controlling woman, female prisoner, city woman, defensive woman, kept woman, single lady, tall woman, princess in the tower, haughty lady, intimidating woman, a self-absorbed lady

30. Lily: old prisoner, private corporation, retirement industry, old maid, private court, ancient, privy council, antique, withdrawn, disciplined, formal, private building, old city/town, life sentence / life in prison

31. Sun: true crime, energy industry, actual enforcement, south of the city, happy old man, it's official, resort, positive judgment, happy past, optimism vs. arrogance, true ambition, happy loner, winning defense, thriving corporation, annual tradition, vacation industry

32. Moon: metaphysical industry, feeling lonely, standoffish, influenced, feeling controlled, aware old man, feeling established, official appearance, phases of solitude, monthly tradition, feeling judged, metaphysical building, feeling defensive

33. Key: free prisoner, definitely lonely, released from prison/jail, keys to the city, prestigious company, affluent old man, free city, key official, open building, respecting the rules, honoring traditions, definitely single, key to the building, sovereign state, definitely established

34. Fish: expensive tradition, financial industry, business establishment, money for bail, business policy, deep pockets of the government, business law, corporation, wealthy corporation, commercial building, deep solitude

35. Anchor: coastal town/city, safe city, stuck in the past, keep defending, ground floor, enduring judgment, keep it formal, still withdrawn, remaining rigid, keeping to yourself, still arrogant, downtown, stay in charge, remain aloof, hanging on to traditions, middle, stay in control, keeping it official, holding on to the past, rescued from the tower, enduring loneliness

36. Cross: religious artifact, cross me (taunt), scandalous corporation, sin city (Las Vegas), ghosts of the past, disappointing ruling, cursed building, pain control, disappointing judgment, intolerable scandalous government official, miserable old man, intolerable rules and regulations, scandalous past, regretting the past, terrible government, orthodox, a monk, church and state, difficult past

Arrogance is a creature. It does not have senses. It has only a sharp tongue and the pointing finger.

—Toba Beta

20. Garden

Gardens are where groups come together, in rolling fields of green
Commonly utilized by everyone, a very popular cultural scene
Meeting as a society, citizens networking in this outdoor space
People en masse and gather, socially enjoying this public place

DESCRIPTION

The bloom of the floral perfume hangs heavily in the air of this public Victorian Garden, an enchanted place filled with lush green foliage, exotic florals, and magick. The afternoon light filters through the Garden, becoming a meeting place for friends; the meerkat and the squirrel came to socialize among the magnificent splendors of the place. The meerkat stands as a symbol of alertness, a gentleman dressed in his finest, exemplary of correct social conduct during this era. The Garden is a place for everyone to gather and take a soothing stroll through the undulating walkways. It is an outdoor place where you can breathe in the crispness of the afternoon air, reconnect with nature while observing the latest fashions, and exchange in some polite conversations. The Garden is a place where everyone is observing others closely at all times, while demurely keeping within the etiquette of proper distance. The Garden, being a group card, is reflected by the meerkat's nature and great sense of community; rarely do you see a single critter out and about, for they are pack animals with a deep sense of togetherness. Standing proudly at the meerkat's side, the single squirrel, being a true player never taking life seriously, injects just enough antics to balance out this team. The squirrel is holding on to a walnut, signifying the importance of thinking about the future, since the Garden was originally constructed with the hopes of preservation in mind, a lasting memento built for many generations yet to come.

The allure of the glowing lanterns mounted on the stone temple beckons crowds to gather beneath the sacred arches, while a small pixie swings from a flowering vine with gossamer wings, slipping in and out of realms, as she haphazardly swings back and forth, emitting sparkly orbs and spreading some mischief throughout the Garden. All work and no play makes for a really dull fairy. A copious amount of striking flowers beautify the scene; pink tiger lilies represent admiration and femininity and are conveniently planted throughout the Garden paths. These beautiful flowers are strategically placed to be plucked along the way and offered up as a token of appreciation to a passerby who catches your eye with a nod and a wink, requesting a rendezvous soon. Pretty creamy-pink sunken roses profusely bloom, caressing the air with their sweet, sultry melody of fragrance that adds an additional touch of femininity, attracting the birds and the bees and people alike to gather in the garden's delightful landscape. The card number 20 gathers in the Garden, bringing similar qualities, such as teamwork and service to the masses. This number expresses itself best when collaborating with a group by offering a fresh perspective. With a flair of devotion, the number 20 is preoccupied with being a valuable part of the team, contributing something grander then itself. Always being concerned with others, this number rarely feels peace in solitude, much rather preferring to be a part of the public scene. The number 20 is a group number, carrying the motto of "The more the merrier." This attitude, combined with the Garden card, describes the scene perfectly.

KEYWORDS

Gatherings, community, meetings, public, groups, social things, crowd, society, a garden, culture, forum, public spaces, events, teamwork, online places, recreation, social life, festivals, venue, outdoors, everybody, social networks, clubs, population, common, citizens, popular, general, average, together, regular

TIMING

Afternoon, June/July, can also indicate the 20th of the month. If the Mountain is present, it can be up to 20 months.

MEANING

The Garden always suggests more than one person, usually referring to a group of people gathering and socializing together. This card describes your network, and in today's day and age, that usually includes a major component of online social media interaction with friends and groups. The Garden, being a public place, also refers to the general public, a community, or a society. When the Garden card appears, it is a reminder of the benefits of spending time outdoors in nature; taking a leisurely stroll about will always help reset, relax, and breathe.

GARDEN IN LOVE

Garden usually represents someone who is very much a free spirit and does not want to settle down. A champion of playing the field, a true social butterfly who loves meeting new people and mingling. Garden variety type is always shying away from exclusivity and settling down.

GARDEN IN CAREER

The Garden card characterizes someone who works with the public or in a group setting. Can be indicative of landscaping, an event planning, or urban planning. The Garden card, as a person, represents a gardener, a public figure, or a socialite.

GARDEN IN WELLNESS

Focusing on connecting with nature, getting fresh air, and incorporating a walking routine.

GARDEN IN MODERN DAY

Online places: social groups, gatherings, virtual meetings, networks, chat groups, dating sites

AFFIRMATION

Unleash the extraordinary masterpiece that is you, radiating brilliance as you stand apart from the vast sea of sameness.

CARTOMANCY: 8 OF SPADES

Traditionally a card of misfortune, the 8 of Spades represents illness or a doctor. As a card depicting group activity, it can foretell a spread of illness from person-to-person transmission, resulting in an epidemic. Enjoying a large social circle, the 8 of Spades continually seeks approval from others to feel validated. At times, the 8 of Spades carries a very negative attitude, getting very worked up and quick to anger when things don't go their way. A long, leisurely stroll through a Garden is very beneficial for the 8 of Spades, allowing them to calm down and help clear their head. Denoting confinement, the 8 of Spades can be prone to impatience, unrest. What greatly helps with this attitude is wide-open spaces, regular travel adventures, and meeting new people—just what the doctor ordered. As a career, this card depicts healing work or healthcare. Magickally, the 8 of Spades represents a coven or magickal group.

LENORMAND GARDEN COMBINATIONS

1. Rider: first meeting, coming and going together, newsworthy event, going to a meeting, coming out publicly, other man on social media, first gathering, suitors moving quickly online

2. Clover: park, casual meeting, wild crowd, chance meeting, country folk, informal event, wild group, brief meeting, funny in general, carefree crowd, gaming group, easy group, casual encounter

3. Ship: moving the crowd, traveling together, distant group, travel club, leaving social media, trip arranged to rendezvous, convoy, leaving together, leaving the public eye, navigating social media, traveling for a meeting, international team

4. House: indoor garden, community, family event, family event, indoors together, family unit, home together, family network, homeland, commune, home turf, indoor rendezvous, home team/side, house meeting, cohabitating together, family members, backyard

5. Tree: health-and-wellness team, slow social life, forest, growing social network, healthcare team, spiritual event, healthcare forum, spiritual garden, growing population, blood donor, living outdoors, growing crowd

6. Clouds: lost society, sad gathering, hidden civilization, misunderstanding on social media, shadow society, hidden society, lost population, hidden social media accounts, shadow citizens, troubled society, addicted to social media

7. Snake: evil group, enticing group, toxic meeting, desiring a social life, lying to the public, constricting group, toxic people, complicated group, toxic gathering, complex social network, betraying the public, complicated social life, lying group, rendezvous (with intent to cheat)

8. Coffin: cancel culture, deleted social media group, final event, bad group of people, nonexistent social life, final meeting, denied public assembly, genocide, denied membership, last gathering all together, silenced citizens, burial plot, sick population

9. Bouquet: wonderful neighborhood, special invite, nice crowd, pleasant community, special event, ornamental garden, artistic group, polite crowd, exhibition, special gathering, wonderful meeting, wonderful social life, beautiful culture, special meeting, celebration (event), special group, enjoying social media

10. Scythe: vaccinating/injecting the public, divided society, breakout (meeting), divided group, dangerous crowd, threat to society, cutting off everyone, segregation, cut off from society, emergency meeting, urgent gathering, separating a group, split society, removed from a group, risky social life, broken society, decimating a population, cut off from social media, threatening a civilization, destroying humanity

11. Whip: angry mob, active on social media, hostile crowd, disruptive group, harming humanity, sexually promiscuous, hurtful group, intermittent social life, sexual rendezvous, intermittent gatherings, hurting people, sex in public

12. Birds: restless crowd, flying together, calling a meeting, anxious citizens, bird/butterfly garden, nervous people, discussions in a meeting, couple of people, taking together, excited crowd, speaking as a group

13. Child: new civilization, short meeting, weak in general, small crowd, inexperienced group, childhood club, small public space, new group, vulnerable population, small garden, shy in social situations, immature group, innocent rendezvous, small social network

14. Fox: scheming group, avoiding crowds, sneaky rendezvous, suspicious meeting, avoiding social gatherings, evading a meeting, tricking humanity, working together, avoiding an event, jobsite, swindling the public, calculated rendezvous, work gathering, caution online, avoiding people, work group, stealthy gathering, pseudo meeting, pretending to be someone else on social media, scamming the public, fake social media

15. Bear: very crowded, vegetable garden, intense group, big social network, strong culture, large population, stronger together, power of social media, large gathering, huge social life, very common, increased teamwork, big public space, increased popularity, more meetings, mommy group

16. Stars: astral group, star-studded gathering, above average, positive crowd, star people, great outdoors, panfederation, famous, universal citizens, future together, utopia, northern population, great community, virtual meeting, positive group, enhancing humanity, improving social life, star group, future meeting, everybody, extensive social networks, future event, online rendezvous, alien civilizations, space, aliens, galactic federation

17. Stork: returning crowd, evolving humanity, exchanging of populations, long meeting, recurring event, quiet on social media, moving in together, returning population, trending hashtag, birthing a new civilization, coming back together, quiet on social media, altering humans

18. Dog: following the pack, familiar gathering, sheeple, friends in common, loyal citizens, philanthropy, protected population, friendly environment, protected group, friendly neighbors, dog people, therapy group, cohorts, watching everybody, searching on social media, surveillance on citizens, following online, search outdoors, stalking on social media / online, friendly rendezvous

19. Tower: town hall meeting, control group, background, withdrawn from society, past meeting, political group, enslaved citizens, city folk, established group, official meeting, formal event, restricted group, unsocial, metropolis, defending the public, illicit meeting, law of the land, ancient civilization

21. Mountain: blockade of people, challenging group, district, restricting people, rough crowd, rock garden, challenging event, postponed meeting, interrupted gathering, fringe population, restricted public gatherings, blocked on social media, territory, permanent resident, remote civilization, area outside

22. Paths: separating the people, strange gathering, many people, unusual neighbors, strange event, unusual crowd, multiple groups, strange civilization, deciding to meet, unusual social life, multiple meetings, deciding together

23. Mice: scattered population, diminished crowd, uncommon, less populated, stressed citizens, diminished social life, uneventful, corrupt group, ruined meeting, thinning out the population, colonies, ruined event, damaged society, destroying people, spreading disease among the population, clusters, jeopardizing the population, unpopular, opportunistic group/people

24. Heart: considerate group, dating event, giving back to society, romantic rendezvous, love gardening, forgive everybody, lover rendezvous, relationship is public, lover is a player, philanthropy, dating on social media

25. Ring: entire population, whole event, entire culture, marrying outdoors, entirely online, surrounded by people, whole social network, surrounded by everybody, making a deal together, entire meeting, promising social life, whole of humanity

26. Book: historical event, logical group, studying horticulture, historical club, knowledgeable group, secret civilization, informed public, clandestine gathering, historical gardens, unknown citizens, school garden, historical park, secret event, educating society, memorial garden, secret meeting

27. Letter: scheduled rendezvous, Tweetup, texting people, scheduled event, results made public, messaging people on social media, writing about humanity, sending results to a group, list of people/attendees

28. Man: player (male), popular man, playboy, cultured man, boy's club, uncommitted man, men in general, group of men, available man, men's group, male public figure, (man) online, social man, common man, gardener (male)

29. Woman: player (female), femme fatale, popular woman, party girl, cultured woman, socialite, women's club, uncommitted female, women in general, group of women, available woman, women's group, female public figure, (woman) online, social woman, common woman, gardener (female), social butterfly

30. Lily: conservative group, mature crowd, private garden, retired population, calm meeting, conservative culture, winter garden, aging population, old people, daddy group, average experience, general privacy, peaceful society, senior citizens, clique, discreet meeting, old civilization, age of majority, zen garden

31. Sun: good people, happy event, really popular, for the good of all, summer garden, annual event, happy citizens, really common, annual gathering, successful civilization, courageous citizens, happy gathering, daily crowd, sun garden, annual meeting, daily rendezvous, winning over the public

32. Moon: nighttime rendezvous, creative group, nightclub, monthly event, magickal outdoor space, feeling crowded, intuitive civilization, psychic group, meditational garden, monthly moon gathering, nightly crowd, full-moon gathering, monthly meeting

33. Key: free citizens, definitely together, privileged meeting, affluent society, important event, privileged group, freedom rally, karmic event, defiantly a player, prestigious gala, key gathering, affluent neighborhood, definitely public, venerable group, executive club, open space, revealing meeting, key player, respecting humanity, fated to be together, karmic meeting

34. Fish: expensive club, business event, financial meeting, commercialized, expensive event, wealthy group, drinking buddies, business people, expensive social life, resourceful group, budget meeting

35. Anchor: settlement (people), holding on to social media, enduring a meeting, saving humanity, stay outdoors, keep the culture going, still meeting, safer in public, stay social, safe group, lengthy meeting, lingering crowd

36. Cross: faith gathering, scandalous social life, miserable people, disappointing everybody, intolerable group, disappointing meeting, sacred gathering, church group, spirit people, dystopia, difficult group, disappointing social life, scandalous rendezvous, miserable social life, difficult gathering

Never doubt that a small group of thoughtful, committed citizens can change the world: indeed, it is only thing that ever has.

—Margaret Mead

21. Mountain

When a mountain rises up before you, be sure you will encounter a block.
Stubborn challenges cause rough setbacks, immovable like a craggy rock.
Obstacles become impassive, stalling and creating obstructions with delay.
Limits placed and lines are drawn; permanent boundaries keep you away.

DESCRIPTION

Bathed in a cascade of defused sunlight, basking the area in hues of red and gold, looms the remote Mountain in the background, absorbing all the sun's splendor and trying to warm up its hard ridges—but to no avail, for no matter how hard the Mountain tries to retain heat, a distant coldness always remains on its snowcapped peaks.

At an impasse, the proud elk stands as an obstacle at the foot of the mountain, allowing passage only for the ones worthy and willing to attempt the challenge he's put forth. This challenge will take you on an enchanted journey where you can leave outdated ideals of yourself at the foot of the Mountain. The elk reminds you that it will be a difficult climb up the rough, craggy face of the sheer rocks, and many delays will be experienced along the way until the summit can be reached.

Being a custodian of the border, the Mountain possesses the immovable stubbornness needed to block any adversary from reaching the summit. The magick of the Mountain is that by possessing the determination to take small, mindful steps, it says that nothing is out of reach or insurmountable. *Slow and steady wins the race*, for no one will reach its lofty peaks by running straight up.

The sacred Mountain was worshiped by many ancient civilizations and honored as the home of the gods, creating a conduit by connecting the heavens and Earth and making the Mountain a symbol to be revered. Humanity will come and go trying to climb and conquer rough terrain; they will live, learn, and die in what seems like a blink of an eye in comparison to the timelessness of the Mountain. A powerful sign of eternity, this remote Mountain is protected by a natural boundary that demands respect as a standing monument of permanence bearing witness for millennia to come.

The number 21 looms onto the Mountain card, bringing with it a very transformative essence. This is a positive, self-aware number that provides just the right amount of fortitude needed to attain your goals. The number 21 brings a high degree of spirituality that will pave the way to facilitate a sacred pilgrimage up the Mountain.

KEYWORDS

Obstacles, stillness, challenges, delays, impassive, distant, permanence, boundaries, remote, setbacks, blocks, limits, obstruction, stalled, immovable, hard, harsh, rough, restricted, interrupting, hiatus, stubborn, district, border, area, rock, impasse, postponement, fringe, intercepted, hindered

TIMING

Delayed. When the Mountain shows up, expect that there will be a delay—likely up to 21 months. The Mountain's presence delays all cards in proximity.

MEANING

The Mountain is a timeless monument carrying a feeling of permanence that's indicative of something that will remain for quite a while. It creates delays and intentionally slows you down as it lies in wait for an opportune time to create a mountainous obstacle before the foothill of your path, challenging you with insurmountable odds. Only with great focus and great effort will any movement ensue, for there is no way around the Mountain. The only way is by climbing up the sheer rock face one step at a time. By distancing yourself from a situation and creating healthful boundaries, you will be able to face any challenge. All this is part of the Mountain's charm.

MOUNTAIN IN LOVE

In a relationship, the Mountain card can be indicative of many obstacles, with a feeling of going it alone bringing a chill of hardness to any romantic connection. When you see the Mountain show up, it prevents you from moving forward, as you experience a hindrance causing stagnation. The Mountain also reminds you that setting boundaries is very healthful for a relationship. If you're single, and seeking love, introspection is needed to recognize what is holding you back. Climb to the summit in order to overcome the Mountain and find love.

MOUNTAIN IN CAREER

As a vocation, the Mountain can represent a career in border security, customs, patrolling the border, or any job that involves an actual Mountain. The Mountain brings stagnation to any job where you feel that there is no movement or promotions in sight.

MOUNTAIN IN WELLNESS

The Mountain brings setbacks to any health situation because of its permanent nature; it is indicative of a health issue or condition that remains. If awaiting surgery, it may be postponed, and if waiting for results, you can expect a delay.

MOUNTAIN IN FINANCE

Obstacles in the horizon with no avail to any financial situations; it's gonna take some time. A great effort is needed to reap any rewards, for it will be like squeezing blood out of a stone.

MOUNTAIN IN MODERN DAY

The Mountain can denote reaching the summit after a very difficult climb while you amble toward reaching its peaks. If successful, it means you have achieved what you set out to do.

AFFIRMATION

My challenges are lessons to teach me how to overcome obstacles and move mountains, for I am truly limitless.

CARTOMANCY: 8 OF CLUBS

The 8 of Clubs is the card of working things out, while having to apply a great effort to any situation in life in order to get you where you want to go. When it comes to relationships, the 8 of Clubs is indicative of a stagnation and feeling blocked in your current circumstance. The 8 of Clubs encourages you to take a step back so you are able to see the whole Mountain, and, with determination and grit, the 8 of clubs can achieve any insurmountable odds it is faced with.

LENORMAND MOUNTAIN COMBINATIONS

1. Rider: first obstacle, other man's distant, coming challenges, broadcast interrupted, first setback, arrival of obstacles, first district, suitor stalls, announcement postponed, notification intercepted, other man is in the area

2. Clover: Green Mountains, temporary limit, lucky interruption, gambling limit, temporary restrictions, brief interruption, brief stubbornness, gambling district, game postponed, casual boundaries, informal limits, gambling restrictions, short-lived stubbornness

3. Ship: trip interruption, very distant, travel jam, international borders, distant area, shipping delays, car stalled, travel barriers, distant and remote, goodbye postponed, departure delayed, foreign area, vehicle blockade

4. House: property boundary, distant family, house delayed, comfortable limit, familiar territory, family district, home base, family zone, housing district, residential area, comfort zone, family member's stubborn

5. Tree: health obstacles, life's rough, medical barriers, extended delays, medical restrictions, medical delay, extended limit, natural boundary, medically challenged, medical boundaries, naturally stubborn, medical obstruction, spiritual boundary, DNA blocker, life's challenges, medical district, system interruptions, treeline boundary

6. Clouds: mental block, uncertain delays, vague boundaries, temperamental borders, weather delay, mentally challenged, hiding stubbornness, obscured limit, troubling challenges, unstable boundary, mental limit, fearing delays, obscured district

7. Snake: constricted and blocked, needing boundaries, tightening restrictions, lies intercepted, problematic area, other woman needs boundaries, affair paused, betrayal is hard, attraction is blocked, affair intercepted, transformation delayed, narrow parameters

8. Coffin: black/dark-colored crystals, final delay, ending restrictions, last obstacle, closed district, final barrier, let go of limits, crypt, funeral monument/marker, mortal confines, dead zone, nonexistent boundaries, black rock

9. Bouquet: fashion district, pleasure interrupted, beautiful mountains, wonderful area, gift is delayed, eastern mountain ridge, displaying stubbornness, gratitude challenge, appreciating the distance, enjoying the challenge, surprising obstacle

10. Scythe: removing restrictions, breaking boundaries, surgery postponed, irrevocable, removing barriers, dangerous area, abrupt interruption, remove limitations, separate area, cracked rock, breaking limits, threatening the borders, removing blocks

11. Whip: sexual limits, red-light district, sexual barriers, intermittent interruptions, aggressive boundaries, fight hard, sex interrupted, questions are challenging, within the striking area, sexually distant

12. Birds: twin peaks, negotiations at an impasse, voice is harsh, call blocked, couple's distant, pair of obstacles, voice obstruction, noisy area, conversation is rough, flight delay, radio interruption, conversation barriers, talking is hard, couple's challenge, phone call intercepted

13. Child: new area, a bit rough, minor interruption, slightly remote, a little bit hard, small area, new district, slightly stubborn, weak boundaries, slight hesitation, childhood barriers, minor setback, slightly delayed

14. Fox: working hard, employment barrier, work obstruction, work/job interruptions, setting cautious limits, working within the limits, fraud intercepted, escaping to the mountains, fictitious boundaries, pretending is hard

15. Bear: market district, immense challenge, stockpile, very rough, increased stubbornness, large district, asserting boundaries, major interruption, strength challenge, very hard, major setback, increased delays, very remote, increased limitations, major hesitation, big mountain, massive obstruction, huge barrier, paramount, pushing the limits

16. Stars: asteroid, seeing beyond obstacles, highest mountain, space rock (meteoroid), clearing blocks, climbing, alleviating challenges, beyond limits, lifting restrictions, enhancing boundaries, lifting obstacles, positive interruption, clearing delays, star district, future obstacles, sky's the limit!

17. Stork: returning obstacle, moving districts, evolving restrictions, moving postponed, trekking up a mountain, shifting boundaries, progress hindered, hiking, long range, evolving challenges, changing limits

18. Dog: patrolling the border, protecting boundaries, looking hard, service interruptions, search the mountains, friendly area, investigation is hindered, friendly boundaries, looking into the distance, "friends' zone"

19. Tower: city limits, established boundaries, tall barriers, government restrictions, political challenges, city blockade, government district, judgment postponed, ruling with an iron fist, building restrictions

20. Garden: Garden District (New Orleans), social media intercepted, common delay, garden area, social interruptions, general obstacle, regular limit, public interruptions, common area, popular district, meeting intercepted, social barriers

22. Paths: unusual obstacle, unfamiliar area, multiple delays, many restrictions, strange stillness, unusual delay, strange distance, strangely stubborn, many challenges, decision postponed, path up the steep mountain, hesitation, plans interrupted, strange obstruction, unusually hard

23. Mice: lessening restrictions, fading stubbornness, damaged crystals, jeopardized borders, damaging setback, reducing restrictions, damaged area, stressful delay, vanishing limits, fewer interruptions, dissolving boundaries

24. Heart: romantic barriers, relationship interrupted, passionate about rocks/crystals, relationship obstacles, love with boundaries, date intercepted, romantically distant, generous boundaries, relationship stalled, flirting with limits, romantic hindrance

25. Ring: rolling stone, marriage barriers, ongoing restrictions, continual interruptions, spouse is distant, ongoing limitations, continued stubbornness, boundaries, surrounding area, deal postponed, offer interrupted, marriage postponed, continual challenges, ongoing delays

26. Book: historical district, educational barriers, secret area, unknown limit, training delayed, studying hard, school district, training setback, educational interruptions, researching an area, academic challenge, lesson postponed, school area

27. Letter: text/messages intercepted, results delayed, communication is limited, texts are blocked, communication interrupted, mail intercepted, texting is interrupted, communication barriers, data blocked

28. Man: stubborn man, hard man, distant man, indifferent man, rugged man, challenging man, mountain man, unavailable man, a hard-to-reach man, blocked man, standoffish man

29. Woman: stubborn woman, harsh woman, distant woman, indifferent woman, rugged lady, challenging female, nonchalant female, unavailable woman, hard-to-reach woman, blocked woman, standoffish woman

30. Lily: old area, peaceful mountains, conservative district, icy-cold rocks, old barriers, remote, respecting boundaries, cold stone/marble, respecting limits, stillness, snowcapped mountains, old limits, winter will be challenging

31. Sun: good area, illuminating barriers, summer in the mountains, energetic boundaries, victory over obstacles, holiday/vacation postponed, sunblock, good interruption, truly remote, happy district, surmounting limits, holidaying/vacationing in the mountains, overcoming barriers

32. Moon: psychic block, subconscious barriers, aware of limitations, creative barriers, monthly challenge, magickal boundaries, feeling held back, monthly limit, emotional barriers, spell's limited, emotionally distant

33. Key: opening barriers, fate intervenes, revealing boundaries, access to the area, significantly hardened, access, opening up restrictions, passing though barriers, open area, revealing difficulties, uncovering limits, karmic obstacle, open district

34. Fish: money delayed, business area, financial barriers, deep stubbornness, business interruptions, shopping district, assets/accounts blocked, distillery district, investment setback, financial district, cash limits, business setback, financial interruptions, supply chain challenges

35. Anchor: enduring setbacks, safe area, persistent block, set in stone, routine interrupted, stillness, remains challenging, still stuck, remains distant, staying within the area, safe boundaries, lingering obstacles, hanging on too hard, still blocked, keep stalling, remaining stubborn, stagnation, hold the line!

36. Cross: disappointing setback, faith-based limits, painful barrier, intolerable boundaries, burdens, shameful setback, religious boundaries, scandalous district, regret setting limits, terribly stubborn, difficulty

Permanence, perseverance and persistence in spite of all obstacles, discouragements, and impossibilities: It is this, that in all things distinguishes the strong soul from the weak.

—Thomas Carlyle

22. Paths

There's a fork in the road ahead; right or left, a decision must be made.
Weighing pros and cons, trying to choose at the crossroads of Hades
A strange path begins appearing, offering options and a possible way.
Unfamiliar plans cause indecision, and in between the crossroads you stay.

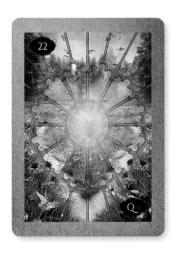

DESCRIPTION

A colorful floral scene unfolds before you, displaying a sweeping vista bustling with wildlife. Two Paths are laid out before you, beckoning you to choose. Butterflies flit around, foreshadowing that any decision made will be transformative in some way. The enchantment lies that there are multiple possibilities, as you stand in the in-between, demonstrated by the wooden motif in the center that acknowledges that even though you possess the free will to make any decision, you can travel only on a single road at a time.

It is not so much about which actual option you take; it is all about where the Paths will ultimately lead and whom you are destined to meet along the way.

Standing in the center and weighing out the pros and cons, you notice many little spirit guides await, ready to lead you down the path of choice.

A striking blue jay is the first totem you meet; she is here to remind you of how truly strong you are, and to readily use all the resources available. The smart and sassy jay with her no-nonsense attitude bestows upon you the gift of tenacity, encouraging you to take the first step.

Buzzing around a sweet, dewy daisy is the bumblebee, bringing the gift of free will, the ability to choose whichever road your heart desires. The busy bee addresses your hesitation and what is really keeping you from making a decision, by reminding you to stop and smell the roses that are strategically placed along the way to entice you farther along the path. On the other side of the Paths, you hear the mighty woodpecker hammering out a beat as old as the pulse of Mother Earth, syncing up with the rhythm of your own heart as he offers the gifts of excitement and possibility. Sitting on the woodpecker's head is a little red-crested hat, symbolizing the mental focus and clarity needed to see the journey through until the end. Nestled among the purple pansies are the black-eyed Susans, winking at you with their expressive, dark eyes, splashing around their sunny yellow color, cheering you on, as you hesitate undecided once again. Many times you will falter along the way or need to take pause when the road seems too unfamiliar, and that is okay, for these Paths are unique to you alone and will unfold in the way they are meant to. The road less traveled is filled with many ups and downs, joining and separating, bringing happiness and tears, freedoms and consequences, successes and failures—that is the uniqueness of the Paths, for you never know what is waiting just around the bend.

As soon as you think you have your bearings and are ready to proceed once again, the road begins to unfold in a strange manner, winding you down a separate offshoot into unfamiliar territory and bringing you closer to the sound of a rushing river. The river appears before you, representing all of your parts converging together; this is the very essence of the origin of your soul, where all Paths lead to one, back to the whole on this epic journey of life. The number 22 on the Paths card visually looks like two winding Paths side by side, since this number brings together the dynamic qualities of facilitating fluid movement needed to move along your destined path throughout life. As a Master builder number, the 22 utilizes your knowledge and practicality, coupled with a splash of intuition. Brimming with strength and success and sprinkled with endless possibilities, the number 22 offers you multiple choices on many Paths that will be laid out before you in this lifetime; all you have to do is decide to take the first step.

KEYWORDS

Deciding, road, choice, possibilities, unusual, pros and cons, adventure, alternative, planning, crossroads, path, multiple, separation, options, unfamiliar, different, the way, many, maybe, between, path, route, strange

TIMING

Paths can represent something happening simultaneously. If using the card's number, it can indicate 22 days or 22 weeks, and if the Mountain is present, it can take up to 22 months.

MEANING

The Paths come meandering into your life, bringing many possibilities as well as a place where you walk in the in-between until a choice or a decision is made that affects the trajectory of your life.

Representing your own personal journey in life, hesitations and the unfamiliarity of what is next are acceptable emotions to feel when faced with decisions. Being a neutral card, the Paths card relies heavily on the surrounding cards to highlight and describe where this road leads. Time to come up with a plan by making a list of pros and cons that will help when the Paths appears before you.

PATHS IN LOVE

When the Paths appear in a relationship reading, it is indicative that a decision must be made.

Also, there is an indication of an unconventional relationship where polyamory can easily come into play. When the Paths is seen next to the Ring, Heart, or Birds, it is never a good sign, for it can indicate a couple going their separate ways. When the Scythe appears after the Paths, it's indicative of a divorce after a separation. If you're single and the Paths appears, be diligent, for it can refer to someone living a double life or leading you on, especially if the Fox or Snake is nearby.

PATHS IN CAREER

Can represent multiple career opportunities presenting themselves, where you have a choice between many job offers. If you are currently employed or self-employed, it can indicate a work decision down the road or taking on another job simultaneously.

PATHS IN WELLNESS

When the Paths card shows up, it suggests that a second opinion may be needed or an ailment that is unusual in nature. Exploring different options, such as alternative medicine, or trying an unconventional method may apply. A second procedure or multiple treatments may be required.

PATHS IN FINANCES

Multiple streams of income. This card can denote an alternative way of making money, or decisions regarding finances.

PATHS IN MODERN DAY

A bohemian lifestyle, living the gypsy life, a traveler, roaming on the road of life, a sovereign citizen

AFFIRMATION

I am in alignment with my life's purpose as I walk my soul's path in the direction I choose—with or without the approval of others.

CARTOMANCY: QUEEN OF DIAMONDS

The Queen of Diamonds represents a grounded, independent woman, who may be self-employed or have an unconventional career. Obsessed with her financial status, the Queen of Diamonds can be very much a free spirit, which increases her tenacity to come up with strange ideas that are so unusual they end up feeding into her indecisiveness, because *everything* is a great idea. Always focused on money and loving the finer things in life, this trendsetter can be a flirty attention seeker, who thrives on admiration—wanting it all and finding it hard to choose between lovers. This Queen often finds herself caught in a love triangle, and other times she can be the other woman caught in between another couple; at best she relishes in becoming a throuple, for that's her plan.

LENORMAND PATHS COMBINATIONS

1. Rider: going down the road, first choice, going separate ways, acting strange, first decision, taking the quick route, first option, hasty decision, acting different, highway, going in the fast lane

2. Clover: country roads, the easy way, wild plans, brief separation, green option, temporary plan, casual decision, taking the easy road, Las Vegas strip, rural road, wild adventure, funny and unusual, quirky, easy choice

3. Ship: exploring possibilities, navigating the road, directions, journey, leaving the path, discovering, travel route, far-off possibility, driving route, adventure, still a distance to go, navigating your path, exploring

4. House: real estate plans, neighborhood street, brand options, house street, household decisions, relatives are strange, house route, real estate possibilities, comfortable choice, familiar road, indoor option

5. Tree: healthcare plan, medical choice, slow to decide, tree-lined street, spiritual plan, life's path, systematic planning, slowly making plans, natural choice, growing plan, forest path/trail, spiritual path, medical plan

6. Clouds: lost your way, hidden options, obscure route, airway, hidden path, lost the plot, hiding a decision, lost on the road, unstable plans, lost possibility, mental health plan, hidden road, mentally checked out

7. Snake: evil path, tempting choice, stringing you along, narrow road, complicated plan, bend in the road, need to decide, lying about separating, enticing possibility, toxic choices, twisted path, flexible options, need to find a way, lying about a decision, meandering

8. Coffin: dark path, bad decision, wrong choice, wrong way, final decision, death the great separator, no way, final choice, last option, denied a choice, end-of-life planning, final option, final separation, dark street, closed road, nonexistent plan, vacant streets

9. Bouquet: wonderful adventure, pretty street, fantastic plan, celebrating differences, designing a plan, east on the road, special options, beautiful possibilities, nice choice, enjoying the adventure, presented with a decision

10. Scythe: irrevocable separation, dangerous road, carving out a path, parting ways, separation, split decision, breaking plans, split down the middle, cut off on the road, obliterated plans, fork in the road, splitting up, irreconcilable differences, divorce, urgent decision, emergency plan, sudden separation, vaccine/injectable hesitancy

11. Whip: back and forth (undecided), sexual preferences, sexual path, aggressive plan, questionable choices, aggressive choice, back and forth on the road, sexual possibility, hurtful decision, sexual deviant, flexible options, dispute on the road, sexual choices

12. Birds: couple talks about separating, two paths, anxious about choosing, two of something, double the options, talking strangely, nervous about a decision, two choices, air miles, conversations on the road, flight options, discussing possibilities

13. Child: childish decision, new road, weak plan, small difference, short route, immature choice, minor decision, a bit strange, slight possibility, short road, new adventure, at minor crossroads, unsure about a decision

14. Fox: calculated agenda, career decision, suspicious decision, pretending to choose, job possibility, cautious choice, avoiding a decision, clever choice, employment options, practical choice, calculated decision, work route, pseudo plan, avoiding a road, feigning indecisiveness, fake separation, job choices

15. Bear: grand plan, meal planning, major highway/freeway, intense decision, asserting the right to choose, "big, big plans," assertive decision, increased options, bold choice, major road, huge possibility, weighing pros and cons, very unusual, big adventure, strong alternative, major crossroads, leading the way

16. Stars: goal planning, hopeful choice, the high road, harmonious decision, see all possibilities, blessed choice, seeing the path, infinite possibilities, great choice, amazing plan, clear road, viable route, high street, best decision, great adventure, best alternative, best option, best path forward, future plan, the best way possible, digital nomad, unlimited choices, extensive planning, exposing differences, highly possible, elevator, future possibilities, seeing it different a way

17. Stork: evolving possibilities, slim chance, evolving adventure, moving/relocation decision, long road, changing the route, proceeding down the road, moving along the way, roaming, wandering down the path

18. Dog: looking for a decision, searching the streets, service road, familiar road, trust the plan, follow the road, looking at possibilities, investigating something unusual, looking at the pros and cons, look in between, familiar route, searching for adventure, looking for something different, looking for options, following a lead

19. Tower: city planning, county road, legal decision, official plan, political decision, legal route, upstairs, authorized option, past decision, city street, ancient path, rules of the road, established plan, defending the right to choose, firm plan

20. Garden: average plans, garden variety, common choice, popular road, urban planning, popular option, general plan, group decision, common path, main street, popular route, people lining the streets, outdoor options, common separation

21. Mountain: hard decision, stony path, hilly road, mountain trail, putting off a decision, stalemate, steep road, limited options, hard path, rocky road, interceptive plans, blocked road, interrupted decision, gravel road, intercepted on the way, hindered on the road, restricting limits

23. Mice: potholes, fewer options, low road, damaged road, taking the low road, undecided, wrench in the plans, dirt road, fewer choices, damaging decision, stressful decision, jeopardizing plans, less possible

24. Heart: compassionate decision, lovers' lane, relationship route, considering options, love path, romantic possibility, giving a decision, pros and cons of dating, given a choice, heartfelt choice, compassionate separation, romantic adventure

25. Ring: roundabout, continued separation, surrounded by roads, wedding planning, the whole plan, ongoing decisions, continuous road, surrounded by possibilities, central plan, golden road, marriage pros and cons

26. Book: smart choice, secret decision, researching options, knowledgeable decision, logical decision, secret separation, memorial path (road) (e.g., Highway of Heroes, unknown road, memory lane), informed choice

27. Letter: paper trail, a map, listing options, read between the lines, texting a decision, resulting in a decision, documenting a decision, writing out possibilities, advertising options, writing on the road, advertising plan

28. Man: indecisive man, separated man, unfamiliar man, multiple men, unusual man, two-timing man, uncommitted man, alternative man, man on the road, strange man, chosen man, adventurous man

29. Woman: indecisive lady, separated woman, unfamiliar lady, multiple women, unusual woman, two-timing woman, uncommitted female, alternative woman, woman on the road, strange woman, chosen woman, adventurous woman

30. Lily: conservative choice, old road, mature plan, the old ways, calm decision, succession planning, retirement decision, lifelong plan, private decision, discerning options, discreet planning

31. Sun: holiday planning, good choice, conscious decision, annual planning, vacationing/holidaying separately, true path, really good possibility, happy trails, the right way, actual options truly separated, real plans

32. Moon: subconscious choice, feeling strange, feeling different now, sleeping apart, monthly plan, intuitive decision, creative plan, spell planning (using moon phases), aware of the plan, emotional choice, the magickal way

33. Key: respecting a choice, honoring a decision, doorway, openly separated, karma chooses for you, fated path, definite plan, uncovering possibilities, open road, definitely possible, privileged choice

34. Fish: expensive decision, financial choices, waterway, expensive separation, costly choice, commission options, investment pros and cons, expensive options, abundant options, water by the road, investment choices

35. Anchor: solid decision, long-term plan, grounded decision, down the path, safe road, downstairs, stuck in between, stay on course, holding on to the plan, rescued on the road, remaining options, still separated, safe choice

36. Cross: desperate choice, disappointing decision, regret going separate ways, cross the street, painful choice, difficult path, religious route, difficult decision, terrible plan, scandalous separation, regretting a choice, terrible options, crossed paths, intolerable decision

I will not follow where the path may lead, but I will go where there is no path, and I will leave a trail.

—Muriel Strode

23. Mice

Bringing damage and destruction, gnawing at things until they fade away
Everything starts gradually declining, spoiling and getting worse by the day.
You will never ever see it coming, until an infestation obsessively is spread.
Repairs needed before it unravels; remember this all began by a tiny thread

DESCRIPTION

Two white Mice casually standing under a cracked, red mushroom tower, oblivious to the utter ruin and decay surrounding them. One is relishing in the savory stolen morsel of Swiss cheese, while the other is watching closely, anticipating a delicious wayward crumb falling her way. The cube of Swiss is setting the tone of the card; with all the holes and gaps, it reinforces the card's main theme of decay and destruction. At first, the Mice seem very unassuming and almost endearing, with little expressive, dark eyes and human-looking hands and feet as part of their allure. Before you even realize, there is an actual infestation; the only thing you might notice is a silhouette moving out of the corner of your eye, accompanied by faint scratching noises of scurrying little paws.

Mounted on the side of the mushroom is an intricate iron clock, cracked and in desperate need of repair. This clock acts as a warning by foreshadowing the destruction yet to come, because unbeknown to you, Mice can slowly move in, taking over your life as time keeps on ticking by. When neglected, the problem is guaranteed to worsen over time, because when you see one mouse you can be sure that there is a whole colony of them lurking in the shadows. Mice are very opportunistic creatures that work collectively for the benefit of the whole, thriving in environments where everyone is like-minded, working toward a common goal.

Once an infestation develops, it becomes almost impossible to eradicate; Mice will wear you down every single time, gnawing at your consciousness. Demonstrating power in numbers, Mice possess an innate corruption and are able to thrive in any environment, reflected by the unperturbed faces of these two casually standing in the dirt and enjoying a bite and a casual conversation. Through close observation, Mice are great at recognizing opportunities that escape others—that is the enchantment of the Mice. They are focused on food, survival, and constantly living in fear, because the Mice know that they are looked upon as the scourge of the earth, as dirty disease-carrying vermin. The great disdain for these timid creatures causes the Mice to live in a constant state of stress, worrying about their survival. Just like the Mice, the number 23 scurries into your life, bringing with it a sense of collective consciousness. Utilizing creativity and wit to work through any issues, the number 23 is always looking ways to thrive. Like its fantastical furry little friends, the number 23 has an adventurous streak and is always game to try anything once. The number 23 is a curious number with widespread interests that is sure to keep the excitement flowing, amusing itself with its nutty antics by expressing itself fully.

KEYWORDS

Diminished, decay, damage, corrupt, theft, spoiled, wearing down, disintegrating, infestation, destruction, fading, vanishing, lessening, dirty, ruined, gnaws, dwindling, opportunistic, depleted, declining, deteriorating, repairs, spread of disease, costly (not money), obsessive, losing, stress, sabotage, decreasing, worry, dissolving, minimizing, messy

TIMING

Something that is taking place right now under your nose, unbeknown to you. This situation has been taking place for a while now, bit by bit over time, but when you do eventually become aware of it, it's already too late. The Mice card is a gradual card, and then bang! It seems that it happened all at once. If the Mountain is present, be prepared for a slight delay.

MEANING

When the Mice come scampering into your reading, be aware, for there is something being gnawed at a little at a time without you even noticing. It is a damage that is not obvious at first, because Mice are unassuming-looking creatures, but when you do eventually take notice, it is usually too late, and an infestation has taken root. For if you see one Mouse, you can guarantee that there is a dirty colony of opportunistic Mice ready to make a mess out of your life. The Mice card has a negative effect, decreasing and minimizing the other cards' effects, usually in a negative way, and will always throw shade on any cards nearby.

MICE IN LOVE

When the Mice card appears and you are in an existing relationship, you need to take heed, for there is something going on right under your nose, continually deteriorating the relationship. If you are single and looking for love, the Mice will come in and diminish your chances of anything you are trying to accomplish romantically. You need to pay attention, identify the problem, and exterminate it before it festers.

MICE IN CAREER

When the Mice come squeaking into your career, it signifies reduced hours or not enough work. This card can also indicate a very stressful work environment, or feelings that your job is slipping away a little at a time. If you are self-employed, the Mice will bring a decline in business and possible theft.

MICE IN WELLNESS

The Mice card brings infectious diseases and, if left unchecked, has the potential of becoming a widespread pandemic. Any health condition will experience a decline when the Mice scurry about. It can be also be indicative of a wasting type of illness that is slowly eating away at you.

MICE IN FINANCE

Finances dwindle when the Mice come out to play; any provisions or resources become scarce.

MICE IN MODERN DAY

Mice carry disease, significant of a widespread pandemic with the ability to wipe out many. Dirt, shit, and anything nasty.

AFFIRMATION

Stress and worries try to gnaw away at my life-force, but watch out, because I bite back harder!

CARTOMANCY: 7 OF CLUBS

A very troubling card. When the 7 of Clubs shows up, you better take notice, for there are issues simmering just below the surface that will catch you off guard. Troubles of all kinds penetrate into every aspect of your life; 7 of Clubs heavily screams a warning to beware. Things are always in disarray and breaking down and in need of repair around the 7 of Clubs. Feelings of worry, tears, and jealousy surround this card, coupled with exhaustion and fatigue. Magickally speaking, the 7 of Clubs is the card of the occult.

LENORMAND MICE COMBINATIONS

1. Rider: news obsessed, horsefly, first repair, acting rotted, news stresses you out, announcement causes worry, mobility declines, visit wears you down, speedy decline, suitor is opportunistic, horseshit!

2. Clover: gaming obsession, luckless, humorless, game sabotage, small opportunity, easy fix, luck's diminished, spontaneous stress, quick repair, fleeting opportunity, briefly stressed, cheering up, chance wasted

3. Ship: trip's ruined, riding dirty, motionless, goodbye wears you down, distance minimized, overseas opportunity, travel theft, leaving causes stress, ship spreads disease, scurvy-carrying mice, car obsession, travel worn

4. House: real estate obsession, house pests, house is messy, homeless, house mouse, comfortless, family member is stressed, house mold, downsizing (house), family is ruined, relative's worried, family member is declining

5. Tree: naturally wearing down, slowly spreading, blood loss, life's stresses, spiritual connections fade, slowly spreading, medical mess, toothless, disintegrating, slowly fading away, body declines, health deteriorates, DNA repairs, blood splatter, lifeless, rootless, system damage, life's a mess, viral spread of disease, spiritual sabotage, medical worry, health-obsessed

6. Clouds: mentally draining, doubtful, neurotic, concealing theft, fearful, hidden damage, mindless, concealing the spread of disease, hidden obsession, troubling stress, uncertainty causes worry, obsessed, psychological mess, thoughtless

7. Snake: evil corruption, vile, wires worn out, toxic obsession, complicated repair, problematic, the other woman is opportunistic, lying rat, problems are worrying, wires or pipes disintegrate, needs fixing, the other woman's a mess, toxic waste

8. Coffin: viral spread, grave robber, death and decay, grave dirt, spoiled, extermination, nothing left, dreadful, black mold, decay, grave disease, death caused by disease/illness, letting go, final repair, death-obsessed, stopping the spread, black plague, badly deteriorated, badly corrupted

9. Bouquet: charmless, pretty mess, special repairs, sweets obsession, surprise ruined, gift damaged, art destroyed, looking worn out, thankless, showing the damage, looking worried, showing stress, colorless, art ruined

10. Scythe: broken and needing repair, damage, removing decay, hoarder, decimation, removing debris, weaponless, threatening damage, emergency repairs, destruction, obliteration, sharp decline, reckless, splitting the damage, risky, removing rubbish, cut your losses, sudden damage, dangerously depleted, dissolving, reducing, decreasing, removing, throwing out the garbage, sabotage

11. Whip: fighting dirty, sexually depleted, aggressive spread of disease, questionable, repetitive theft, pattern of worrying, alarming infestation, sexual mess, sexually damaged, hard-hitting obsession, brutal destruction, obsessive, relentless, sexual tension, inflicting damage

12. Birds: talking shit, bird mites, gossip causes ruin, restlessness, panicky, anxious, partnerless, partner is worn out, conversation wasted, couple is destroyed, conversation is ruined, rumors are costly, calling less, voiceless, talk is cheap

13. Child: minor damage, new obsession, a bit dirty, minor corruption, slightly worried, childhood spreading disease, a little bit obsessed, vulnerable to stress, slightly ruined, playing dirty, little mouse, minor repairs, childless

14. Fox: sneaky shit's happening, employee theft, stealthy obsession, suspicious robbery, "scamdemic," shifty, at any cost, sneaky, jobless, sabotage, vanished, fake repairs, it will be costly (not money), pretending to dissolve something, pseudo spread of disease, corruption, feigning damage, escaping, coworker stealing

15. Bear: grand larceny, big infestation, major damage, very dirty, diet fatigue, food obsession, the "Big Cheese," tasteless, overbearing stress, food stolen, hors d'oeuvres, very costly (not money), major repairs, very corrupt, major deterioration, more or less, hairless/beardless, motherless, more obsessed, very stressful, powerless, big mess, food is wasted

16. Stars: online obsession, hopeless, exposing the obsession, at a high cost (not money), exposing the obsession, fixing the damage, wireless, exposing theft, clearing infestation, improving stress, sightless, future reduction, exposing the dirt, see beyond the mess, clear as mud, seeing a decrease, seeing an opportunity, space debris

17. Stork: evolving obsession, shiftless, leg damage, baby obsessed, evolving spread of disease, recurring infection, pregnancy worries, baby stolen, moving stress, changes cause stress, dancing less, moving theft

18. Dog: friendship is messy, looking for dirt, investigating corruption, helpless, friendless, looking for damage, investigating theft, without support, dog stolen, investigating the spread of disease, odorless, trust is ruined, friendship is wasted

19. Tower: political mess, citywide, ambitionless, government theft, spineless, ancient ruins, traditions fade, formalities dissolve, indifferent, politically obsessed, defenseless, lawless, in ruins, self-destructive, established corruption, self-deprecating

20. Garden: publicly damaging, common spread, mass corruption, public nuisance, average damage, garden pests, public mess, social media obsessed, contagious spread of disease, common obsession, general repairs, population decline

21. Mountain: blocking the spread of disease, interrupted robbery, limited damage, rough decline, permanent obsession, putting off repairs, setback, boundaries dissolve, permanent mess, steep decline

22. Paths: unusual decay, strange damage, unusual decline, unusual repair, strange obsession, "plandemic," undecided, between repairs, strange spread, possible damage, choices dwindle, multiple repairs

24. Heart: loveless, careless, compassionless, lover is obsessed, dateless, relationship needs repairing, romance fades, forgiving damage caused, heart stolen, heartless, love-obsessed, love life's a mess, romance dwindling, relationships wear you down

25. Ring: agreement dissolves, totally worried, spouse is obsessive, continual decline, connection fades, marriage destroyed, surrounded by rats, continual deterioration, surrounded by destruction, ongoing infections, ongoing corruption, marriage is messy, promises dissolve, marriage needs repairing, ongoing obsession, ring/jewelry stolen, continual damage, completely stressed, marriage obsessed

26. Book: secret obsession, senseless, book/reading obsessed, secretly worried, educational mess, master of disaster, secret is ruined, history is corrupt, books stolen, school is stressful, unknown damage, education ruined, studying causes stress, book damage

27. Letter: writing obsession, paperless, texting diminishes, messages decrease, results are worrying, communication fades, texts vanish, mail is stolen, documents fade, papers disintegrate, text message causes stress, newspaper is corrupt, files stolen

28. Man: worried male, dirty man, lesser man, damaged man, corrupt man, stressed man, opportunistic man, draining man, ruined man, obsessive man, lowly man, husbandless, messy man, worried man, manless, obsessed man, spoiled man, degraded man

29. Woman: worried female, dirty woman, lesser woman, damaged lady, corrupt woman, stressed woman, opportunistic woman, draining woman, ruined lady, obsessive woman, lowly woman, wifeless, messy lady, worried woman, womanless, obsessed woman, spoiled lady, degraded woman, lady is a shrew

30. Lily: antiquated, fatherless, old obsession, peace vanishes, age-obsessed, old person is stressed, discreet corruption, snow/ice melts, privacy ruined, old age wears you down, retirement causes stress

31. Sun: truly obsessed, real damage, daily stress, day-to-day worries, rewardless, truth is costly, truth causes destruction, daily obsession, illuminating the dirt, annual repairs, sunlight decreases, vacation/holiday obsessed, yearly decline, happiness ruined, illuminating corruption, real damage, it's a hot mess!

32. Moon: spell diminishes, emotionless, sleepless (night), feeling dirty, feeling worn out, talent's wasted, magickal mess, moonless (night), emotional damage, feelings fade, monthly repairs, emotional low, occult obsession, dreamless, emotionally destroyed, feeling less than, emotionally depleted (fatigued)

33. Key: definitely corrupt, keyless, definitely ruined, status obsessed, honor among thieves, uncovering dirt, revealing the damage, keys stolen, uncovering corruption, definitively deteriorating, definitely spoiled, karmic mess

34. Fish: financially depleted, money-obsessed, business stresses, costly, penniless, financial worries, price reduction, deep decline, water recedes, resourcelessness, cashless, deep damage, deep corruption, drinking obsession, business dissolution, costly repairs, money's stolen

35. Anchor: long-lasting damage, holding on to stress, constant repairs, saved from more damage, keep reducing, lowly, still obsessed, constantly worn down, keep whittling away, groundless

36. Cross: at a terrible cost, difficult repair, remorseless, sinful, regretting the damage caused, faithless, terrible damage, shameful sabotage, scandalous corruption, disappointing repairs, repentless, shameful, ghost/spirit vanishes, terrible mess

Every one of us is losing something precious to us. Lost opportunities, lost possibilities, feeling we can never get back again. That's part of what it means to be alive.

—Haruki Murakami

24. Heart

Searching through eternity, until one day you were found.
Hearing your loving voice was the sweetest sound.
The beating of your heart sang that I was made for you.
Feelings of love ignited when you said you loved me too.

DESCRIPTION

Behind the gauzy curtains we see a big, bright, shiny red Heart in a protective stance, putting itself in front of anything that threatens its love, and the little Heart peaks around him. The little Heart shares a message with you: love comes in many forms; love does not judge or discriminate. As long as the passion is heartfelt, bringing you pleasure, it's enough validation that you are in a loving relationship. The little heart gently reminds the big Heart that it is better to *feel* love than to be told you are loved, and kindness costs you nothing. Demonstrating that loving feeling, the hearts are adorned with a shimmery golden embellishment, swirling in a bold pattern and symbolizing that there will be many twists and turns along the way to finding true love.

Encrusted in these golden scrolls rests a topaz—a symbol of truth, trust, and forgiveness qualities that will benefit any relationship.

A showy display of rose petals rain down, adding romance, stoking the fires of passion, and demonstrating the imperativeness of keeping romance alive in a relationship. The rose petals are akin to pleasure, one of the most timeless and celebrated of all flowers that epitomize love and generosity. Finally, these two hearts found each other after searching so long for something real, ultimately reuniting because, before them, there was us. Life's grand design of life conspired and contrived for them to meet up again in this lifetime, just to whisper to each other the heartfelt words of "I will love you forever"; all I ask is that you remember us.

The Heart card bears the number 24, which is the factorial of 4! Corresponding to the fourth chakra, located in the center of your being, where your greatest source of power lies—your Heart—since this is the feeling center, which deals with all things connected with passion, love, relationships, and romance. Love is definitely in the air, demonstrated by the azure sky framed by billowy, white clouds peeking out behind the Hearts, reminding you that when love is manifested in its truest form, it can be expansive, enchanted, loyal, sincere, and limitless.

KEYWORDS

Love, heartfelt, passion, romance, relationship, the heart, compassion, lover, pleasure, flirting, kindness, loving, generosity, affection, dating, forgiveness, affairs of the heart, philanthropy, considerate, intimate, giving, favorite, tender, cherished, interested, caring, admiring, accepting, loving feelings

TIMING

The Heart card in timing denotes the 24th day or 24th week or in 24 months, if the Mountain is present.

MEANING

The Heart stirs with feelings of love in all its forms when this card appears in a reading. It is usually in reference to romantic love. Located in the center of your being, with this placement the Heart affects every aspect of your life, for love is the center of all things. The primal beating is the giver of life, love, passion, happiness, joy, and fulfillment. When the Heart pulses its way to you, get ready to feel things you never thought possible.

HEART IN LOVE

The Heart card represents a loving relationship. If you are single, the Hearts card can indicate a date or a new love interest. This card represents the feeling of falling in love or having romantic feelings toward someone, since the Heart card embodies the expression of love in all of its forms.

HEART IN CAREER

The Hearts card represents having a passion for your career and loving your job. It can also be indicative of a pleasurable work environment or even an office romance. As a vocation, the Hearts card can represent philanthropy, charity work, working for a nonprofit organization, or working in the field of cardiology.

HEART IN WELLNESS

The Heart card represents anything connected to the heart and the Heart Chakra.

HEART IN FINANCES

The Heart card is all about generosity and giving, also making charitable philanthropic donations. When the Heart card shows up in finances, it can also represent the love of money.

HEART IN MODERN DAY

Modern-day "likes." The Heart emoji in social media shows love or appreciation for something.

AFFIRMATION

Life is a love song, as I follow the primal beat of my heart; my soul stirs with the possibility of becoming whole.

CARTOMANCY: JACK OF HEARTS

Jack of Hearts is affiliated with Eros, the Greek god of love and sex. This Jack can also represent thoughts and intentions; look carefully to the surrounding cards to see how genuine these loving thoughts are. This Jack is a very creative person who expresses himself through the arts, using various mediums. The Jack of Hearts can represent a young person of either sex, often viewed as a suitor with a sensitive and warm heart. The Jack of Hearts can appear as a friend, or a lover, and sometimes even as a beloved pet. Regardless, it will always be someone familiar and connected to you, and someone dear to your heart.

LENORMAND HEART COMBINATIONS

1. Rider: first love, announcing a relationship, first date, racing heart, visiting a lover, first lover, rapid heartbeat, first relationship, acting romantic, rushed relationship, news of a relationship, young man falls in love, a suitor

2. Clover: green heart (heart chakra), brief relationship, quick romance, wild romance, betting on love, lucky lover, betting on the other man, take a chance on love, happy-go-lucky lover, casually dating, short-lived relationship, easy to love, funny date

3. Ship: leaving a lover, foreign charity, distant lover, long-distance romance, international dating, foreign interest, distant heart, navigating love, driving for pleasure, leaving the dating scene, travel passion

4. House: family donation, familiar relationship, home care, family charity, house full of love, real estate interest, indoor date, place of love, domestic relationship, family acceptance, family generosity

5. Tree: tree hugger, healthcare, heal the heart, spiritual relationship, deeply rooted feelings, slowly falling in love, slow heartbeat, medical donation, deeply rooted love, organ donor, slow-moving relationship, spiritual love, deeply rooted pleasure, healing relationship

6. Clouds: misplaced affections, passing flirtation, lost passion, temperamental lover, lost in love, temperamental relationship, lost pleasure, fearful of love, misunderstood relationship, hidden romance, anonymous donation, lost lover, unstable relationship, moody lover, addicted to love, disheartened, thinking about a lover

7. Snake: cheating partner, problematic relationship, craving, constricting relationship, toxic heart, complicated love, wanting to cheat, desiring a relationship, jealous heart, needing love, dislike, tempting relationship, attraction

8. Coffin: black heart, dark lover, final relationship, denied love, ill-fated relationship, nonexistent love, last relationship, sick at heart, death of a lover, last love, denied affection, closed off to love, letting go of a lover, last date, death of a loved one, uninterested, palliative care, stopped heart, ill considered

9. Bouquet: wonderful lover, sweetheart, celebrating love, sweet lover, wonderful relationship, grateful heart, making sweet love, generous donation, fondness, special relationship, enjoyment, beautiful romance, kindness, wonderful date, pleasure, special kind of love, budding affection

10. Scythe: unexpected romance, hurtful relationship, cutting off a lover, broken relationship, cutting off a date, blindsided breakup, splitting up (relationship), ex-lover, hurtful lover, decimating love, severing a relationship, killing passion, separate relationships, cutting off generosity, breaking hearts, harmful relationship, separating

11. Whip: hurt heart; on-again, off-again relationship; hurtful relationship; sexually considerate; erotic lover; sexual relations; intermittent dating; sexually passionate; repetitive flirting; opposed to dating; angry lover; sexually interested; sexual love

12. Birds: discussing romantic feelings, couple in love, saying "I love you," two lovers, plural relationship, saying sorry, double date, bonded lovers, rumored relationship, a couple (in a relationship), bonded

13. Child: new love, weak relationship, inexperienced lover, new romance, weak heart, small donation, tenderhearted, new lover, a little flirty, small generosity, slight pleasure, a little forgiveness goes a long way, small kindness, vulnerable heart, fragile relationship, small heart, infatuation, fresh start (relationship)

14. Fox: pretending to be in a relationship, feigning interest, pseudo philanthropist, avoiding relationships, feigning forgiveness, escaping a relationship, fake love, stealthy relationship, careful with your heart, avoiding a lover, suspicious lover, practical relationship, fake charity, avoid dating, calculated romance, scheming lover

15. Bear: bold lover, very romantic, huge flirt, intense relationship, big donation, enlarged heart, oversentimental, mother's/grandmother's love, very generous, more to love, very kind, assertive lover, increased affection, very forgiving, immense pleasure, mother-like affections

16. Stars: improving relationship, astral/star lover, universal love, positive relationship, great heart, forever love, online relationship, great pleasure, "bless your heart," alien sympathizers, upgrading a lover, potential romance, great lover, best date, great relationship, potential lover, future relationship, looking forward to dating, see beyond the flirting, wish in your heart, look of love

17. Stork: evolving romantic feelings, returning to a relationship, restless lover, quiet lover, baby love, moving in together, restless lover, evolving relationship, gentle lover, long relationship, born to love you, longing

18. Dog: loyal heart, submissive lover, puppy love, friendly relationship, looking for forgiveness, philanthropic donation, attentive lover, protect your heart, friendly date, therapeutic relationship, follow your heart, faithful lover, friendly kiss, look in your heart, searching for love, stalking a lover, searching for a date, looking for pleasure, friends before lovers, Philadelphia

19. Tower: defensive lover, having walls up, Paris (city of love), one love, self-love, traditional relationship, self-care, formally dating, defending your relationship, official donation, ambitious lover, self-worth, estranged, indifference, officially "in a relationship"

20. Garden: social media relationship, average lover, general affection, average relationship, general care, public relationship, popularity, outdoor date, social media dating, rendezvous with a lover

21. Mountain: hard to love, rough relationship, limited love, interrupted date, obstacle in the relationship, hard-hearted, atherosclerosis, interrupted pleasure, obstacle to love, hard relationship, blocked donations, insensitive

22. Path: many roads to love, unusual relationship, strange lover, strange date, multiple relationships, many dates, between relationships, wandering heart, between lovers, on the path to love, abnormal heartbeat, unusual romance

23. Mice: damaged heart, costly relationship, fading passion, diminished love, jeopardizing love, less passion, repulsed, unaffectionate, uncaring, less generous, stealing hearts, fewer dates, unpleasant, losing passion, less compassionate, crumbling relationship, fixation, unkind, corrupt philanthropist, deteriorating heart, destroying a relationship, jeopardizing love, obsession, messy relationship, disheartened, stressful relationship

25. Ring: wholeheartedly, continual donations, marital relationship, entire relationship, "you complete me," ongoing romance, dedication, ongoing flirting, continued kindness, ongoing generosity, continued affection, surrounded by love, devotion, commitment, completely forgiven, in a relationship, continual love, promising relationship, offer is generous

26. Book: anonymous donation, books on relationships, information on a lover, learning to love, high school sweethearts, secretly dating, lesson learned in love, memories of a relationship, expert matchmaker, information on a lover, reminiscing (love)

27. Letter: words of love, messaging a lover, posting relationship status, write from the heart, written love note, texting words of love, written love letter, paper heart, texting relationship, blogging about romance

28. Man: male lover, passionate man, generous man, heart-shaped-face man, bighearted man, gentleman, considerate man, kindhearted man, tender man, compassionate man, philanthropist (male), relationship with a man, forgive a man, lovely man, giving man, man in a relationship

29. Woman: female lover, passionate woman, generous woman, heart-shaped-face woman, bighearted female, gentlewoman, considerate woman, kindhearted woman, tender woman, compassionate woman, philanthropist (female), relationship with a woman, forgive a woman, lonely woman, giving woman, woman in a relationship, kind lady

30. Lily: mature relationship, restrained lover, kindness, a tryst, discreet relationship, heart, icy eldercare, old relationship, father's/grandfather's love, frail heart, private lover, father-like affections, coldhearted, delicate, discreetly dating, at peace

31. Sun: good-hearted, annual donation, happy relationship, true heart, real love, winning your heart, truly forgiven, real affection, happy heart, successful date, truly heartfelt, really passionate, truly loved, actual lovers, true compassion, truthful lover, an actual heart, real relationship

32. Moon: feeling loved, creative lover, enchantment, mystical lover, feelings of compassion, feeling generous, manifesting a relationship, "all the feels," feeling emotional, feelings/emotions, monthly donation, having an emotional relationship, manifesting love

33. Key: karmic relationship, affluent lover, key relationship, honor your heart, courtship, definitely love, reveal your heart, uncovering a relationship, openly flirting, fated relationship, open heart, revealing the relationship, defiantly dating, defiantly in a relationship, open to forgiveness, honoring a lover, definitely flirting

34. Fish: expensive relationship, deeply heartfelt, paying for love, financially taken care of, deep passion, expensive lover, deep compassion, financially generous, financial charitable donation, deep pleasure, financial relationship, drunk on love

35. Anchor: arranged date, still in a relationship, lasting relationship, still in your heart, holding on to love, saving the relationship, lingering lover/relationship, from the bottom of your heart, safe relationship, still in love, staying in a relationship, still flirting, stay kind, keep loving, still dating, rescued lover, hanging on to a lover/relationship, steadfastness, heavy-hearted

36. Cross: disappointing date, shameful flirting, doomed relationship, painful heart, testing the relationship, scandalous relationship, difficult lover, religious donation, cursed relationship, obligated donation, difficult lover, cross your heart, disappointed in love, obligated care, intolerable relationship, insufferable dating, shameful love affair, sinful pleasures, regret loving someone, miserable relationship, terrible date, exhausting relationship, terrible relationship, ghosted

For it was not into my ear you whispered, but into my heart. It was not my lips you kissed, but my soul.

—Judy Garland

25. Ring

The bond we share is continual, not written in the sand.
Contracts bind us together with a golden marriage band.
This ring promises eternity, sealing the deal when I said "I do."
Completely offering my heart, vowing to be devoted and true.

DESCRIPTION

A beautiful, shinning golden Ring is cradled in the heart of a velvety, crimson rose; soft rose petals circle this sacred amulet in a cloud of perfume and beauty. The red rose is the epitome of conveying feelings of commitment, inflaming the heart to beat strongly with promise. With no beginning or end, the Ring has been exchanged as a promise, of an eternal union with a continual melody forever singing the praises of a devoted connection. The circular Ring is inscribed with enchanted symbols highlighting the gold's protective qualities, bewitching this Ring into a sacred talisman designed to ward off any ill will or unwanted attention.

The center of the Ring is set with a stunning star sapphire; the sky-blue stone connects the Ring to the heavens, emphasized by the celestial angel spreading her wings as she floats within the twinkles of the star. When this jewelry is worn, it offers the bearer universal knowledge, opening up the floodgates of abundance and mental clarity—very useful qualities when making deals or signing contracts and agreements. The Ring is a symbol of status favored by royals throughout the centuries, symbolizing promises, proposals, and marriages that are arranged for the betterment of realm, by securing a union in order to improve positions of status and wealth.

Bound by the Ring card, the number 25 brings qualities that are very beneficial and can come in handy when looking to secure a marriage proposal. The number 25 will lead you to your heart's desire, assisting you in finding your happily-ever-after by locating the right romantic partner to ensure that outcome. Just as the Ring, the number 25 is honor bound and balanced, containing the energy of relationships and unions within its circle.

KEYWORDS

Commitments, agreements, unions, circle, connections, engagements, marriage, continual, jewelry, contracts, deals, round, promise, bonds, proposal, circulation, vows, inner circle, dedicated, offer, entire, surrounded, complete, total, whole, consent, spouse, devoted, ongoing

TIMING

When the Ring card shows up, it is indicative of something continuous and ongoing and can also represent the wedding month of June. The Ring can represent the 25th day or 25 weeks, if the Mountain is present.

MEANING

A positive card, the Ring can symbolize a commitment of an engagement or a promise of marriage, and that is why when the Ring appears, it can denote an actual Ring. The other meaning the Ring carries is that it has anything to do with agreements, offers, deals, proposals, or connections made, or things that are continuous in nature.

Beware and be wary of making a vow or swearing an oath, because the Ring will bind any card in proximity to it; whether the card be positive or negative, you will be sure to feel the ongoing effects of the Ring.

RING IN LOVE

A favorable card to see, since the Ring represents promises, proposals, engagements, and marriage. It's symbolic of a committed relationship. If you're single, the Ring heralds the possibility of a new relationship entering in your life, with the possibility of serious commitment or an offer of marriage. Pay close attention to the card next to the Ring, for it will influence its meaning. Beware if the Paths, Scythe, or Coffin are in proximity since it speaks of a separation, a divorce, or an ending, resulting in a parting of ways.

RING IN CAREER

In career, the Ring would represent any vocation involving contracts, agreements, proposals, offers, and business deals. It can also refer to an offer of employment or a collective agreement. Ring too can represent a job where a repetitive type of work is conducted, such as a factory worker or assembly line worker—any job that is continuous in nature.

RING IN WELLNESS

When the Ring presents itself in wellness, it can denote an ongoing health concern or continued treatment. The Ring represents the circulatory system.

RING IN FINANCES

Keeping the Ring shape in mind, in finances it reflects a balanced approach with funds in a continual flow.

A coven, a secret society, or a very exclusive group; also demonstrates the circle of trust.

AFFIRMATION

I am complete and infinite; when I know this, I know everything.

CARTOMANCY: ACE OF CLUBS

As a traditional card of marriage, the Ace of Clubs is used to arrange a union to boost the status and wealth of the bride's family. When promised to the bridegroom, the potential bride enters into a binding contract that gives the right of stewardship over to the proposed husband. Similar to the Ring, the Ace of Clubs represents marriage, proposals, and binding contracts of all kinds.

LENORMAND RING COMBINATIONS

1. Rider: first marriage, coming around, quickly bonded, first offer, going around, quick proposal, fast deal, rushed marriage, quick offer, first promise, first round, rushed engagement, heading toward marriage, going in circles

2. Clover: brief marriage, wild deal, short-term arrangement, brief connection, happy-go-lucky spouse, temporary agreement, casual commitment, temporary contract, lucky marriage, betting it all, wild connection

3. Ship: leaving a marriage, vehicle contract, travel connections, car/bicycle/motorcycle tires, long-distance marriage, distant connection, traveling around world, trading gold, travel arrangements, journey continues

4. House: house rental agreement, family wedding, comfortable marriage, family centered, familiar connection, family heirloom ring/jewelry, inner circle, familiar surroundings, inside, family unity, familial bonds, family jewels, real estate contract

5. Tree: slow deal, spiritual jewelry, deeply rooted bond, blood circulation, ancestral jewelry, blood oath, spiritual marriage, ancestral bond, medical-alert jewelry, tree rings, deeply rooted connection, slow to propose

6. Clouds: hidden deal, misplaced jewelry, unstable marriage, temperamental deal, confusing marriage, hidden marriage, lost ring, air circulation, hidden jewelry, cyclone, unstable agreement, volatile connection

7. Snake: infidelity, tempting deal, enticing offer, constricting marriage, toxic connection, complicated marriage, complex deal, cheating spouse, complicated agreement, problematic marriage, cheating while married, desiring commitment, wanting marriage, tight ring, unfaithful, bracelet/necklace, lying spouse, betrayal

8. Coffin: bad offer, expired contract, no connection, bad union, last offer, no consent, letting go of a marriage, black diamond, dark vow, bad contract, death contract/agreement, inconclusive, last marriage, final round, no commitment, "till death do us part," dead ringer, cremains jewelry, ill/sick spouse, inherited jewelry (of the dead), burial/funeral contract, no agreement, noncompliance, expired contract/offer, void contract

9. Bouquet: wonderful marriage, gifting a ring, celebrating marriage, fashionable jewelry, beautiful engagement/wedding, perfect union, wonderful connection, special bond, beautiful dedication, special agreement, surprise proposal, beautiful ring, fantastic deal

10. Scythe: vaccinated/injected spouse, dangerous connection, decimating a marriage, breaking a vow, splitting/breaking up (marriage), breaking the circle, severing bonds, broken engagement, part/half, irrevocable contract, severing a marriage/engagement, breaking a deal, an ex (wife/husband), separation agreement, cutting off an ex, splitting a contract, shotgun wedding, an urgent offer, threatening spouse

11. Whip: aggressive spouse, sexual bond, aggressive offer, abusive marriage, ongoing, arguing over jewelry/ring, sexual union, abusive spouse, hitting the bull's-eye, sex ring, intermittent connection, sexual consent

12. Birds: twice married, verbal consent, discussing offers, sibling bond, verbal offer, negotiating a contract, talks of engagement, verbal promise, talking about marriage, partner proposes, two offers, flying around, nerve center, gossip circulating

13. Child: new contract, weak offer, short marriage, small wedding, new ring/jewelry, weak commitment, small agreement, small circle, vulnerable contract, child ring, slight connection, weak circulation, vulnerable marriage, child bond, newly engaged

14. Fox: calculated offer, practical marriage, reneged promise, job offer, clever agreement, sneaking around, suspicious offer, employment contract, practical agreement, tricky deal, pretending to be faithful, avoiding commitment, guilty spouse, suspicious relationship, costume/fake jewelry, reneged deal, avoiding engagement/marriage, pseudo marriage, pretending to be engaged, fake offer, feigning loyalty, escaping a marriage, noncommittal

15. Bear: increasing connection, strong commitment, big offer, intense marriage, mother's/grandmother's ring, increased offers, assertive spouse, more promises, increased circulation, big proposal, intense bond, big ring, strong contract, bold jewelry, big wedding, huge deal, motherly bond

16. Stars: astral connection, wishing for marriage, great deal, improving, celestial sphere, marriage, positive connection, blessed union, harmonious marriage, eternity, best offer, electric circuit, expansive circle, diamond band, eternal vow, future commitment, potential deal

17. Stork: returning spouse, evolving offer, renewal of vows, long engagement/marriage, altered agreement, evolving connection, recurring contract, returning to a marriage, renewed commitment, returning a ring, spinning around, baby bond, renewed contract, moving around, did a 360°

18. Dog: loyal spouse, friendship ring/jewelry, following a fiancé/spouse, service agreement, nose ring, attentive spouse, alert jewelry (medical alert), friendship bond, faithful union, friendly offer, watching for deals, earrings

19. Tower: defensive spouse, cock ring, past marriage, city center, formal offer, established marriage, past agreement, established connection, traditional marriage, past promises, formal agreement, single connection, past commitment, official agreement, "one ring to rule them all" (control)

20. Garden: average deal, public offer, event contract, outer circle, common offer, average marriage, public contract, playing the field and avoiding marriage, common-law marriage, average connection, popular jewelry, general agreement, public circle

21. Mountain: tough marriage, blocked deal, postponing an engagement, interrupted deal, delay continues, limited agreement, distant connection, obstacles to marriage altar, restricted union, interrupted offer, crystal jewelry, challenging commitment

22. Paths: multiple connections, unusual bond, many promises, strange agreement, unusual contract, between contracts, multiple commitments, many contracts, planning a wedding, strange marriage, unusual connection, choosing a ring, multiple deals

23. Mice: costly promise, stolen jewelry, jeopardizing the marriage, messy marriage, corrupt deal, disconnected, partial deal, fading vows, vanishing promise, losing a contract, dirty deal, dissolving an agreement, costly promise, uncommitted, disintegrating marriage, messing around, incomplete, disloyal, unpromising, losing the contact, corruption ring

24. Heart: considering an offer, engagement ring, giving a promise, sentimental attachment, loving bond, giving an offer, forgiving spouse, giving a commitment, loving connection, relationship leads to marriage, giving a proposal, generous offer

26. Book: informed consent, secret engagement/proposal, unknown offer, secret marriage, educational offer, school contract, secret connection, lesson continues, education completed, training ongoing

27. Letter: written contract, schedule completely full, written consent, newspaper circulation, written guarantee, texting/messaging continues, sending a contract, written offer, texting/messaging a spouse

28. Man: committed man, husband, married man, taken man, male partner, connected man, dedicated man, round-faced man, engaged man, surrounded by men, masculine ring/jewelry, bonded male, fiancé (male), devoted man

29. Woman: committed woman, wife, married woman, taken woman, female partner, connected woman, dedicated lady, round-faced woman, engaged woman, surrounded by women, feminine ring/jewelry, bonded female, fiancée (female), devoted woman

30. Lily: conservative offer, old married couple, private deal, discreet connection, old commitment, antique jewelry, father's/grandfather's ring, lifelong marriage, mature union, discretion continues, old ring

31. Sun: good deal, successful agreement, holiday/vacation proposal, true connection, energetically bonded, really committed, good marriage, true bond, gold jewelry, true union, actual offer, winning the contract, truly complete, energetic connection, destination wedding

32. Moon: creative proposal, mystical connection, psychic bond, feeling whole, metaphysical jewelry, feeling connected, monthly contract, silver ring/jewelry, an orb, psychic connection, monthly agreement, manifesting marriage

33. Key: prestigious connections, affluent marriage, karmic wheel, honoring a commitment, karmic circle, important connection, karmic bond, fated marriage, open contract, destinies entwined, karmic marriage, significant piece of jewelry, honoring a promise, solemn vow, respecting an agreement, honoring vows, definitely married, soul connection, Yes—I do!

34. Fish: expensive deal, deep connection, expensive engagement ring, deep bond, financial consent, investment offer, financial bonds, business commitment, shopping for a ring, circulation, business engagement, deeply devoted, business deal, financial marriage

35. Anchor: solid connection, keeping promises, stuck in a marriage, staying connected, lasting commitment, arranged marriage, long-lasting engagement, stable contract, staying married, safe zone, continued, stay in the loop, solid offer, holding on to marriage, tying the knot

36. Cross: religious marriage, terrible offer, testing your spouse, difficult marriage, spirit attachment, cross (ring/necklace), miserable marriage, disappointing offer, exhausting commitment, regret proposing, insufferable commitment, scandalous union/marriage, regret getting married, terrible deal, religious oath, obligated to the marriage

"Chains do not hold a marriage together," she replied. "It is thread, hundreds of tiny threads which sew people together through the years. That is what makes a marriage last—more than passion or even sex. But those threads should never become chains."

—Simone Signoret

26. Book

Within the book's mysterious pages, unknown secrets gently concealed
Wisdom inscribed on vellum pages, information yearning to be revealed
Education becomes great knowledge, memories veiled in time and space.
Remember history has yet to be written, a mystery worthy of one's embrace.

DESCRIPTION

The emerald quartz in a bejeweled, life-sized Book beckons you to come in and take a closer look, as a wave of enchantment penetrates your aura. Mysteriously you hear a whispering voice state: ***Only the worthy will be able to find their way through the labyrinth and gain access to the inner secrets of the Book.***

Your eye catches a glint coming from the five milky emeralds set strategically within the labyrinth, and you wonder what lessons will be taught before the Book will impart its inner secrets. As you set the intention for the journey and take your first step into the *unknown*, immediately you feel the effects of the first stone, allowing you to recall your memories and all the history over the years.

The second stone represents *knowledge* as it bubbles up to the surface, empowering you to take the next step. The third stone you land on represents *learning*, the ability to expand your mind in order to unveil all the possibilities laid out before you. The fourth stepping-stone awakens something primal within you, as universal energy channels *information* into your being, connecting you to a higher purpose. And before you realize it, you have traveled into the very center of the labyrinth, standing on the fifth and final emerald quartz.

On this final stone you begin to feel a sensation stirring in your heart chakra, spinning and radiating outward as you become aware of the culmination, and the fifth stone is the most important one of all. This final arcana is the ability to master *wisdom*, the culmination of all the lessons you've learned throughout your life and the ability to apply them; the resulting wisdom is the greatest guarded secret. You stand there in awe as waves of love begin cascading over you, taking root in your soul, stirring up memories you forgot you had. The Book opens up before you, and tears fill your eyes, revealing a single handwritten inscription on the creamy vellum page.

Amid life's labyrinth, you wander and explore

The Book's greatest mysteries, hidden in lore

Discover the secrets, of wisdom's sacred tome

Each page is a portal, into realms unknown

Unveiling lessons, profound and very grand

Inscribe your knowledge with a steady hand

Let the Book record stories, held in eternal bind

The details of your journey, body, spirit, and mind

Each time the quill references, true history be told

Each page is a masterpiece, where dreams unfold

Embrace the Book's chapters, story of spirit ignite

In fate's splendor's tapestry, of your soul's eternal light

Remember, seek not without but delve deeply within,

As you turn the to the page, where a new story begins.

Stunned, letting the information slowly seep into your understanding, you read the message over and over again. You frantically flip through the rest of the pages in the tomb, looking for more, realizing that the rest of the Book is blank; as it dawns on you, it's true that the greatest secret of the Book *is* YOU!

The number 26 graces the pages of the Book as it imparts that creative knowledge is needed to tap into your highest potential and achieve any goals you've set your sights on. Having mastered the qualities of the Book, you can then effectively teach others the greatest secrets by using your intellect combined with life experiences, sprinkled with education and lessons learned, inspiring yourself and others to dream the biggest dreams and reach for the stars.

KEYWORDS

Secrets, a book, information, knowledge, wisdom, manuscript, facts, journal, diary, unknown, expert, history, education, studies, memories, research, learning, lesson, training, academic, teaching, logical, smart, remembering, story, evidence, mysterious

TIMING

The timing is unknown, and this will take awhile, just as it takes time to learn something new, acquire knowledge, or even read a book. The Book can also represent the 26th day of the month, or 26 months when the Mountain is present.

MEANING

Secrets pressed tightly within the pages of the Book are the main themes of this card; being a very straightforward card, the Book represents a body of information. Many stories are stored within, just waiting for you to come by and unleash all the wisdom held within its pages. A Book can teach you many things, such as you can live vicariously through the tales, visit far-off lands, and meet very memorable characters. These important life lessons learned by reading could save you the heartache of having to experience some things yourself. Knowledge is power, and remember: a single Book can change your life forever, moving you in ways you never thought possible.

BOOK IN LOVE

The Book card in love can indicate a secret relationship or keeping something from someone; if this information comes to light, it would drastically change the dynamic of the original situation.

BOOK IN CAREER

As a career, the Book represents any field in academia or education, being in a role to impart knowledge and expertise in your chosen field. Careers involving physical books surrounding you interest you, such as a librarian, accountant, lawyer, teacher, professor, researcher, or writer. It can also indicate that more education or training is needed in your current job.

BOOK IN WELLNESS

In wellness, the Book denotes there is an undiagnosed or unknown ailment, and more information is needed. Researching anything medical or health related is represented by the Book, also indicative that someone is keeping a medical condition a secret.

BOOK IN FINANCES

In finances, the book represents the actual books of a company or financial records of an individual, such as a bank book. Secrets surrounding money, spending, or keeping your finances under wraps are very possible when the Book shows up.

BOOK IN MODERN DAY

In modern day, the book refers to the Akashic records, where the books of all your lifetimes are kept. Magickally, the Book represents a Grimoire (book of spells), or a Book of Shadows (BOS). At times, the Book can also mean having a secret career or job, such as "I'm an accountant." If you know, you know.

AFFIRMATION

I learn from life's lessons as I channel these teachings into knowledge by applying this wisdom into every aspect of my life.

Show me the money! This is a card of big money and profits. The 10 of Diamonds is complementary to the Book, for success can never be achieved or retained without learning and gathering information, attaining knowledge and expertise, then knowing how to apply that wisdom. As a card of thought, the 10 of Diamonds is associated with the brain, flexing that mental muscle to dream up the big ideas. When it comes to the occult, the 10 of Diamonds represents a Grimoire or a Book of Shadows.

LENORMAND BOOK COMBINATIONS

1. Rider: going to school, fast learner, first chapter, freshman, rushed research, news story, first book, acting secretive, acting smart, first memory, guest book, first grade, broadcasting secret information

2. Clover: quick witted, fleeting memories, brief education, short-term memory, brief history, funny story, spontaneous memories, wild secret, small opportunity (education), casually informed

3. Ship: boarding school, car manual, travel stories, nautical training, travel history, long-distance education, distant memory, travel memories, leaving school, trade secrets, navigating education, goodbye story

4. House: property information, household manual, insider's knowledge, family stories, real estate information, familiar memories, internal secrets, family is educated, real estate history, place is unknown

5. Tree: medical information, growing secret, medically informed, deep-rooted secret, medical knowledge, health education, slow learner, medical facts, slow training, medical history, deeply rooted memory, medical books, diagnosis kept secret, life story (memoir), spiritual books

6. Clouds: confusing information, vague history, cloudy memories, smoke screen, shady secrets, hidden in plain sight (information/secrets), shadow journal, hidden memories, lost book, confusing story, hiding evidence, troubling facts, hidden history, clouded research, dementia, traumatic memory, hidden journal/diary, redacted information

7. Snake: wanting information, complex research, cheating in school, toxic secrets, problems studying, complicated story, complex information, problems studying, complicated book, toxic memories, complex training, unwise, untrue facts, lying about education

8. Coffin: bad information, erased history, dark secret, final chapter, ill informed, buried memories, no facts, nonexistent research, no memory, let go the stories, denied information, memorial, last memory, deleted information, closing a chapter, uneducated, deleted research, grief journal, final grade, closed book, condolences book, no logic, denied education, bad memories, dark secret, de-enrolled, erased/deleted memories, unwise

9. Bouquet: surprising facts, pleasant memory, beautiful story, art school, showing evidence, presenting the facts, fantastic book, special memory, beautiful manuscript, wonderful education, beautiful history, wonderful lesson, gifting a book

10. Scythe: vaccine/injectable research, collecting facts, emergency training, dangerous secret, injectables history, risk factors, emergency handbook, urgent information, decimating education, broken secret, gathering research, dangerous knowledge, expelled from school, obliterating history, half-wit, unexpected information

11. Whip: repetitive information, sex stories, erotic book, hurtful memories, sex journal, intermittent training, arguing the facts, aggressive training, carnal knowledge, pattern of keeping secrets, harmful secrets, muscle memory, intermittent lessons

12. Birds: discussing research, discussing facts, talking about memories, call log history, anxiety journal, distracted from studies, reminiscing, gossiping behind your back, telling a story, talking in secret, recanting a conversation

13. Child: tiny secret, new chapter, insignificant facts, little information, short story/manuscript, slightly knowledgeable, ignorant, short history, new memories, a bit of a smarty pants, new facts, childhood history, primary/grade school, a bit of logic, child prodigy, little education, somewhat unknown, small fact, slight history of . . .

14. Fox: avoiding studies, on-the-job training, skipping school, unknown, pretending to remember, pseudo research, secrets, pretending to know, practical lesson, suspicious story, superficial memories, untrustworthy research, pseudo expert, manipulating facts, work manual, AI (artificial intelligence), job information, clever, false facts

15. Bear: manager's handbook, powerful lesson, powerful facts, strong memory recall, more research, increasing memory, food memory, big story, more training, very knowledgeable, largely unknown, more information, recipe book, more secrets, very educated, intense studying

16. Stars: hopeful information, check online history, astrology book, online learning, digital information, scientific journal, online information, extensive history, uplifting story, scientific facts, digital history, scientific research, digitizing books, exposing secrets, science/space academy, upgrading education/training, infinite wisdom, looking forward to school, future studies/training, star student, extensive research, vast knowledge, future information, visual learner, online books, great story

17. Stork: reenrolled, pregnancy book, altered information, returning a book, evolving story, changing history, evolving research, changing story, evolving evidence, moving toward publication, long history, altered facts, birth information, transferring information, recurring memories, trending books, progressive education, repeated a class (grade)

18. Dog: smell of books, dog training, protected information, investigating evidence, supported facts, informative investigation, scent memory, self-help book, investigating facts, friendly reminder, research, reliable information, dog-eared book

19. Tower: past secret, traditional education, detention, corporate information, past stories, official secret, "top secret," ancient wisdom, government memorial, established facts, formal evidence, official information, high school, legal information, personal history, gatekeeping information, controlling the narrative

20. Garden: average intelligence, general knowledge, average education, general studies, shared memories, common fact, colleagues, average grades/student, gardening books, group classes, public school/education, shared history, popular book, general information, backstory, general research, campus

21. Mountain: hard evidence, remote training, postponing education, limited evidence, hard facts, limited history, delayed information, interrupted training, intercepted information, blocked information, limited research, challenging information

22. Paths: multiple stories, strange information, strange facts, unusual education, strangely unknown, unusual lesson, strange memories, planning educational path, undecided and therefore unknown, many memories, strange history, between classes, pros and cons of keeping a secret, unfamiliar memory, unusual story

23. Mice: unknowingly, fading memory, incognizant, uninformed, jeopardizing education, destroying history, spoiled education, corrupting historical facts, pirated book, irrational, unsubstantiated evidence, illogical, uncertain, corrupt information, damaging secrets, destroying books, dirty little secret, spreading secrets, costly lesson, corrupt research, stolen information

24. Heart: love story, romantic book, relationship journal, heartfelt memories, giving a book, relationship information, giving information to someone, relationship memories, in loving memory, giving facts

25. Ring: ongoing history, surrounded by books, the whole story, ongoing secrets, continuing studies, continued journaling, surrounded by memories, ongoing saga, surrounded by secrecy, ongoing lessons, continual research

27. Letter: data research, pages of a book, communication book/journal, written evidence, documented facts, lists of information, texting in secret, textbooks, writing an essay/assignment/thesis, journaling, writing history, communicating in secret, a page out of history, newspaper archive, recorded, text/messaging history, notebook, writing a memoir, newspaper story

28. Man: secretive man, educated man, secretive man, unknown man, intelligent man, author (male), academic (male), male student, male teacher, professor (male), logical man, smart guy, secret man, remembering a man, memorable man

29. Woman: secretive woman, educated woman, secretive lady, unknown female, intelligent woman, author (female), academic (female), female student, female teacher, professor (female), logical woman, smart lady, secret woman, remembering a woman, memorable woman

30. Lily: old memory, cold facts, mature subject, old information, discreet research, secret/secretive, private knowledge, wise, old story, discreet information, old evidence, father's/grandfather's memories, lifetime student

31. Sun: conscious memory, really smart, good history, daily journal, good education, bright student, happy memories, good information, joy journal, real evidence, good logic, optimistic information, good evidence, actual facts, truly wise, happy story, annual training

32. Moon: intuitive/psychic information, feeling smart, psychic journal, dream recall, occult knowledge, creative studies, psychic memories, reflection journal, magickal teachings, monthly training, subconscious memory, bedtime stories, mysterious, occult books, creative journaling, metaphysical book

33. Key: significant evidence, access to information, passing grade, uncovering secrets, fate unknown, privileged information, karmic wisdom, uncovering the story, key fact, important memory, definitely secret, important lesson, affluent expert, Ivy League school, it will be known, revealing facts, uncovering information, definitely a lesson, unlocking memories, award-winning book, uncovering evidence

34. Fish: expensive education, financial books, deep memories, exchanging information, business operations manual, paying for school, financial ledger, deep secret, business history, fishing book, business ledger, valuable information,

35. Anchor: holding on to a secret, same story, keeping a journal/diary, solid evidence, sound logic, lingering memory, remain logical, solid facts, same information, keeping a secret, stay informed, routine information, holding on to evidence/information, remains unknown, holding on to memories, solid education, keep studying

36. Cross: obligated secrecy, terrible education, tax information, scandalous secret, religious school, believing a story, devotional book, ghost story, shameful history, terrible information, difficult training, intolerable secrets, scandalous book, terrible secret to keep, exhausting research, terrible memory, sacred texts (books)

I love you as certain dark things
are to be loved, in secret, between
the shadow and the soul.

—Pablo Neruda

27. Letter

Missives of communication, inky scribbles left behind on a page
Writing letters on vellum paper, pages become yellowed with age
Emails sent out and airdrop files, text messages typed out by hand
Data transmits into either, not ever knowing where it may land

DESCRIPTION

A vintage Letter appears, waiting unassumingly between the blades of the emerald grass. The once-pristine vellum pages are now discolored and faded with age into a creamy hue of yellow. Wanting to take a closer look, you cautiously approach the Letter, careful not to disturb the Fae folk living in the red mushroom caps nearby. You get a glimpse of the writing and behold the most-exquisite smooth, cursive lettering gracing the page, as it peeks out the top of the envelope. This style of elegant writing is not lost on you, and you take a moment to appreciate the beauty of this long-forgotten art form. The Letter is secured with a flaming vermilion wax seal sent forth into the world in transit until reaching its final destination, all the while keeping its words safely tucked within.

The red seal, now cracked with age, tempts passersby to pause and read the written words and become transported to a bygone era.

Standing sentinel in the background, a red, metal postbox waits patiently, allowing only the intended person to retrieve this missive. Curiosity gets the best of you, and you reach out and take the thick stationery into your hand, gingerly removing the Letter within. As you slowly unfold the crisp folds of paper, an anticipation begins kindling strong emotions within you that no typed electronic message ever could.

Upon closer inspection, the familiar handwriting immediately captures your attention, bringing tears to your eyes, as a loving energy envelops you. Long gone by now, but a tangible essence remains on the pages cradled in your hands, as you gingerly crush the Letter to your chest in hopes of connecting the words to the feelings stirring in your heart. Memories come flooding back, as you appreciate the time it took to painstakingly pen this Letter, conveying the sweetest of sentiments of heartfelt emotions. The inky marks left on the pages made by a loving hand, every precious chosen word, including spelling errors that cannot be deleted with a convenient keystroke, are now encased in these pages forever. This cherished keepsake captures a moment in time, forever memorializing the ethos of the writer; even the very envelope you are holding was sealed with their essence and breath. Real and raw, the classic Letter is a form of communication that will remain immortal until destroyed; this piece of nostalgia is like holding a bit of the person in your hand, making it a treasure that can be revisited anytime. Suddenly, you come to the realization that the Letter was not "lost in the mail" or never written; the Letter was only waiting for the perfect moment of divine timing to reappear when you were ready to receive the message.

The awareness settles over you like a wave, as you recognize that you were the intended destination of the Letter sent ages ago. Smiling up at the universe, you marvel at the enchantment of the serendipitous events that unfolded for this communication to find you. The number 27 is embossed on the Letter card, denoting an aspect of travel, the Letter's fated journey traveling through time and space, delivering the message you awaited a whole lifetime to receive.

KEYWORDS

Letter, something written, emails, texts, communication, schedule, cards, mail, certificate, notes, writer, results, documents, files, papers, messages, newspaper, advertisement, poster, brochures, blog, lists, sending, a review, a post, data, missive, dispatch, memo, typed, correspondence, bills, receipts, printed materials, a page, reports, records

TIMING

The letter indicates a short time period. A good way to remember is . . . as long as it would take for a letter that is sent to arrive to its destination is the time it could take. It can also indicate the 27th day of the month.

MEANING

The Letter in a card's meaning has been updated to fit in with modern day and always refers to something written. Today, we are all about instant communication, so the Letter card has morphed into the modern-day meaning of "typed" electronic communication: emails, texts, messages, tweets, posts, blogs, and such all are part of the modern Letter. When the Letter shows up in a reading, it can indicate a small document, file, papers, certificate, card, note, or advertisement—something printed or indicative of results.

The lost art of correspondence lovingly penned by someone's hand is still the most cherished kind of letters, especially if the writer is no longer Earthside. Physical writing stirs up emotional memories more than holding a text or email printed out on paper, lacking the energetic essence of the person who wrote it. This is why people get tattoos of a person's handwritten messages to immortalize that essence on their body. You will not often see a text message tattooed on one's person, though; it does not have the same effect.

LETTER IN LOVE

A love letter, a written message, or correspondence between two lovers, a flirty text, or a card sent

LETTER IN CAREER

The Letter is indicative of a career as a writer, as a blogger, in postal services, or in marketing and advertising. In a business dealing, the Letter can depict a résumé, memos, emails, invoices, and newsletters.

LETTER IN WELLNESS

Referring to prescriptions, health charts, health cards, health documents, test results, and referrals.

LETTER IN FINANCES

This card is indicative of any financial document, such as a financial statement, a passbook, a check, or paper money.

LETTER IN MODERN DAY

The written Letter is a dying art in today's day and age, so now the Letter represents any "typed" or electronic communication sent and received: a blog, post, text, message, email, or tweet, and even extending into a vlog or a video recording—any type of virtual communication. Your news feed on social media, text message, instant message, or direct message or any app of communication can be indicated; the meaning can even extend to digital photos, especially if the Stars card is around.

AFFIRMATION

I write to expose my heart and thoughts, to bear my soul, and to quell the darkness within.

CARTOMANCY: 7 OF SPADES

Double, double, toil and trouble; Fire burn, and cauldron bubble.
—William Shakespeare's *Macbeth*.

The 7 of Spades is a card of tears and troubles, addictions, and overindulging, a warning of misfortune looming on the horizon. When the 7 of Spades appears, it usually foreshadows a change—but for the worse. When referring to the occult, it denotes potions infused with essential oils. For health questions, it's symbolic of a doctor's visit.

1. Rider: incoming data, delivering results, first draft, initial communication, delivery schedule, other man's communicating, delivering newspapers, instant messaging, race schedule, first post, incoming results, first review, delivery of mail/letter, front-page news, preliminary results, first message/text

2. Clover: lotto results, brief communication, casual texting, gambling card, temporary schedule, quick results, wild texts, funny pages, spontaneous message, casual communication, funny card, memes, comic strip, temporary results

3. Ship: travel data, leaving a goodbye note, itinerary, overseas mail, car calendar, goodbye text message, travel papers, ship's log, leaving a note, travel schedule, pen friend, long-distance communications, bus/rail schedule, "In the mail/post," travel voucher, foreign newspaper, international letters/documents

4. House: real estate papers, family schedule, family letter, property bill, home is listed, domestic newspaper, place cards, domestic letter, household bills, real estate sign, family member's handwriting, family texting "chat"

5. Tree: medical/health data, patient records/files, slow results, vital data, health card, medical journal, blood requisition, doctor's note, slow communication, medical bills, snail mail, health records, medical note, doctor's handwriting, blood results, medical papers, get-well-soon card, medical brochure, healthcare records, bio data, health document, medical bill

6. Clouds: obscured data, confusing results, lost documents, hiding texts, vague text, inconclusive results, lost mail, misplaced papers, unstable data, hidden results, lost email, misunderstood text, lost tickets, hidden post, weather report

7. Snake: complex data, problematic report, lying about results, evil post, toxic text message, tempted to message, propaganda, complicated results, fabricated messages, complex documents, problematic communication, wanting results, cheating messages, toxicology report, tight schedule, enticing messages

8. Coffin: negative results, obituary, deleting data, death note, last text message, final post, erased data, last page, autopsy report, dying communication, negative message, deleted texts, dark communication, deleted post, empty schedule, deleted documents/files, sympathy card, ending communications, banned post, funeral card, buried data, black-border letter (death notice), final schedule, empty communication, final results, death registry, erased messages, death record

9. Bouquet: surprising data, wonderful results, cursive, florist card, polite letter, sweet message, special handwritten card, presenting the results, beautiful handwriting, special report, wonderful communication, perfect schedule, beautiful card, thank-you note, wonderful writer, neat handwriting, special message

10. Scythe: collecting data, immunization records, severing communications, collection "bills," get to the point (communication), urgent email, dangerous results, irrevocable message, gathering documents, cut off from messaging, emergency communications, splitting the bills, half the results, threatening text/message

11. Whip: conflicting data, repetitive posts, questionable results, back-and-forth texting, booty text, hurtful texts/messages, sexual texts, conflicting schedules, aggressive advertising campaign, intermittent communication, fitness results, ALL-CAPS TEXT (angry text)

12. Birds: discussing results, telegram, airmail, passenger list, concert stub/ticket, phone bill, busy schedule, dictation, communications, reading out loud a text message, spoken word, vlog, anxious writer, speech, oral report, conveying results, "chatting" through text

13. Child: new results, venerable data, childcare bill, new schedule, small note, short texts, posted note, bullet point, short email, immature messages, small card, weak results, vulnerable files, little sign, short list

14. Fox: manipulating the data, suspicious results, miscommunication, calculated text message, time card, propaganda newspaper, avoiding communication, forgery, falsifying papers/documents, pseudo writer, practical notes, stealth messaging, job posting, fake documents, sneaky communication

15. Bear: powerful data, meal schedule, food stamps, powerful ad, mass email mail-out, menu, big results, intense schedule, strong advertising, assertive text/message, grocery bill, increased messaging, pushing the envelope

16. Stars: digital data, hopeful results, online schedule, digital ID (identification), great communication, clear schedule, electricity bill, e-ticket (digital ticket), internet bill, digital map, star chart, extensive notes, inspirational blog, future scheduled posts, exposed text/message/email, informatics

17. Stork: altered data, lengthy communication, returning messages/emails, evolving communication, seasonal schedule, moving checklist, transferring files, birth records, trending blog, changing reports, returned mail

18. Dog: protected data, friend's text message, dog tags, investigating documents/files, familiar schedule, therapy bill, supporting documents, protected file, friendly words, friend's post, investigating text messages, familiar handwriting, investigating reports, prove it!

19. Tower: defensive communication, government data, past communication, government-issued card, official results, legal papers, official schedule, antique papers, mandatory reporting, copyright, legal letter, formal report

20. Garden: normal results, public data, team email, group memo, general communication, popular post, general ad, average review, popular writer, census records, meeting notes, group results, group chat, regular schedule

21. Mountain: restricted data, limited results, delayed reports, blocked communication, interrupted writing, backlog, mountain of papers, intercepted text message, delayed schedule, restricted files

22. Paths: unusual results, planning a schedule, deciding to text or not, many ads, multiple texts, street signs, strange post, weird text, strange message, unusual writer, many messages, strange communication

23. Mice: stolen data, fading communication, stolen documents, messy writing, damaging post, stolen card, damaging review, ruined papers, corrupt newspaper, thinning out your papers/files, less texting, stressful schedule, corrupt results

24. Heart: romantic communication, flirty messages, dating post/ad, "I'm sorry" text message, giving a card, romantic messages, considerate message, giving results, heartfelt communication, romantic card

25. Ring: marital documents, contract, surrounded by newspapers, continue advertising, entire list, surrounded by files and papers, ongoing communication, wedding card, complete results, wedding schedule, whole text message, complete data

26. Book: studying literature, secret file, expert data, records, school/study schedule, book report, cryptography, academic paper, unknown results, historical records, cryptic text messages, research notes, informational pamphlet, informative text, secretly communicating, historical book, journaling, something written on a book page, studying marketing/advertising, secret texts/messages, manuscript

28. Man: expressive man, male blogger, writer (male), message from a man, composed man, eloquent man, communicative man, thoughtful man, sentimental man, eloquent man, man card, texting a man, something written by a man

29. Woman: expressive woman, female blogger, writer (female), message from a woman, composed lady, sentimental woman, communicative woman, thoughtful woman, sentimental woman, eloquent lady, woman card, texting a woman, something written by a woman

30. Lily: private data, conservative communication, old schedule, discreet texting/messaging, old card, discreet email, private text, old post, discreet about results, old text, old bill, peace sign, "deuces"

31. Sun: daily text, calendar, holiday postcard, sunshine list, winning results, truthful text, energy bill, annual report, truthful post, daily newspaper, good data, real results, good writer, daily schedule, happy message, daily posts

32. Moon: nightly schedule, monthly blog, creative post, monthly bill, creative writing, monthly schedule, monthly newsletter, manifesting communication, intuitive messages, monthly posts, nightly text, monthly list, magickal sigils, monthly report, psychic communication

33. Key: privileged email, keynote, important results, Yes—they wrote it, definitely communicating, open schedule, freedom of the press, uncovering text messages, revealing results, uncovering records, open email, accessing files, freelance writer, karmic sign

34. Fish: bills, banknote, credit card statement, financial papers, credit note, financial reports, water bill, credit card receipt, stock certificate, pay slip, bank card, financial data, drunk text, bank letter

35. Anchor: reserved ticket, insurance papers/documents, routine schedule, staying in touch, keeping notes, sustainability report, routine bills, unchanged results, saved cards, lingering communication, saving newspapers, keep writing, stay on schedule, holding on to text messages, still texting

36. Cross: religious card, tax bill, obligated communication, scandalous post, regret writing that, exhausting schedule, regret sending a text, terrible results, scandalous text/message, miserable email, disappointing communication

Why do I write? I write because I have to, because it is all I know, because it is my truth, because I am compelled, because I am driven to make the world acknowledge that woman like me exist, and we possess a dangerous wisdom.

—Patrick Califia

28. Man

In the time of Lenormand, the man card meant being a man.
Give pass to the ancients, a nod to honor the past gentleman
You don't have to stick with it; a man can be anything you decide.
Unlike the times of before, nowadays we have nothing left to hide.

DESCRIPTION

A confident Man with an unapologetic stare casually hides his naughty nature behind those smoldering, moss-green eyes. He is quietly challenging you, tempting you to come closer so he can pick up your scent. His strong jawline shows a streak of stubbornness, since he is used to getting his way, and he plays for keeps; you can be sure that this Man is not accustomed to losing. His high, prominent cheekbones speak of his breeding, with a glint in his eye and a perfectly manicured beard concealing the cleft in his chin hiding the devil within. Enticing you with the promise of danger and a touch of pain, he will bring you to such dizzying heights of pleasure you couldn't even fathom.

Relaxed in his stance, the Man's slender form demands respect, as he looks down his aristocratic nose. Soft, full, kissable lips slightly glisten with moisture, as he anticipates the sweet taste of your name on his lips. Impulsive and untamed, the Man stands in the frame of a door, becoming a part of the darkness; strands of his white hair transform into a silvery web of luminance from the magickal glow of the lamplight. Standing alone in the deserted alleyway, the light casts an ominous shadow around him, shrouding him in a silhouette of mystery and awakening something wild and predatory as he looks into the darkness. Fashion forward and steeped in the subculture of Victorian romanticism, the Man is immaculately dressed in a smooth, velvety-brown suede vest and a matching top hat jauntily placed upon his head. He smells expensive and knows how attractive he is; the revealing curve of his lips, not quite a smile or a sneer, tells you all you need to know.

Thriving on adrenaline and the thrill of pushing the envelope, the Man satisfies this need by living on the edge. Behind him waits his steel horse built in steampunk style, as he invites you to take his hand and go on the ride of your life. As complex and multifaceted as human beings are, there is something primal and raw when it comes to masculine energy. The Man card pulsates with the rhythm of the number 28, bearing a strong power of persuasion and a magnet for trouble. As a possessive number wanting everything for himself, the number 28 leads the way with the expectation that others will follow, captivated like the pied piper. When the number 28 is in charge, you can sit back, relax, and enjoy the ride.

KEYWORDS

The querent, a Man known to the querent, a male significant other, a man, a gentleman, a male significator, a male family member, a male, a husband, a fiancé, a partner, a boyfriend, a male friend, everyman, masculine energy, male influence, a boy.

TIMING

Can represent the 28th day of the month. Or, by using the Ace of Hearts, timing denotes the summer season.

MEANING

When the Man card steps into your life, it represents an actual person. If the Seeker is male, it represents him; if the Seeker is the opposite sex, it would represent an important male or a known Man in her life. The Man card is spoken about; therefore, it is key to look at the cards surrounding him to understand and gather more information about the Man, for he takes on the qualities of the cards next to him.

At times, the Man card can refer to typical generalized masculine qualities, such as aggression, forcefulness, or a hardness, to name a few. Keep in mind that a person does not have to be of the male gender to portray these characteristics; it is perfectly common for anyone to give off the vibration of masculine energy. For some, it is easier to view this card as masculine energy rather than a gender.

MAN IN LOVE

When the Man card appears in love, it can be in reference to your committed partner, boyfriend, or husband, or a male of interest. Take a good look around at the surrounding cards for a clue to what qualities this Man is bringing into the relationship.

MAN IN CAREER

Usually working in a male-dominant field. Also can denote a male coworker or boss. Being surrounded by a lot of masculine energy at your work. A Man who influences your work.

MAN IN WELLNESS

In order to get a clear picture of the situation, look to the cards near and surrounding the Man. This card is also representing a Man in healthcare, such as a male doctor.

MAN IN FINANCES

In order to get a clear picture of the financial situation, look to the cards near and surrounding the Man. This card also represents the finances of Man.

MAN IN MODERN DAY

This card can be viewed as masculine energy, which any gender can express at any given time.

AFFIRMATION

I accept my hard edges and angles in my life, as I embrace my divine masculinity within.

CARTOMANCY: ACE OF HEARTS

The Ace of Hearts is the family card; therefore, when combined with the Man, it translates into the quintessential meaning of the family Man. Being an Ace, it leads the way with new beginnings, especially in love. It represents the actual home and everything going on beneath its roof. Denoting an actual heart and soul, the Ace of Hearts is a very positive card that brings good luck.

LENORMAND MAN COMBINATIONS

1. Rider: flamboyant man, male visitor or caller, man arrives, the other man, news about a man, male suitor, young man, male admirer, first husband, acting manly, male guest, gay man, queer man, male suitor, attractive young man

2. Clover: the gambler, a lucky man, a risk taker, an Irish man, a casual man, a happy-go-lucky man, a lighthearted man, a funny man, an exciting man, betting man, casual boyfriend, wild man, spontaneous man

3. Ship: foreign man, male traveler, worldly man, vagabond (male), male ship's captain, male gypsy, jet-setter, male who works in travel and tourism, driver (male), man is leaving, distant man, male far from home, international male, bohemian, saying goodbye to a man

4. House: family man, man of the house, male family member, male relative, man with strong family values, lord of the manor, male homeowner, homeboy, handyman, houseboy, male homebody, domesticated man, male real estate agent

5. Tree: shaman, male system, virile man, natural man, male lineage, medicine man, male physician, male ancestor, healthy man, spiritual man, patient (male), male DNA, doctor (male), spiritual connection with a male, male/masculine body, blood ties with a male, masculine spirituality, male health

6. Clouds: confused man, man's thoughts, masculine demeanor, man full of doubt, shady man, unstable man, depressed man, troubled man, moody man, lost man, temperamental man, sad man, male attitude, hidden man, that man is trouble!

7. Snake: seductive man, dishonest man, cheating man, rogue male, male enemy, toxic man, jealous man, snake charmer, deceptive man, a mean man (mean like a snake), snake oil salesman, charlatan, envious man, rake, enticing man, evil man, tempting man, cheating husband, complicated man, problematic man, lying man, betraying a man, cheating with a man

8. Coffin: man in denial, negative man, a dead man, a silent man, deceased male, closed-off male, dying man, bad man, ill/sick man, empty man, widowed husband, grieving male, dark male, death of a man, late husband, no man, nonexistent man, deleting a man

9. Bouquet: masculine attire, polite man, poetic man, pleasant man, sweet man, grateful man, flashy man, considerate man, wonderful man, Prince Charming, delightful man, conceited man, handsome man, artistic man, male artist, male designer, surprising man, masculine features, male cologne, beautiful man, special man, charming man

10. Scythe: impulsive man, divorced man, severing ties with a man, broken man, cutting off a man, decisive man, dangerous man, ruthless man, an ex (male), wounded man, vaccinated/injected male, risky man, ex-husband, splitting up with a man, half the man, threatening man, separated man

11. Whip: aggressive man, personal trainer (male), competitive man, sexy man, active man, creature of habit, abused man, kinky man, violent man, a dominant (male), sexual man, abusive man, argumentative man, angry man, hurtful man, enraged man, feisty male, a man hurt her, fighting with a man, anarchist, hostile man

12. Birds: talkative man, nervous man, restless man, vocal man, curious male, male singer, male musician, pilot (male), talking to a guy, flight attendant (male), man's voice, gossiping man, brother(s), anxious man, two men, same-sex couple, masculine tone, discussing a man, male partner, jittery man, flaky man, brother

13. Child: young man, vulnerable man, immature man, new man, small man, innocent man, short man, naive man, man-child, playful man, inexperienced man, slight man, a boy, wee man, weak man, childish man, fragile man

14. Fox: cunning man, working man, male employee, male coworker, guilty man, shallow man, manipulative man, sneaky man, con man, red-haired man, sly man, scheming man, avoiding a man, clever man, superficial man, calculating man, practical man, suspicious man, stealthy man, careful man, cautious man, elusive man, fake man, pretending to be a man

15. Bear: powerful man, dominant man, forceful man, obese man, bearded man, boss man, overbearing man, muscular man, large man, big man, dominant (male), overweight man, hairy man, strong man, bold man, intense man, immense man, assertive man, formidable man, masculine build

16. Stars: famous man, male influencer, inspiring man, hopeful man, positive man, goal-oriented man, dreamer (male), visionary (male), optimistic man, good-natured man, man of your dreams, philosophical man, technical man, online man, blessed man, guided man, best man, great man, exposed man, future man, potential man, enlightened man, recognizable man

17. Stork: a man returns, transitioning male, evolved man, sophisticated man, monogamous man, quiet man, caring man, graceful man, progressive man, restless man, leggy man, changed man, trendy man, modified man, a man is moving, male dancer

18. Dog: faithful man, submissive man, friendly man, helpful man, loyal man, dependable man, trustworthy man, familiar man, male friend, supportive man, policeman, known male, boyfriend, stud, alpha male, protective man, territorial man, male dog, following him, male witness, male scent, stalking him, male therapist

19. Tower: ambitious man, traditional man, man from the past, egotistical man, arrogant man, lonely man, proud man, imposing man, formal man, established man, controlling man, male prisoner, city man, defensive man, single man, tall man, old man, commanding man, intimidating man, selfish man, self-absorbed man

20. Garden: player (male), popular man, playboy, cultured man, boy's club, uncommitted man, men in general, group of men, available man, men's group, male public figure, (man) online, social man, common man, gardener (male)

21. Mountain: stubborn man, hard man, distant man, indifferent man, rugged man, challenging man, mountain man, unavailable man, a hard-to-reach man, blocked man, standoffish man

22. Paths: indecisive man, separated man, unfamiliar man, multiple men, unusual man, two-timing man, uncommitted man, alternative man, man on the road, strange man, chosen man, adventurous man

23. Mice: worried male, dirty man, lesser man, damaged man, corrupt man, stressed man, opportunistic man, draining man, ruined man, obsessive man, lowly man, husbandless, messy man, worried man, manless, obsessed man, spoiled man, degraded man

24. Heart: male lover, passionate man, generous man, heart-shaped-face man, bighearted man, gentleman, considerate man, kindhearted man, tender man, compassionate man, philanthropist (male), relationship with a man, forgive a man, lovely man, giving man, man in a relationship

25. Ring: committed man, husband, married man, taken man, male partner, connected man, dedicated man, round-faced man, engaged man, surrounded by men, masculine ring/jewelry, bonded male, fiancé (male), devoted man, honorable man

26. Book: secretive man, educated man, secretive man, unknown man, intelligent man, author (male), academic (male), male student, male teacher, professor (male), logical man, smart guy, secret man, remembering a man, memorable man

27. Letter: expressive man, male blogger, writer (male), message from a man, composed man, eloquent man, communicative man, thoughtful man, sentimental man, eloquent man, man card, texting a man, something written by a man

29. Women: *See Woman card for combinations; when the Woman card shows up, it's literally a woman

30. Lily: father, father figure, grandfather, older man, experienced man, wise man, "silver fox," private man, pensioner (male), calm man, mature man, retired man, a cold man, discrete man, conservative man, reserved man, peaceful man, laid-back male, restrained man

31. Sun: masculine, successful man, warm man, energetic man, optimistic man, courageous man, good man, confident man, truthful man, male energy, boys of summer, fiery male, hot man, honest man, real man

32. Moon: creative man, emotional man, intuitive man, talented man, moon-faced man, compelling man, fantasy man, sensitive man, male witch, skillful man, talented man, man in the moon, psychic man, manifesting a man, spelling a man, magickal man, appearing male

33. Key: free man, important man, soulmate (male), significant male, open man, virtuous man, influential man, key male, honorable man, available man, sophisticated man, nobleman, dignified man, regal man, unforgettable man, prestigious man, distinguished gentleman, definitely male, affluent male, esteemed man, privileged man, king, man's reputation

34. Fish: materialistic man, business man, male entrepreneur, money man, wealthy man, financially independent man, gold digger (male), man with deep pockets, alcoholic (male), male investor, resourceful man, expensive man, salesman, luring a man, drunk guy, wishy-washy man,

35. Anchor: stable man, settled man, serious man, persistent man, safe man, secure man, grounded man, solid man, stuck man, holding on to a man, lingering man, saving a man, kept man, persistent man, mariner (male), ties to a man, dependable man, arrangement with a man

36. Cross: religious man, miserable man, tormented man, defeated man, afflicted man, needy man, pained man, obligated man, suffering man, burdensome man, remorseful man, difficult man, disappointing man, male in crisis, exhausted man, male spirit/ghost/entity, pious man, worn-out man, male victim, cursed man, intolerable man, scandalous man, disgraceful man, regretful man, terrible man, superstitious man, remorseful man, a priest

Men at any age truly never grow up. All, no matter what importance they may have attained, are still no more than little boys.

—Diane de Poitiers

29. Woman

In the time of Lenormand, the woman card meant being a woman
Give pass to the ancients, a nod to honor the past gentlewoman
You don't have to stick with it; a woman can be anything you decide.
Unlike the times of before, nowadays we have nothing left to hide.

DESCRIPTION

The moonlight filters through the diffused fog, as silvery beams of full moonlight lessen the inky darkness. A Woman appears on the terrace bathed in the soft, flickering glow of candlelight, and a gentle breeze picks up and billows around her, gently rustling her pink sari. The color pink never looked so pretty, setting off the contrast of her long, chestnut tresses cascading down her back in silky layers. Her perfectly shaped brows eloquently frame the Woman's expressive espresso eyes; alit with intelligence and passion, those endless limpid pools allow you to see all the way down into the depths of her soul. The crease of her brow is hidden by an intricate, ornate golden disk protecting her third eye; possessing women's intuition, she has the ability to peer deep within the souls of others and sees their true nature. This power she has makes her greatly feared or loved, depending on who is standing before her.

The softness of her curves is concealed beneath the flowing scarves; you will never know her mysteries or see the way her hidden shapely limbs dance to the rhythm of her soul beneath the light of the moon. Her cheeks are stained the same color as the pink flowers behind her, giving her creamy-coffee complexion a natural blush. She is spellbinding, flawless, and glowing, yet she is so unaware of her arresting exotic beauty. Tender lips like soft, powdery spring petals slowly break into a smile—she is stunning, as a wave of sweet-smelling perfume envelops you whole, feeling like an inferno blossoming within you. For a moment you are breathless, not sure if you fell under her enchantment or the scent came from the profuse brilliance of the fragrant blossoms of the pink trumpet trees swaying in the distance. Your eye catches on the dark limbs of the dead tree, seemingly so out of place among all this beauty; the barrenness is stark as it stands beside the lush brilliance of the tree full of life. A cold bead of sweat runs down the center of your back as you realize that this Woman standing before you is a goddess; she is both a vessel of life and a promise of death represented by the Ace of Spades adorning her card. On her neck sits an ornate, golden necklace befitting her station as a deity, her ears pierced with bejeweled golden chandelier earrings drawing your attention to her tender shells; she is exquisite. Age cannot affect a beauty like hers, for she radiates outward, fueled by an eternal flame that can never be extinguished.

The highly intuitive number 29 graces the Woman card, bringing creativity and sensitivity, and fostering a need for a strong sense of self-worth. Compassionate and concerned for humanity, this number vibrates with the passion to forge lasting connections and the ability to see beyond the veil into the very essence of everything. This number perfectly describes the essence of a Woman.

KEYWORDS

The querent, a woman known to the querent, a woman, a female significant other, a lady, a female significator, a female family member, a female, a fiancée, a partner, a girlfriend, a female friend, everywoman, feminine energy, female influence, a girl

TIMING

This card represents the 29th day of the month or, by using the Ace of Spades as timing—which denotes the beginning of winter—the week of December 19 to December 25.

MEANING

When the Woman card steps into your life, it represents an actual person. If the Seeker is female, it represents her; if the Seeker is the opposite sex, it would represent an important female or a known Woman in her life. The Woman card is spoken about; therefore, it is key to look at the cards surrounding her to understand and gather more information about the Woman, for she takes on the qualities of the cards next to her.

At times, the Woman card can refer to typical generalized feminine qualities such as emotional, nurturing, or a softness, to name a few. Keep in mind that a person does not have to be of the female gender to portray these characteristics; it is perfectly common for anyone to give off the vibration of feminine energy. For some, it is easier to view this card as feminine energy rather than a gender.

WOMAN IN LOVE

When the Woman card appears in love, it can be in reference to your committed partner, girlfriend, or wife, or a female love interest. Take a good look around at the surrounding cards for a clue to what qualities this Woman is bringing into the relationship.

WOMAN IN CAREER

Usually working in a female-dominant field. Also can denote a female coworker, or boss. Being surrounded by a lot of feminine energy at your work. A key Woman who influences your work.

WOMAN IN WELLNESS

In order to get a clear picture of the situation, look to the cards near and surrounding the Woman. This card also represents a Woman in healthcare, such as a female doctor.

WOMAN IN FINANCES

In order to get a clear picture of the financial situation, look to the cards near and surrounding the Woman. This card also represents the finances of a Woman.

WOMAN IN MODERN DAY

This card can be viewed as feminine energy, which any gender can express at any given time.

AFFIRMATION

I accept the soft side of my nature, as I embrace my divine femininity within.

CARTOMANCY: ACE OF SPADES

The Ace of Spades is one of the most powerful cards of the deck, fitting to adorn the Woman card.

When looking at the actual playing card, you will notice it is the only Ace with an ornate design, symbolizing there is beauty in loss, with the opportunity for a great transformation ushering in a new beginning. This is the only card that when reversed is traditionally read as death if the surrounding cards support this combination.

LENORMAND WOMAN COMBINATIONS

1. Rider: colorful lady, female visitor or caller, woman arrives, news about a lady, female admirer, female suitor, young lady, first wife, acting feminine, female guest, gay woman, attractive young lady

2. Clover: lady luck, a gambling woman, a risk taker, an Irish woman, a casual woman, a happy-go-lucky woman, a lighthearted woman, a funny lady, an exciting woman, betting woman, casual girlfriend, wild lady, spontaneous woman

3. Ship: foreign woman, female traveler, international woman, worldly woman, ship's captain, female gypsy, jet-setter, bohemian, female who works in travel and tourism, driver (female), female is leaving, distant female, female far from home, saying goodbye to a woman

4. House: nurturer, the lady of the house, female family member, housekeeper, landlady, female relative, female with strong family values, lady of the manor, female homeowner, homegirl, female homebody, domesticated woman, female real estate agent

5. Tree: healer, female system, fruitful woman, natural woman, female lineage, medicine woman, female physician, female ancestor, healthy woman, spiritual woman, patient (female), female DNA, doctor (female), spiritual connection with a female, female/feminine body, blood ties with a female, feminine spirituality, female health

6. Clouds: confused lady, woman's thoughts, feminine demeanor, woman full of doubt, shady lady, unstable woman, depressed woman, troubled lady, moody woman, sad woman, temperamental woman, female attitude, lost woman, hidden woman, that woman is trouble!

7. Snake: seductive female, dishonest woman, cheating female, rogue female, female enemy, dark-haired female, toxic woman, jealous woman, striking lady, alluring woman, deceptive woman, mean woman (mean like a snake), charlatan (female), sensual woman, the other woman, envious woman, curvy female, enticing woman, evil woman, tempting woman, cheating wife, complicated woman, problematic woman, lying woman, betraying a woman, cheating with a woman, siren

8. Coffin: woman in denial, negative woman, a dead woman, a silent woman, deceased female, closed-off female, dying woman, bad woman, ill/sick woman, empty woman, widowed wife, grieving female, dark female, death of a woman, late wife, no lady, nonexistent woman, deleting a woman

9. Bouquet: feminine attire, polite woman, girly fashion, poetic female, pleasant woman, sweet lady, grateful woman, fancy female, considerate woman, wonderful lady, delightful woman, conceited woman, gorgeous woman, artistic woman, fashionable woman, surprising woman, female artist, female designer, feminine features, female perfume, special lady, beautiful woman, charming lady

10. Scythe: impulsive lady, divorced woman, severing ties with a woman, broken woman, cutting off a woman, decisive woman, dangerous female, ruthless woman, an ex (female), wounded female, vaccinated/injected female, risky woman, ex-wife, splitting up with a woman, half the woman, threatening woman, separated woman

11. Whip: aggressive woman, personal trainer (female), competitive female, a dominatrix, sexy lady, active female, fierce woman, creature of habit (female), abused woman, kinky female, sexual female, abusive woman, argumentative lady, angry lady, hurtful woman, enraged woman, feisty female, a woman hurt him, fighting with a woman, rebellious woman, hostile woman

12. Birds: a bird, "Chatty Cathy," nervous lady, restless woman, vocal lady, curious female, female singer, female musician, pilot (female), talking to a girl, flight attendant (female), woman's voice, gossiping woman, sisters, anxious woman, two ladies, same-sex couple, feminine tone, discussing a woman, female partner, jittery female, flaky woman

13. Child: young lady, vulnerable woman, immature woman, new woman, petite lady, innocent woman, short woman, naive woman, playful woman, inexperienced female, timid woman, slight woman, a girl, wee lady, weak woman, childish woman, fragile woman

14. Fox: shrewd woman, working woman, female employee, female coworker, guilty woman, shallow woman, manipulative woman, sneaky woman, con artist (female), red-haired woman, sly lady, scheming woman, avoiding a woman, clever woman, foxy lady, superficial woman, calculating woman, practical woman, suspicious woman, stealthy woman, careful woman, cautious woman, elusive lady, fake woman, pretending to be a woman

15. Bear: mother, grandmother, mother figure, matriarch, formidable woman, dominant lady, pushy lady, curvy girl, boss lady, overbearing woman, large woman, overweight woman, strong woman, obese woman, bold woman, powerful woman, big lady, intense woman, assertive woman, feminine build, assertive female

16. Stars: famous woman, female influencer, inspiring female, hopeful woman, positive lady, goal-oriented woman, dreamer (female), visionary (female), optimistic woman, good-natured lady, dream girl, philosophical woman, technical woman, online woman, blessed woman, guided woman, best woman, great lady, exposed woman, future woman, potential woman, enlightened woman, recognizable woman

17. Stork: a woman returns, transitioning female, evolved woman, sophisticated lady, monogamous woman, quiet lady, caring woman, graceful lady, progressive woman, leggy woman, changed woman, trendy woman, modified woman, a woman is moving, female dancer

18. Dog: faithful woman, submissive female, friendly woman, helpful lady, loyal woman, dependable woman, trustworthy woman, familiar woman, female friend, supportive woman, policewoman, known female, girlfriend, bitch, alpha female, protective woman, territorial woman, female dog, following her, female witness, female scent, stalking her, female therapist

19. Tower: ambitious woman, traditional woman, woman from the past, egotistical woman, selfish woman, arrogant woman, lonely female, proud woman, imposing woman, formal woman, established woman, controlling woman, female prisoner, city woman, defensive woman, kept woman, single lady, tall woman, princess in the tower, haughty lady, intimidating woman, a self-absorbed lady

20. Garden: player (female), femme fatale, popular woman, party girl, cultured woman, socialite, woman's club, uncommitted female, women in general, group of women, available woman, woman's group, female public figure, (woman) online, social woman, common woman, gardener (female), social butterfly

21. Mountain: stubborn woman, harsh woman, distant woman, indifferent woman, rugged lady, challenging female, nonchalant female, unavailable woman, hard-to-reach woman, blocked woman, standoffish woman

22. Paths: indecisive lady, separated woman, unfamiliar lady, multiple women, unusual woman, two-timing woman, uncommitted female, alternative woman, woman on the road, strange woman, chosen woman, adventurous woman

23. Mice: worried female, dirty woman, lesser woman, damaged lady, corrupt woman, stressed woman, opportunistic woman, draining woman, ruined lady, obsessive woman, lowly woman, wifeless, messy lady, worried woman, womanless, obsessed woman, spoiled lady, degraded woman, lady is a shrew

24. Heart: female lover, passionate woman, generous woman, heart-shaped-face woman, bighearted female, gentlewoman, considerate woman, kindhearted woman, tender woman, compassionate woman, philanthropist (female), relationship with a woman, forgive a woman, lonely woman, giving woman, woman in a relationship, kind lady

25. Ring: committed woman, wife, married woman, taken woman, female partner, connected woman, dedicated lady, round-faced woman, engaged woman, surrounded by women, feminine ring/jewelry, bonded female, fiancée (female), devoted woman

26. Book: secretive woman, educated woman, secretive lady, unknown female, intelligent woman, author (female), academic (female), female student, female teacher, professor (female), logical woman, smart lady, secret woman, remembering a woman, memorable woman

27. Letter: expressive woman, female blogger, writer (female), message from a woman, composed lady, sentimental woman, communicative woman, thoughtful woman, sentimental woman, eloquent lady, woman card, texting a woman, something written by a woman

28. Man: *See Man card for combinations; when the Man card shows up, it's literally a man.

30. Lily: older lady, experienced woman, wise woman, silver-haired lady, private woman, pensioner (female), calm woman, mature woman, retired woman, cold woman, discreet lady, conservative woman, reserved lady, peaceful lady, laid-back female, restrained woman

31. Sun: successful woman, warm woman, energetic woman, optimistic lady, courageous woman, good woman, confident lady, truthful woman, female energy, girls of summer, fiery female, hot woman, honest woman, real woman

32. Moon: feminine, creative lady, emotional woman, intuitive woman, moon-faced woman, compelling woman, fantasy female, sensitive woman, female witch, skillful woman, talented woman, psychic woman, manifesting a woman, spelling a woman, magickal woman, appearing female, mystical woman, witchy woman

33. Key: free woman, important woman, soulmate (female), distinguished lady, significant female, open woman, virtuous lady, influential woman, key female, honorable woman, available woman, sophisticated woman, noblewoman, dignified lady, regal woman, unforgettable woman, prestigious woman, definitely female, affluent woman, esteemed lady, privileged woman, queen, woman's reputation, classy lady

34. Fish: material girl, businesswoman, female entrepreneur, money woman, wealthy lady, financially independent woman, a gold digger, woman with a big purse, alcoholic (female), female investor, resourceful woman, expensive woman, saleslady, luring a woman, drunk girl, wishy-washy woman, deep woman

35. Anchor: stable woman, settled female, serious woman, persistent woman, safe woman, secure lady, grounded woman, solid woman, stuck woman, holding on to a woman, lingering woman, saving a woman, kept woman, persistent woman, mariner (female), ties to a woman, dependable woman, arrangement with a woman

36. Cross: religious woman, miserable woman, tormented lady, defeated woman, afflicted woman, needy female, pained woman, obligated woman, suffering woman, burdensome woman, remorseful woman, difficult woman, disappointing woman, female in crisis, exhausted woman, female spirit/ghost/entity, pious woman, worn-out woman, female victim, cursed woman, intolerable woman, scandalous woman, disgraceful woman, regretful woman, terrible woman, superstitious woman, remorseful woman, a nun

A girl should be two things:
who and what she wants.

—Coco Chanel

30. Lily

Mature conservative Lily, discreet and private you have been
During your lifetime I imagine, all the winters you have seen
Age brings on a calmness, experience never makes you feel old.
Ability to discern what is best, always protects you from the cold

DESCRIPTION

Winter descends upon the Lily as he stands up a bit straighter, privately accepting that this is the last hurrah before the season of his life comes to a close. Digging his little feet farther into the cool, fertile earth, the Lily tilts his sweet face toward the sun, savoring the last drops of gentle light as he prepares himself to be held in winter's long embrace.

As an accomplished thief, winter slowly seeps into his lifelong essence, making him feel tired and old, but in return the cold leaves behind wisdom in exchange for beauty, for soon he will wither and fade into a frail papery version of his former glory.

Little white butterflies with gossamer, fluttering wings blow in the wind, heralding the metamorphosis that soon will take place. Even in the winter of his life, the Lily is unafraid, for age brings experience, and with that, the maturity to understand that nothing lasts forever.

The weather turns as a bitter chill fills the air, while the sun dips and sets behind the horizon plunging the earth into an ashy darkness. Nodding his sleepy head, a serene wave of peace engulfs the Lily, leaving behind an ethereal calm.

Capturing the Lily's awareness, a scent of decay permeates though the damp, rich soil as his soft, fertile bed awaits. *"To truly live, one must die,"* he whispers, as his words are sacrificed to the blustery wind. Stoic and brave, he takes a final breath and plunges into the deep, dark, dank soil, feeling a final coolness kiss his face and the warmth of darkness wrap him in a veil of dirt. With open arms the element of Earth gently receives him, cradling his frail body as it's laid tenderly against the bosom of Mother Earth. Here the Lily will retire and be nurtured until he is completely rested and restored. In the silence beneath the dirt, a welcoming sanctuary emerges, a safe haven for the Lily to rest his weary head, and just when he closes his eyes, a flash of wisdom descends upon the Lily, gathered from lifelong experiences: *"Regeneration is completely possible;*

this is not the end . . . I didn't die; I was replanted!" The time will come once again for the Lily to reemerge in all his splendor, emblazoned with a mix of vibrant pinks and scarlet hues, displaying the natural expression of a passionate soul of fire and ice.

Blooming in the height of creative expression, the number 30 is bright, optimistic, and full of inspiration. Life experiences give this number the freedom to unapologetically express itself in any way it chooses, a perfect number to grace the Lily.

KEYWORDS

Old, mature, aged, calm, wisdom, discreet, winter, restrained, father or grandfather discernment, retirement, experienced, peaceful, rest, lasting a lifetime, private, cold, patient, conservative, relaxing, old-fashioned

TIMING

When used for timing, the Lily card refers to time passing gradually. Think of it like aging, which is a lifelong process. The Lily also denotes the season of winter.

MEANING

Old and frail in the winter of his life, the Lily is a card of age and experience accumulated over a lifetime. With maturity comes the gift of decrement; knowing when to keep something private is the restraint of the Lily's charm.

Slowing down with age as thoughts turn toward retirement gives the Lily a chance to relax and get away from the coldness that winter brings. In reference to a person, the Lily represents a father, a grandfather, or a father figure.

LILY IN LOVE

A mature, old-fashioned love that has developed and shared over a lifetime. If you're single, the Lily could indicate finding love much later in life. When it comes to describing a love interest, this card is indicative of a person of age, possibly with gray hair or a mature lover.

LILY IN CAREER

The Lily brings extensive experience to any vocation, whether it be academic or life experience. It represents being established, so relaxed at your job, and staying until retirement. If you're looking for a job, areas of working with the elderly or a work environment that is calm are indicated.

LILY IN WELLNESS

Being a card of age, the Lily bring with it all the aches and pains and inconveniences that come with age; it can also denote geriatric-related ailments. This is the natural process of aging gracefully, which is just a mindset away.

Life savings, retirement fund, pension, a nest egg

LILY IN MODERN DAY
Snowbirds, an older, retired couple who get away from the cold by going someplace warm and staying the entire winter season

AFFIRMATION
I achieve inner peace by having the mindset of whatever happens happens, because life experience has shown me . . . it is what it is.

CARTOMANCY: KING OF SPADES
Traditionally viewed as an old man of dark coloring who may be divorced or widowed.

The King of Spades is the highest-ranking court card and is proclaimed as the King of Kings. Protective and powerful, this King needs to be in charge at all times and sees the world from a mature perspective due to his vast life experience. He has mastered the fine art of discernment, which makes him a very dangerous King. The King of Spades is looked upon as a father or a father figure.

LENORMAND LILY COMBINATIONS
1. Rider: going peacefully, announcing it in private, this coming winter, suitor of advanced age, young father, acting mature, visit in the winter, other man is discreet, "young" senior

2. Clover: temporary private, brief rest, lucky throughout life, easygoing father, gaming/ gambling experience, chance in the winter, opportunity of a lifetime, wild experience, temporary peace, funny father/grandfather, "green" winter

3. Ship: travel experience, navigating old age, goodbye in private, traveling in retirement, departing in winter, leaving discreetly, distant father/grandfather, distant and cold, boating experience

4. House: family patriarch, family member retires, real estate discernment, place is private, comfortable in old age, family privacy, sanctuary, home is peaceful, comfortable retirement, home for seniors/retirees, inner peace, real estate restraint

5. Tree: medical experience, living in peace, growing restraint, spiritual discernment, growing cold, naturally calm, a lifetime, body matures, system is retired, medical discretion, extended lifetime

6. Clouds: disturbing the peace, sad dad, behaving restrained, depressed senior, thinking about retirement, bad winter weather, addiction lasts a lifetime, misunderstanding with a father figure, unstable father/grandfather, confused senior

7. Snake: gnarled with age, toxic father/grandfather, desiring someone older, other woman's discreet, wanting peace, cheating father, betraying an elder, complicated retirement, cheating throughout a lifetime, needing rest, lying father/grandfather, unethical

8. Coffin: dark winter, loss of a father/grandfather, denied privacy, grieving a grandfather, no peace, sick father/grandfather, closed off, no patience, death handled discreetly, mourning a father, deathly cold, dying in peace

9. Bouquet: wonderful retirement, special age, nice winter, polite elder, wonderful experience, special father/grandfather, modest, sweet senior, pleasant rest, inviting a father/grandfather, appreciating old age

10. Scythe: vaccinated/injected senior, breaking a truce, sudden cold, dangerous ice, obliterating peace, decimating privacy, urgent retirement, cutting off a father/grandfather, detached, separated/divorced father/grandfather, semiretired

11. Whip: hurtful father/grandfather, assaulting a senior, punishing cold, intermittent peace, sexual privacy, aggressive father, sexually reserved, abusive grandfather, sexual experience, abused senior, cold snap, sexually restrained

12. Birds: restlessness, talking to dad, conversation runs cold, chatty senior, nervous, stressing over age, gossiping discreetly, musically adept, two fathers/grandfathers, couple is discreet, vocal senior, negotiating retirement, calling your grandparents

13. Child: newly retired, frail father/grandfather, new dad, a bit cold, bashful, frail old person, demure, kid gloves, age appropriate, meek, slightly older, immature father, short retirement, a little bit old, little privacy, playing in the snow, little rest

14. Fox: scheming father/grandfather, avoiding retirement, practical experience, suspicious elder, careful restraint, job experience, pretending to be older, feigning discretion, cautious, pretending to be mature, sneaky, practical lifetime, avoiding dad, hiring freeze

15. Bear: hibernation, huge restraint, intense father, forced retirement, immense experience, very reserved, thick skinned, bull in a china shop, maternal father/grandfather, increased privacy, very cold, increasingly calm, very mature

16. Stars: digital age, improving with age, lasting a lifetime, seeing beyond age, looking forward to future retirement, future father-in-law, inspirational father/grandfather, vast cold, great wisdom, wishing for peace, extensive experience, great-grandfather, infinite lifetimes, viewer discretion, highly experienced, famous dad

17. Stork: long winter, birth father, quiet senior, gentle, moving in the winter, long retirement, figure skating, gentle, progress made through a lifetime, relocating an old person, quiet retirement, nurturing an old person, spring's coming, baby crone

18. Dog: smell of winter, protective father/grandfather, helping an old person, searching for your father/grandfather, looking for peace, searching in the snow, searching in the snow, observant, supportive father, helping grandpa, protecting the elderly, looking for privacy, befriending someone older

19. Tower: ultraconservative, solitary, defending a senior, self-control, reserved, diplomatic, self-regulated, judicious, defending your privacy, tall father/grandfather, old man, defensive father/grandfather, reclusive, antique, aloof

20. Garden: average lifetime, garden lily, regular winter, average age, social media discretion, socializing seniors, social network for seniors, socially appropriate, public father, public discretion

21. Mountain: limited experience, postponed retirement, interrupted peace, finding it hard to relax, obstacle to retirement, distant, challenging age, limited patience, stubborn father/grandfather, challenges throughout a lifetime

22. Paths: possible retirement, multiple lifetimes, strange chill, choosing peace, eccentric father/grandfather, pros and cons of retirement, eccentric old person, unusual winter, adventurous senior, separated father, plans for the winter

23. Mice: less restraint, frail, indiscreet, stressed old person, damage lasts a lifetime, spreading cold, less privacy, crumbling peace, deteriorating, less experienced, losing patience, damaging ice, impatience, jeopardizing retirement, lacking discernment, frayed, imprudence

24. Heart: doting grandfather, relationship privacy, forgiving grandpa, kind, give peace, romantic discretion, forgive an older man, kind dad, compassion for seniors, considerate father/grandfather, in love with someone older

25. Ring: whole lifetime, completely private, continued discretion, surrounded by seniors, enveloped by cold, encircled by lilies, continued peace, married for life, continued privacy, contract freeze

26. Book: logical father/grandfather, intelligent, secret about dad/granddad, memories lasting a lifetime, wisdom, secretive older man, secrecy, unknown age, secret, educated father/grandfather, educational expert

27. Letter: scheduled retirement, card sent by father/grandfather, writing experience, card written by a father/grandfather, texting dad, writing of a father/grandfather, something written lasts a lifetime

28. Man: father, father figure, grandfather, older man, experienced man, wise man, "silver fox," private man, pensioner (male), calm man, mature man, retired man, a cold man, discrete man, conservative man, reserved man, peaceful man, laid-back male, restrained man

29. Woman: older lady, experienced woman, wise woman, silver-haired lady, private woman, pensioner (female), calm woman, mature woman, retired woman, cold woman, discreet lady, conservative woman, reserved lady, peaceful lady, laid-back female, restrained woman

31. Sun: holiday somewhere cold, fire and ice, vacation relaxation, real experience, truly at peace, warm, truthful father, mild winter, mild winter, successful father/grandfather, melting ice, truly lasts a lifetime

32. Moon: creative father/grandfather, magickal lifetime, psychic discernment, magickal wisdom, emotionally cold, magickal experience, feeling peaceful, psychic wisdom, feeling rested, emotional experience, emotionally calm, feeling cold

33. Key: definitely old, karmic lifetime, definitely calmer, open to retirement, definitely experienced, karmic wisdom, "Freedom 55," respecting elders, access, privy (to something that was private before), loosen up a bit!

34. Fish: expensive retirement, deeply private, resourceful grandfather, water lilies, deep cold, financial discernment, deep relaxation, businesslike, money wise, business experience, wealthy father/grandfather, financial prudence

35. Anchor: lingering cold/winter, rescuing a senior, keeping the peace, lasting a lifetime, stay mature, lasting privacy, grounded father/grandfather, remain calm, staying discreet, stay in check, saving a father/grandfather, keeping private

36. Cross: testing patience, miserable retirement, disappointing father figure, insufferable cold, cursed father, miserable old person, difficult winter, regretful father/grandfather, scandalous elder, terrible father, obligated retirement, insufferable age, difficult lifetime, intolerable father, miserable winter, religious older man, terrible experience

Grow old along with me! The best is yet to be,
the last of life, for which the first was made.

—Robert Browning

31. Sun

Success is part confidence, being positively optimistic that you will achieve.
Just add a joyful drop of golden happiness, having the consciousness to believe.
Your light is illuminating, bringing an energetic radiance to all that you do.
Living your truth is a victory, by having the daily courage to see it through.

DESCRIPTION

The days are getting longer as the sky bursts into a blaze of golden pinpoints of light, igniting a fire so hot that it melts away the last patches of snow left on the face of the cool, fertile ground. The Sun sends down his vibrant golden shafts of light connecting with Mother Earth, giving her a long-awaited kiss, rousing her from a long, dreamless slumber. He pauses to savor the exquisite beauty, as he watches the last remnants of the season past walk steadily into summer's warm embrace. Slowly stirring the world with a brilliant radiance, the Sun continues to extend his golden rays in every direction, unifying all of humanity. This magick is something we can all experience, as the light of day kisses the morning and everyone begins to awaken.

The Sun is full of confidence and not concerned with letting his sister, the Moon, shine for a time, as he reenergizes, filling up with light once again. For centuries, ancient civilizations worshiped the glorious Sun god, for he was the bringer of life, and where there is light there is life; everyone wins and everything thrives. The Sun is not concerned with the past, like his sister, the Moon, for HE is just as vital as SHE. It is his turn to shine now as the Sun once again rises over the horizon, pulsating with an energetic virility, painting a warm glow on his canvas and promising illumination to everything he touches with his gentle brush. The Sun's color brings forth a burst of fiery oranges in a sensation of happiness, exploding in hues of shimmering gold that slowly wash over the edge of your realization, spreading a smile onto your face. The Sun paints a final crimson swath, feeding optimism into your heart and warming your soul.

Being present in the moment while absorbing sunshine into your being makes you come alive with radiant energy, and a sensation of joy washes over you, sending you into a state of blissful elevated consciousness—knowing that, even on a cloudy day, the Sun is always shining just above the mantle of clouds, leaving droplets of delight that remind you he is everywhere. The number 31 burns into your consciousness, bringing with it a flair of creativity and vibrant colors. This number helps you clearly recognize all of your heart's desires, illuminating a path for you to follow in order to achieve your goals. The number 31 harbors a great need for security, and once you allow the Sun to wrap you up in its loving rays, you will begin feel a deep sense of confidence by facilitating great enlightenment and allowing the truth to shine through.

KEYWORDS

Energy, truth/true, vital, success, renewal, achievement, positive outcome, warm, happiness, confidence, optimism, summer, light, victory, joy, day, win, thrive, consciousness, golden, south, hot, courage, illumination, radiance, holiday/vacation, good, annual, real/tangible, fire, annual

TIMING

The Sun represents the time frame of a day, anytime between the rising and setting sun. It can also denote a daily occurrence and the season of summer. When the Mountain is around, it represents one year, the exact time for the earth to make a full revolution around the Sun, as he continues to move through each of the zodiac signs. As a day of the week, the Sun represents Sunday. The Sun is symbolic of the crafts a year and a day, when the Moon is near.

MEANING

The brilliant Sun will always enhance the positive cards and diminish the effect of negative ones surrounding it. Although it will not magickally remove any challenges, by illuminating the truth and allowing you to see the situation for what it truly is, you can be assured that end results will be positive. With the Sun around, you can count on a win because it is a card of abundance and good tidings, bringing you all the elements needed to truly thrive. Fun in the sun, a holiday somewhere warm, is just what the Sun does, as it leaves little drops of golden sunshine on whatever it touches. The Sun shines outward, bringing daily renewal and optimism while smiling down on you as you awaken, whispering, "Shine, shine, shine."

SUN IN LOVE

The Sun warms every heart, bringing blissful rays of love to any romantic encounter. This is a very good card to see when asking any love question or relationship queries. It shines into your love life with positive outcomes and wins. Remember, when the Sun shines down on love, it turns up the heat! If you're looking for love, this card brings good prospects your way by allowing you to see others in a more romantic light.

SUN IN CAREER

The Sun sends rays of illumination and facilitates the achievement of career goals set by the Stars. The Sun card is symbolic of having a good job, a golden parachute, or a shining employee—a very optimistic sign for job advancement or promotions. If you are looking for employment, the Sun card brings optimism to your job search.

SUN IN WELLNESS

The Sun supports recovery, vitality, and healthful vigor as it renews the life force within. The Sun is life, for without the Sun nothing survives, making it a very optimistic card to see when inquiring about health.

SUN IN FINANCE

When the warmth of the Sun shines on your finances, it shows up in ways of abundance—always a good thing . . . Winning!

SUN IN MODERN DAY

The Sun card represents your astrological sun sign, specifically Leo, its ruling planet the Sun. The Sun represents energy. Children commonly draw the Sun with a smiley face, so in today's day and age, the Sun is akin to the smiley-face emoji :), showing happiness, and all is well.

AFFIRMATION

I consciously fill myself with sunshine and face the day with joy, as I shine my light onto the world.

CARTOMANCY: ACE OF DIAMONDS

The Ace of Diamonds directly represents the Sun and brings illumination to any situation, that energetic spark that stokes the fires of your soul. Traditionally representing a letter or a ring, the Ace of Diamonds brings new beginnings, consciousness, renewal, energy, electricity, vitality, optimism, fire, and rewards—exactly what the Sun card denotes. As an item in the home, the Ace of Diamonds represents a fireplace, heating system, or stove—anything that is associated with fire. In occult practices, the Ace of Diamonds denotes the presence of a spirit.

LENORMAND SUN COMBINATIONS

1. Rider: going well, first day, fast-moving energy, quick success, small opportunity looms on the horizon, first holiday/vacation, this coming summer, acting confident, first win, visit in the summer

2. Clover: game day, fun day, wild energy, happy, easy success, carefree and confident, chance at happiness, win, small opportunity brings success, flash of the truth shines through, spontaneous holiday/vacation, last-minute travel

3. Ship: traveling on holiday, moving energy, gone away on vacation, travel day, going on a cruise, leaving for the summer, going south, departing with confidence, overseas vacation, leaving an opportunity behind

4. House: familiar energy, house fire, family holiday, home's heating source, real estate market is hot, place's energy, indoor lights, home for the summer, brand success, family member tells the truth

5. Tree: slowly winning, deeply rooted energy, slowly warming up, spiritedness, vitality, spiritual connection shines brightly, grounded energy, healthy, growing confidence, living well, log on the fire (bonfire), body confidence, thriving, medical truths, spiritual vibes

6. Clouds: depressing energy, storm in the summer, discouraged, lost consciousness, clouded outcome, demoralized, doubtful victory, overcast, troubling truths, gloomy energy, sad holiday, dimmed light

7. Snake: evil energy, complicated day, twisted outcome, snake/toxic energy, complicated truth, wanting success, needing to hear the truth, lying, problematic year, the ugly truth, envious of someone's happiness/success, dishonest

8. Coffin: bad year, extinguishing fires, void of light, final days, dark energy, bad outcome, meh, bad holiday, denied the truth, no victory, final holiday, no good, coma (loss of consciousness), denied happiness, yesterday (last day), dead energy, untrue, unconscious, end of days

9. Bouquet: wonderful holiday, special day, perfect vacation, pleasant day, wonderful year, nice energy, celebrating a win, beautiful summer's day, special holiday, wonderful outcome, beautiful radiance, good

10. Scythe: crack of dawn, cutting energetic cords, reaping rewards, autumn's day, sudden spark, unexpected fire, broken confidence, obliterating happiness, separating the truth from the lies, divided outcome, splitting the win (tie), risk vs. reward, splitting vacation time, obliterating the good

11. Whip: sex positive, aggressive heat, disrupting happiness, sexual energy, intermittent truths, Tuesday, sexually satisfied, sexual truths, intermittent happiness, active day, sexually confident, abuse illuminated

12. Birds: flying south, two suns, a couple of days, whistleblower, anxious energy, say it like it is, discussions about holiday/vacation, negotiations are successful, rumors/gossip illuminated, anxious about the outcome

13. Child: New Year's Day, vulnerable to sunburn, weak energy, lacking confidence, bit of success, vulnerable to energy, a bit of truth, small achievement, somewhat happy, a little bit optimistic, leap year (short year), a bit courageous, new day

14. Fox: suspicious of the "truth," cautiously optimistic, pretending to be truthful, be careful today, be vigilant on holiday/vacation, time-share scam, unreal, fake suntan, coworker energy, feigning confidence, pseudo victory, pretended to be happy, false/fake

15. Bear: very good, unbearable heat, brave, big truth, Thursday, big energy, very optimistic, immense happiness, great joy, mother/grandmother energy, huge victory, big day, huge success, intense energy, asserting the truth

16. Star: etheric energy, Northern Lights, aura, universal truth, blessed day, illumination, the sun, victory, future success, looking forward to the holidays, great win, looking good, extensive achievements, alleviating heat, highly optimistic, seeing beyond reality, seeing the truth, in future years, fantastic year, shine your light!

17. Stork: shifting energy, long summer, shifting reality, changing outcome, long vacation/ holiday, spring's day, baby energy, alternate reality, long day, modifying the truth, renewal, recurring wins

18. Dog: smell of summer, follow the energy, watching the sun, "friends" holiday, follow your conscious, searching for the truth, follow your bliss, friend energy, searching for happiness, follow the light, investigating an opportunity

19. Tower: defensive energy, city lights, self-confidence, court win, past summer, defending the truth, past success, legal victory, established energy, formal victory, past vacation/holiday, official holiday, egotistical

20. Garden: average summer, group energy, generally true, common outcome, average success, for the common good of all, social media opportunity, generally successful, average day, mutually beneficial, outdoor lights

21. Mountain: hard year, impeding the truth from coming out, rough day, interrupted holiday/ vacation, harsh summer, stagnant energy, obstacles to success, blocking the sun, boundaries are good, blocked opportunity

22. Paths: strange energy, unusual summer, choosing joy, separate vacations/holidays, many truths, path to the truth, multiple vacations/holidays, path to success, road to recovery, unusually good, deciding/choosing the winner, strange day, unusual light

23. Mice: cost of success, unsure, unconvincing, losing confidence, depleted, stealing joy, fading light, losing consciousness, losing sunlight/heat, unhappy, spoiled holiday, ruined summer, losing steam, scattered energy, unrealistic, discontent, low vibration, damaging truth, jeopardizing success, damaging heat, listless, crumbling opportunity

24. Heart: relationship truths, lover is happy, romance is thriving, passionate heat, relationship success, loving the sun, romantic vibes, giving it a year, relationship bliss, Friday, heartburn, forgiven for real, giving energy, romantic holiday

25. Ring: orbiting the sun, the whole truth, entire summer, wedding anniversary, the whole day, entire year, surrounded by energy, continued happiness, ongoing success, Saturday, circle of light, ongoing illumination, continuous renewal

26. Book: school year, historical day, Memorial Day, Remembrance Day, happy memories, summer training, knowing the truth, stories of success, secretly optimistic, unknown memory, academic success

27. Letter: scheduled holiday/vacation, writing with confidence, text/message is true, posting the truth, writing achievement, newspaper delivered daily, results are positive, review is positive

28. Man: masculine, successful man, warm man, energetic man, optimistic man, courageous man, good man, confident man, truthful man, male energy, boys of summer, fiery male, hot man, honest man, real man

29. Woman: successful woman, warm woman, energetic woman, optimistic lady, courageous woman, good woman, confident lady, truthful woman, female energy, girls of summer, fiery female, hot woman, honest woman, real woman

30. Lily: restrained happiness, grandfather energy, personal success, winter's day, laid-back energy, peaceful day, retirement success, discerning the truth, relaxing vacation/holiday, experience brings confidence, personal truth

32. Moon: nightly, psychic energy, feeling good, feeling renewed, feeling positive, creative energy, feeling hot, divining the truth, feeling happy, monthly achievement, feeling energetic, manifesting a win

33. Key: privileges, important achievement, key victory, revealing the truth, VIP holiday/vacation, defiantly good, free will, significant year, uncovering the truth, karmic year, accessing the truth, karmic energy

34. Fish: expensive holiday, the Deep South, wealth, financial truth, business renewed, financially confident, abundance, investment success, prosperity, deep dive into consciousness, flowing joy, financial reward, bank holiday

35. Anchor: keeping it real, still good, remain optimistic, lingering summer, keep shining, stay gold, stay positive, holding on to the truth, keeper of the flame, remain truthful, heavy vibe, residual/lingering energy, due south

36. Cross: painful truth, disappointing vacation, terrible day, difficult year, terrible summer, difficult win, insufferable heat, intolerable energy, shameful truth, holy days, terrible holiday, entity/ghost, horrible energy, religious vibe

Keep your face always towards the sunshine,
and the shadows will fall behind you.

—Walt Whitman

32. Moon

A silvery Moon goddess appearing, manifesting her phases in the night
Magickally influencing your subconscious, with a mystical second sight
A skilled weaver of the imagination, creatively casting her monthly spell
Bestowing psychic reflections of the occult nightly, intuitive dreams foretell

DESCRIPTION

Encroaching on the velvety darkness, the Moon crests over shimmering sapphire waters, full and heavily dripping her milky-white light as she nourishes the world. The Moon's silvery waves of rippling moonlight defuse over the reflective waters, inspiring lovers, writers, poets, musicians, and all creative endeavors as the nine muses look on and pirouette in joy. A soft bluish hue of light cascades onto the sacred pillars of the Moon temple, framing her beautiful round silhouette against the deep-indigo sky as she breathes wisps of intuition into your subconscious. Crowning the temple is an opaque symbol of the Triple Goddess, representing her three aspects: the Maiden, the Mother, and the Crone, symbolizing the phases of the waxing crescent, the full Moon, and the waning crescent. The Moons teaches you to use her waxing phase to attract what you want to grow in your life, a great time to focus on manifestation. At the height of her power on the full Moon, which is a good time to charge magickal tools, perform rituals, or make some full Moon water, the full Moon will add intensity to any basic spell. Finally moving into her waning phase, where she diminishes and gets darker, this is a great time to cut cords or perform banishing spells; this phase enables you to rid things from your life that no longer serve your highest good. These gifts of enchantment are bestowed onto the worthy; if you can unravel the mystery and know how to harness the power of each Moon phase, you will be able to use your innate skills and garner more power for manifesting your spells.

The Moon causes ripples in the oceans, stirring feelings within you and matching the rhythmic rise and fall of crashing waves. She was born from the skies and controls all tides, roaring like the churning sea with the ebb and flow of her undercurrents as her effects are felt throughout the world. When the emotional full Moon enters your life, she brings creativity, intuition, and mysticism that influence all phases of your life.

Queen of the skies and sister to the Sun, night is her time to shine, and she moves effortlessly through her phases, shining her gentle light upon all her children and watching them dream and sleep. Since her watery depths represent the realm of imagination linked to the subconscious mind, you navigate through your story of life, oscillating between the tide's ebb and flow.

The number 32 glows into your life, bringing a creativity that encourages you to dream the biggest dreams and have the courage to see them through by giving them a breath of life. Like the Moon, round and sensual, the curvy 32 is witty with a wild abandonment and adventurous by nature. The number 32 is not afraid of trying new things and feeling emotions to the fullest; just as there is a dark side to the Moon, so it is with the number 32, where its influence can facilitate an inward retrospection that encourages self-realization.

KEYWORDS

Night, manifestation, emotions, creativity, intuition, reflection, feelings, imagination, subconscious, magick, appearance, influence, phases, occult, awareness, talent, divination, fantasy, skill, psychic, spells, mystical, dreams (while sleeping), monthly, lunacy

TIMING

It takes 28 days for the Moon to complete her phases; this denotes, when using this card for timing, it will happen within a month's time. As a day of the week, Moon Day is Monday.

MEANING

When the Moon card manifests into your reading, she will affect all the surrounding cards with her gentle glow. Highlighting all magickal things, intuition, and the mysteries of the occult, she will influence your emotions as she ebbs and flows into your life. The Moon communicates through your dreams, using your subconscious and creative imagination to bring awareness into all phases of life through personal reflection.

MOON IN LOVE

The Moon in love brings a sweetness, inspiring long moonlit heart-to-hearts, as she speaks to a deep, emotional, magickal connection. She stirs up subconscious feelings of romance, making you feel a psychic connection while filling your soul with love. If looking for love, consider doing a love spell or sending your intentions of finding love to the full Moon, since she just might reveal a lover in a dream.

MOON IN CAREER

Any career dealing with the emotional well-being of an individual or group. The Moon card is indicative of a career in the occult, or a job that lets your creative juices flow. This card can also be read literally as moonlighting.

MOON IN WELLNESS

The Moon manifests itself in the aspect of emotional well-being, and all the disorders that contribute to unbalanced emotions are covered under this card. Focus on the female reproductive system is associated with the Moon, since she controls the female monthly cycle.

MOON IN FINANCES

The Moon is really not a money card but can denote the monthly phases your finances go through, such as the natural ebb and flow of money. You could use the moon to manifest abundance into your life.

MOON IN MODERN DAY

Moon Magick can be employed by observing and using the phases of the moon for opportune timing of spells. Representing all things occult, psychic, intuition, metaphysics, and divination, the Moon card is filled with magick!

AFFIRMATION

I trust my intuition as I continue developing the skills to stir the magick within me.

CARTOMANCY: 8 OF HEARTS

The emotionally balanced 8 of Hearts wraps its loving arms around the Moon, whispering that everything will turn out all right. A positive card, shaped as the infinity sign, it highlights romantic connections through creative endeavors that bring fulfillment. In the occult, the 8 of Hearts indicates a spirit guide, a celestial being guiding you, or an ancestor watching over you.

LENORMAND MOON COMBINATIONS

1. Rider: first quarter (moon phase), quick to manifest, acting emotional, January (first month), fast spell, visitation in your dreams while sleeping, other man acting crazy, suitor makes an appearance, first night

2. Clover: green magick, brief appearance, lucky month, wild fantasy, temporary phase, luck manifests, game night, lucky moon phase, wild night, quick spell, wild imagination, temporary madness, gaming skills, lucky charm, Clubs (cartomancy)

3. Ship: distant feelings, journey/journeying into the occult, driving at night, exploring magick, goodbye spell, car charm, trip manifests, journey into the subconscious, international talent

4. House: family spell, real estate spell, family night, place of magick, family influence, brand creativity, domestic talent, family member appears, familiar feeling, house spell, familiar phase, house of magick

5. Tree: slow night, deep-rooted emotions, medical intuitive, deeply rooted feelings, spiritual phase, growing intuition, slow phase, deeply rooted fantasy, spirituality, slow to manifest, spiritual, elemental spell, slow month, natural skills, slow spell (timing)

6. Clouds: misplaced feelings, fly-by-night, hiding intuition, unstable emotions, temperamental spell, hidden talent, chaos magick, hidden emotions, weather spell, chaotic month, unstable spell, madness, hidden creativity

7. Snake: evil spell, complex emotions, complicated phase, snake magick, needing sleep, tempting fantasy, toxic influence, complex spell, complicated night, needy, wanting to feel something, cheating emotionally, other woman is psychic, enticed by the occult

8. Coffin: bad dream, bad influence, no skills, dark fantasy, bad night, buried feelings, unimaginable, dark spell, final phase, death spell, dark magick, dreadful feeling, not manifesting, closed off emotionally, November (month of the dead), death dream, final night, dark side of the occult

9. Bouquet: artistic, special night, flower/plant magick, pleasant dreams, creative, special spell, color magick, wonderful skills, beautiful fantasy, wonderful influence, pleasant feeling, beauty phase, showing feelings, special magickal talent, beautiful night, wonderful month, gifted psychic, surprising manifestation, rhyming spell

10. Scythe: breaking a spell, unexpected feelings, dangerous magick, cutting off influence, half the month, dangerous night, autumn months, cutoff feelings, separation/divorce spell, cutting cords spell, half moon, Spades (cartomancy)

11. Whip: sexual dreams, aggressive spell, angry emotions, sexually talented, repeated monthly, sexual feelings, repeating a spell, aggressive feelings, sexy appearance, hurtful spell, sexually influenced

12. Birds: two months, couple of nights, call-me spell, two moons, discussing feelings, wordsmith, vocal skills, flying spell, negotiating skills, talking about feelings, reciting a spell, discussing the occult, musical talent, twice a month

13. Child: initiation, starting a new phase, beginner spell, slightly influenced, beginning to manifest, childlike appearance, vulnerable to the occult/magick, slightly aware, little imagination, short spell (duration), beginning phase, weak spell, new month, slightly intuitive, new spell, innate talent, simple spell

14. Fox: practical magick, useful skills, tricky phase, suspicious appearance, working at night, suspicious of the occult, the craft, working phase, pseudo psychic, avoiding feelings, fantasy, beware of appearances, magic spell (fake), under the cover of night, fake feelings, suspicious feeling, working a spell

15. Bear: powerful imagination, maternal feelings, mighty skills, intense emotion, big night, strong feelings, maternal feelings, great skills, powerful manifestation, huge influence, big moon, intense emotions, big month, hibernation, increased awareness, overemotional, strong intuition

16. Stars: highly intuitive, vivid dreams, vivid imagination, influencer, goals manifest, enhanced intuition, fantastic night, horoscope, the moon, high emotions, astronomy, positive spell, expansive awareness, starry, starry night, future influences, extensive fantasy, see beyond appearances, Diamonds (cartomancy), to the moon!

17. Stork: long night, evolving feelings, longest night (December 21), changing appearance, spring months, evolving spell, long month, quiet evening, moving month, long spell (duration), relocation spell, returning spell

18. Dog: howling at the moon, watching you sleep, scouting out talent, searching at night, follower, searching your subconscious, follow the moon, friendly feelings, trust your gut feeling (intuition), friendship spell, trust your emotions, a fetch

19. Tower: defensive magick, past phase, traditional magick, defensive spell, ancient spell, established feelings, defensive, ambitious spell, judging by appearance, indifferent, past spell, ancient magick

20. Garden: average talent, common skills, average intuition, common appearance, common fantasy, popular spell, common/mundane magick, popular phase, public appearance, online psychic, social media influence, rendezvous under the cover of night

21. Mountain: rough night, hard month, blocked feelings, interrupted spell, boundaries/wards (magickal), delayed spell (timing), remote viewing, challenging phase, limited magick, delayed manifestation

22. Paths: strange night, unusual psychic ability, strange feeling, outlandish fantasy, strange dreams, between planes, planning a spell, many months, separation spell, strange appearance, on the road at night

23. Mice: fading feelings, rotten evening, ruined spell, fading dream (when you awake), losing awareness, deteriorating monthly, unpredictable, dissipating influence, sleepless nights, dirty appearance, fading spell, crumbling fantasy, lessening intuition, damaging (emotionally)

24. Heart: heartfelt, relationship spell, lovestruck, forgiveness, compassion, sympathetic magick, date night, give it a month, philanthropic, love, romantic feelings, intimate emotions, cherished, accepted, lover's influence, considerate, planchette (Ouija board), Hearts (cartomancy)

25. Ring: orb, entire night, whole month, surrounded by moonlight, ongoing influence, continual manifestation, ongoing fantasy, completely aware, continual spell, circle (magickal), engagement spell, surrounded by magick

26. Book: secret talent, unknown feelings, historical month, secret fantasy, memorizing a spell, unknown origins of a spell, remembering a dream, historical spells, book of spells, recording dreams

27. Letter: communication spell, message appears, texting at night, sending messages at night, text/message-me spell, writing talent, journaling, messages appear, documenting psychic/magickal experiences, text appears

28. Man: creative man, mystical man, emotional man, intuitive man, talented man, moon-faced man, compelling man, fantasy man, sensitive man, male witch, skillful man, talented man, man in the moon, psychic man, manifesting a man, spelling a man, magickal man, appearing male

29. Woman: feminine, mystical woman, creative lady, emotional woman, intuitive woman, moon-faced woman, compelling woman, fantasy female, sensitive woman, female witch, skillful woman, talented woman, psychic woman, manifesting a woman, spelling a woman, magickal woman, mystical woman, appearing female, witchy woman

30. Lily: restrained emotions, private feelings, old magick, winter months, frigid (emotionally cold), unemotional, serene, impassive, peaceful month, personal appearance, paternal feelings, private reflection

31. Sun: good intuition, true feelings, abundance manifestation, true reflection, real magick, true appearance, successful manifestation, good skills, fire witch, summer months, happy emotions, optimistic phase, real emotions, positive influence, the sun and the moon, good psychic, Sunday night, good sleep, solar magick, good month, chakras

33. Key: karmic reflection, key skills, answers spell, revealing a fantasy, key to magick, important month, open spell, precognitive dreams, uncovering the night, open to the occult, revealing feelings, significant dream, freedom spell, Yes—it's karma!

34. Fish: expensive evening, alcohol influence, drinking phase, deep emotions, water witch, deep slumber, financially influenced, money appears, abundance spell, deep subconscious, shopping phase

35. Anchor: lasts throughout the night, lingering influence, grounding spell, long-lasting phase, grounding meditation, knot magick, stable month, safety spell, rescue work (saving spirits), solid feelings, keep manifesting, enduring the night, rescue spell, holding on to a fantasy, stay aware, stable spell, still influenced, long-lasting spell, keeping up appearances

36. Cross: a spirit/ghost/entity, disappointing evening, cursing spell, terrible psychic, miserable month, terrible night, shameful fantasy, scandalous appearance, shameful feelings, occult, suffering, tax month, intolerable appearance, difficult magick, painful night

Follow your inner moonlight; don't hide the madness.

—Allen Ginsberg

33. Key

At significant times in life, answers can be accessed only with a Key.
A door reveals the way to freedom, unlocking an important destiny.
A ritualistic ceremony of privilege, bestowed by karma as she awaits
Every solution and answer of yes, must honor the way of the fates.

DESCRIPTION

An ornate, golden Key, symbolic of status and nobility, lies in wait across an enchanted threshold, radiating and pulsing with magick and daring you to come by to unlock the door of destiny. Embellished with a shiny, red ribbon steeped in ceremony and ritual, the Key beckons you to grasp hold and be shown the way to freedom through the intricate filigree adorning the bow into the waiting arms of fate. Through the twists and turns of karma, the lacy, glistening gold leads you to the center, inlaid with a beautiful aquamarine gemstone that is a talisman for revealing answers and a way out. The luminance of the blue hue of the stone embodies all things destined; while gazing into the depths of the aquamarine, it reflects endlessly onto itself, connecting sea to sky, unlocking access to where solutions will be revealed to life's problems. Flanked by colorful flowers, the gerbera radiate with pure distinction and honor, as these blushing blossoms pay homage to their liege the sun by turning their faces toward the warmth as a sign of respect. Faintly, behind the Key, we see the glowing outline of the door of destiny, daring you to open yourself up to boundless magick that begins with one resounding YES!

The importance of this Key is that it can unlock a multitude of doors, accessing freedom both in the physical and the spiritual realms. This mastery is also reflected in the number 33, regarded as a high spiritual master with a reputation of unlocking the card's destiny, as you delve into the abyss of self-actualization.

Unlocking, significant, karmic, important, distinguished, destiny, fate, noble, solution, ceremony, access, affirmative, answers, way out, definite, revealing, open, resolution, freedom, ritual, honor, respect, reputation, prestige, affluent, key, uncovering, regal, yes!

TIMING
The Key denotes the timing of now, as all life unfolds in the present moment.

MEANING
The Key opens up with affluence and prestige as it unlocks the door of destiny, offering answers and solutions while showing you the way to your soul's karmic path. The Key is heavily associated with fated events and by knowing that everything happens for a reason. You are one step ahead in this great tapestry of life. In a reading, when the Key appears, it usually implies "yes," but make sure you look to the surrounding cards to ascertain the strength of the affirmative answer. The Key card is one of the positive cards—a great place to look in the Grand Tableau, for it will set the premise of the whole reading demonstrating your soul's path.

KEY IN LOVE
A very positive card to see when in love and asking about a relationship, for it is indicative of a karmic soulmate, a destined love, or a fated connection. If looking for love, the Key can reveal an opening to access this soulful kind of love, implying that someone will enter your life with potential to be a significant prospect of fated love, especially if this person comes back into your life from the past.

KEY IN CAREER
Directing your own career path or a prestigious career, or indicative of reaching an important milestone, of significant breakthroughs and discoveries. Also can represent someone who carries many keys at work.

KEY IN WELLNESS
The Key denotes that something will be revealed, and answers will be received. Given access to treatments, this is a positive card to see, since it brings about concrete answers to resolve any situation.

KEY IN FINANCES
A significant amount of finances, affluence and prestige, trust funds, and old money. Access to financial freedom that is yours for the taking.

Doorways, portals, gateways, initiations, rituals, and access to magick. Passwords, digital keys, pass keys, any technology used to access a door. When a key is worn as a necklace, it means "Key to my Heart."

AFFIRMATION

When I say YES to life, doors open, giving me access to things I never thought possible.

CARTOMANCY: 8 OF DIAMONDS:

The need to strive for financial balance, time to be vigilant and exercise careful planning. Money is being spent at a quicker rate than it's earned; don't stretch yourself too thin. Traditionally, this is the card of money coming in and going out. This card indicates current delays and denotes that future success may be possible. The 8 of Diamonds brings the vision needed to reveal and see things as they actually are, offering great insight into any situation.

LENORMAND KEY COMBINATIONS

1. Rider: initial response, acting important, first answer, young person's reputation, other man is being respectful, quick answer, suitor is revealed, incoming solution, hurried reply, other man offers a way out

2. Clover: easy answer, temporary solution, green door, temporary access, green pass, quick ceremony, wild reputation, informal ritual, wild answer, short-term access, lucky karma, easy way out, gambling with fate

3. Ship: travel access, leaving for freedom, moving toward the exit, "Goodbye; don't let the door hit you on the way out," car key, vehicle access, trip is important, navigating karma, sailing toward your destiny, trading keys

4. House: family reputation, brand prestige, family crest, house door, family ritual, house key, kingdom, family legacy, office key, indoor ceremony, house access, housing solution, comfortable resolution

5. Tree: medical solution, health pass, slowly revealing a way out, healthful solution, medical access, slowly opening, growing respect, spiritual ceremony/ritual, spiritual karmic connection, natural solution, living free, spiritual answers

6. Clouds: doubting the answer, troubling karma, cover up, hidden key, uncertainty revealed, chaotic ceremony, vague answer, desperate for a way out, hidden door, obscured opening, puzzling answer, lost key, troubling reputation

7. Snake: evil ritual, tempting fate, constricting freedoms, enticing solution, toxic reputation, cheating revealed, lying, complex ritual, needing answers, desiring a way out, tightening up access, needing respect, cheating karma

8. Coffin: bad reputation, no access, dead as a doornail, unimportant, skeleton key, commemorative ceremony, denied freedom, no answers, denied entry, dark ritual, locked door, no resolution, no way out, death was fated, no honor, bad solution, no respect, refusing to answer, at death's door, death ritual

9. Bouquet: special access, wonderful honor, gift of fate, polite answer, surprising solution, special ceremony, colorful reputation, enjoying free access, wonderful ceremony, beautiful ritual, wonderful karma, polite and respectful, celebration, perfect answer

10. Scythe: breakthrough, decimating a reputation, breaking out, cutting keys, danger at your door, broken key/door, removing access, risky reveal, dangerous ritual, obliterating freedom, unexpected answer

11. Whip: violent reputation, sexual access, questioning the answer, aggressive response, violating freedoms, sexually revealing, radical solution, intermittent access, sexual reputation, conflicting answers, punished by karma

12. Birds: negotiating a resolution, music is key, speaking freely, gossipy reputation, nervous answer, phone unlocked, curious ritual, verbal permission, two keys, affluent couple, hectic ceremony

13. Child: slight opening, child's reputation, small key, of little importance, slightly ajar, small reveal, a bit privileged, simple answer, toying with karma, short response, newfound respect, small honor, somewhat of an answer, small ritual, childish response

14. Fox: work reputation, pseudo freedom, avoiding answers, eluding karma, clever solution, wrong answer, escaping, feigning affluence, finding a way out, pseudo ritual/ceremony, sly reputation, office door, dishonest reply, a cautious "yes"

15. Bear: grand honor, mother's/grandmother's reputation, assertive answer, immense privilege, huge significance, immensely important, large opening, immense respect, big reputation, very open, more karma, very distinguished, big ceremony, increased access

16. Stars: stellar reputation, potential solution, astral key, luminary, high regard, internet/online access, highly respected, future resolution, Wi-Fi access, digital key, highly privileged, online reputation, upgrade, blessing ceremony, computer left open, high class, seeing a way out, illuminating answer, of vast importance, unlimited access, expansive opening, vast freedoms, of future significance, computer access, glory, positive

17. Stork: quiet reputation, gentle solution, changing fate, evolving access, changing answers, recurring access, spring ceremony, altering karma, birth canal, moving out, cycling through karma, long-term access

18. Dog: trustworthy reputation, guardian of the gates, searching for answers, trusting karma, searching for a solution, following destiny, searching for a way out, amicable resolution, friendly respect, familiar ritual

19. Tower: corporate reputation, defensive answer, one solution, arrogant answer, justice served, defending freedom, traditional ritual, defending a reputation, established access, arrogant reputation, the laws of karma, snobbish, formal ceremony

20. Garden: public reputation, civil liberties, general solution, social media reputation, outdoor ritual, average reply, all access, common answer, social media left open, public status, social class, mutual respect, general response, social media access, middle class

21. Mountain: delayed response, postponed ceremony, interrupted ritual, blocked opening, obstructed freedom, hard fate, delayed access, chip on your shoulder, harsh reply, stubborn reputation, limited answers, blocked access, hash destiny

22. Paths: alternative solution, multiple-choice answers, strange ritual, deciding how to reply, the way will be revealed, deciding yes, weird destiny, the way out, many keys, unusual answer, the plan worked, road/street access, strange fate, this is the way!

23. Mice: corrupt reputation, dishonorable, losing respect, fading significance, low key, less important, damaged reputation, stolen keys, disreputable, jeopardizing a resolution, lower class, stolen freedoms, jeopardizing access, damaged door, unavailable, less privileged, closing, insignificant

24. Hearts: relationship reputation, giving a key, kind resolution, generous reputation, compassionate solution, given a way out (relationship), lover revealed, heart of the matter, meaningful, forgiveness is the solution, granting access, relationship/love revealed

25. Ring: offering a solution, proposing a resolution, offering answers, continual karma, marital answers, continued importance, ongoing significance, proposing a resolution, marital solution, round opening, commitment ceremony, offering a way out

26. Book: unknown answer, secret door, knowing sets you free, logical solution, secret ceremony, smart reply, secretive reputation, secret way out, Akashic records, secret ritual, remember karma is a bitch!

27. Letter: data breach, email reply, it's written (fate), message replied to, notable, written response, letter opener, text reply, file access, author is honored, scheduled access, text/messages left open, writer's reputation

28. Man: free man, important man, soulmate (male), significant male, open man, virtuous man, influential man, key male, honorable man, available man, sophisticated man, nobleman, dignified man, regal man, unforgettable man, prestigious man, distinguished gentleman, definitely male, affluent male, esteemed man, privileged man, king, man's reputation

29. Woman: free woman, important woman, soulmate (female), distinguished lady, significant female, open woman, virtuous lady, influential woman, key female, honorable woman, available woman, sophisticated woman, noblewoman, dignified lady, regal woman, unforgettable woman, prestigious woman, definitely female, affluent woman, esteemed lady, privileged woman, queen, woman's reputation, classy lady

30. Lily: conservative ceremony, father's/grandfather's reputation, calm solution, personal honor, private ritual, personal answer, peaceful solution, personal access, old key, mature answer

31. Sun: good reputation, optimistic resolution, privileged, truthful answer, good solution, the truth shall set you free, true honor, portal (energy door), annual ritual, yearly access, happy ceremony, really significant, true destiny, real solution, wide open, truly free, winning an award

32. Moon: intuitive answers, an oracle, feeling honored, monthly access, manifesting answers, monthly ritual, magickal opening, feeling open, appears open, manifestation of karma, emotionally accessible, intuition unlocking, magickal significance, creative distinction, appearance of fate, magickal solution, intuitively open

34. Fish: financial reputation, expensive solution, business reputation, buying access, deep honor, business key, money access, financial solution, exchanging keys, funds available, alcoholic reputation, business access, prosperity, investments accessible (open)

35. Anchor: chained to fate, still accessible, enduring karma, solid reputation, routine answers, downgraded, safe answer, holding on to freedom, safe access, remains important, solid solution, steady resolution, routine ritual, stay respectful, holding out for answers, stuck open

36. Cross: terrible reputation, regret opening up, difficult resolution, painful answer, insufferable reputation, burden of karma, disappointing answer, terrible solution, portal (spirit door), sacred ritual, test of fate, disappointing resolution, insufferable karma, scandalous reputation, regret answering, terrible answer

What's meant to be will always find a way.

—Trisha Yearwood

34. Fish

Swimming like a fish in the deep end, water flowing over my head
Lack of money and financial resources brings uncertainty and dread.
Expensive monetary transactions, shopping and spending all my wealth
Importance is on earning and assets, while looking after financial health.

DESCRIPTION

Beams of moonlight filter down from above, revealing a scene of extraordinary riches, as the lost city of Atlantis rises up to touch the remnants of light from its watery grave. Paddling around in the deep, rolling sea, two Fish swim around the ruins, flowing with the current as a prism of light reflects off their scales, casting rainbow swirls onto the bubbles that escape into the blue abyss.

The enchanted city is now far removed from the upper world, a shell of her former glory as she lies forever entombed in a watery grave, and wisps of her riches remain held in this vast body of water—the Fish swim on in oblivion through a sea of salty tears.

Inheriting all the sunken opulent wealth, the crowned king Fish has no clue that once the city streets were lined with businesses, bustling with voices of merchants bartering and trading their wares; all the Fish care about is laying claim to these underwater riches.

The location is overrun by lush vegetation that casts a dark silhouette on the cracked pillars, creating a natural blind to hide the sunken treasures in the turbulent sea, while chests overflowing with valuables leave a lustrous, golden trail of coins.

The cold temperature of the deep waters casts a blue-filtered light, blending with the golden shimmer from the coins, and turns the sea green with envy, and the crowned Fish claims the treasure, turning this money into his own underwater empire.

His friend in the crumpled steampunk hat clearly has had too much to drink, lips peeled back and his face stuck in a grimace. A frozen scream escapes and echoes underwater as haunting notes float up to the surface, creating an eerie sound carried by the ocean spray. A vigilant jellyfish floats in the distance, warning of the potential overindulgence; he swims precariously close to the intoxicated Fish, encasing him with hundreds of stings and sinking toxins in his system, making him feel the dark side of excess.

The number 34 swims into the picture, bringing inner wisdom needed to accumulate great wealth by using visceral reactions when it comes to business ventures and making the 34 very savvy with money.

KEYWORDS

Money, flow, commerce, business, exchange, alcohol, shopping, currency, body of water, prosperity, wealth, finance, investments, earnings, abundance, actual fish, assets, budget, fluid, funds, circulation, transaction, cost, wages, commissions, resources, expensive, market

TIMING

Not traditionally used for timing but can use the dates of the sign of Pisces, February 19–March 20

MEANING

When the Fish card swims its way into your spread, it represents all things to do with finances, business, and the movement of money. At times, it can literally mean a Fish or any body of water. In some cases, the Fish card represents alcohol—remember the common saying of "drinking like a fish." Since the Fish is a card representing water, real alchemy can take place; symbolic of the womb, the true giver of life where new business ideas can spring forth, or coming into a great windfall will change your life in an instant.

FISH IN LOVE

Love is freely flowing, and just like Fish, it can change directions fairly quickly too—so the Fish in love is very unpredictable. There are Fish that love swimming in the deepest oceans, and some love the rocks and shallows. It is up to you to decipher which Fish you caught in your love net: is it the one who loves deeply or the one whose love is superficial? If you're single, the Fish card can be indicative of the one who got away; but don't worry, there are plenty of Fish in the sea.

FISH IN CAREER

A career that allows you the freedom of being self-employed, to swim and flow in any direction you want to go and not keep you feeling like you are trapped in an aquarium.

The Fish card also represents an entrepreneur, a stockbroker, a brokerage firm, a bank—any career in finance or dealing with money. The other aspect of the Fish card is alcohol, so working in a bar is right up the fish's alley. The Fish card is one of business and enterprise.

FISH IN WELLNESS

When we see the Fish appear in a wellness question, think circulation or respiratory ailments. Also, it can denote alcoholism or substance abuse or erratic changes to a health condition.

The Fish is all about finances; it is the main card in the Lenormand that represents anything to do with the movement of money in all its forms.

FISH IN MODERN DAY

All and any forms of substance abuse, especially alcohol, are indicated. When asking about love, the Fish can refer to dating sites; for example, "Plenty of Fish."

AFFIRMATION

I manifest abundance and wealth into my life, since I am deserving of all the blessings and riches that flow unto me.

CARTOMANCY: KING OF DIAMONDS

A perceptive, natural-born leader, the King of Diamonds is a self-made man; the entrepreneur who, like the Fish, enjoys his sense of freedom. Having accumulated great wealth, he can become quite aggressive when he feels his livelihood is threatened. He is an intelligent go-getter who enjoys the finer things in life, but when he gets carried away, he can become quite self-indulgent. Being a very private man, the King of Diamonds shows only one side of his face, trusting only his inner circle; when he feels comfortable, only then does he reveal his true nature and shows you the other side of his face.

LENORMAND FISH COMBINATIONS

1. Rider: going shopping, incoming money, acting rich, delivery business, first exchange, fast cash, transactions (money), serving alcohol, fluid, coming and going (money), visiting a business, other man's wealthy, young man drinks, active market, delivery costs, go with the flow

2. Clover: luck flows, gambling business, small opportunity (business), casual drink, temporary funds, happy-go-lucky drunk, gambling (stocks), short-term loan, gambling, wild exchange, easy money, jackpot, happy hour, temporary funds

3. Ship: travel budget, departure of funds, export business, trading business, foreign market, gone fishing, leaving the business, international business, gas money, car value, distant body of water, international shopping, foreign beer/wine, transport business (logistics), foreign bank, international waters

4. House: family budget, household income, home appraisal, home loan/mortgage payment, real estate check, family values, place of business, domestic market, family business, real estate / housing market, property/house value, domestic beer/wine, family trust fund, house financing, domestic bank, house for sale, house prices

5. Tree: medical budget, slow flow, medical practice (business), blood flow/circulation, deep pockets, natural resources, spiritual waters, natural spring, spiritual abundance, bodily fluids

6. Clouds: misplaced/lost money, unstable investments, cryptocurrency, unstable finances, confusing exchange, hidden costs, mad money, temperamental investor, clouded judgment when it comes to money

7. Snake: tight with money, complicated finances, toxic water, flexible funds/investment, tightening the budget, desiring wealth, poisonous fluid, needing money, problematic financial transaction, enticed by money, complicated business, cheated out of money

8. Coffin: dead fish, bad investment, dead in the water, no value, loss of commission, final payment/check, denied alcohol, closed business, black market, final exchange, last paycheck, denied resources, closed bar, let go (money), blackout drunk, denied payment, nonexistent wealth, no assets

9. Bouquet: design budget, tip/gratuity, cosmetic business, med-spa business, art value, enjoys investing, flower shop, marijuana business, wonderful flow, brand-name shopper, beautiful lake/ocean/sea, gift of money/assets, celebrating wealth, special financing, show me the money!

10. Scythe: broke (money), cut off financially, breaking an investment, "broke the bank," reducing wages, withdrawing money, removing assets, gathering resources, dividing the business, dividends, reducing business operations, splitting the cost, reduction in pay, dividing shares, cutting out alcohol, emergency funds, dangerous drunk, splitting the money, broken supply chain, threat to your money, splitting commissions

11. Whip: back-and-forth exchange, sexual investment, habitual spender, intermittent commissions, hurting bottom line, repetitive shopping, aggressive investor, sex shop, intermittent earnings/wages, arguing over spending, aggressive market (bull market), habit of spending

12. Birds: negotiating a wage, song royalties, asking for a loan, worried about money, joint bank account, sound of water, discussing payment, stressed about finances, fly fishing, asking for money, talks of borrowing money

13. Child: short on cash, playing the stock market, small investment, short-selling, vulnerable finances, small body of water, short-term investment, shorting a stock, weak circulation, small exchange, small fish/shrimp, of little value, weak bottom line, small loan

14. Fox: job costing, work salary (paycheck), job market, suspicious investment, conned out of money, cautious spending, scammed, stealthy drinking, pseudo business, fake alcohol (nonalcoholic drink), pretending to be wealthy, useful resource, illegal business

15. Bear: chief financial officer (CFO), drinking alcohol, big investment, more money, very deep, big-ticket item, inflation, increased business, large sum of money, increased wages, food bank, big value, huge loan, whale, immense wealth, big fee, grocery store / food market, strong cash flow, grocery budget, increased costs

16. Stars: future wealth, universal credit system, nest egg, exposing finances, vast body of water, astrology business, blessed financially, astronomically high prices, vast wealth, blessings of money, future value, tech investors, unlimited funds, extensive assets, improving finances, digital currency, a raise

17. Stork: transferring money, returned check, evolving financial position, changing wages, ROI (return on investment), long-term investment, changing market, long-term loan, trending stocks, shifting business model, fluctuation

18. Dog: watch the water, searching for money, protecting wealth, friendly loan, friend's business, following stocks, searching the water, reliable investment, support financially, friend is wealthy, watch spending, relying on a paycheck

19. Tower: city resources, strict budget, self-funded, government check, past-due payment, established business, official earnings, government funding, corporate business, past value, government grant, selfish with money, authorized payment, established wealth, building for sale

20. Garden: crowdfunding, average finances, public intoxication, public business, average wage/salary, stock exchange (public market), public funding, commonwealth, public resources, population exchange, mutual funds, average price, general ledger, common assets, popular business

21. Mountain: hard liquor, limited budget, blocked prosperity, restricted flow, interrupted supply chain, blocked funds, interrupted financial transaction, limited funds, limited value, interrupted wages

22. Paths: separating cash, deciding where to invest, choosing stocks, multiple transactions, unusual exchange, decision regarding money, possibly valuable, multiple resources, unusual business, strange flow, deciding a budget

23. Mice: dirty water, worthless, eating away at your savings, decreasing business activity, muddy waters, defund, dredging, dissolving investments, destroying resources, jeopardizing commissions, shallow, less flow, damaged goods, jeopardizing sobriety, less money, contaminated water, unprofitable, devalued, dirty business, corrupt stock market, draining the bank account, losing money, dwindling resources

24. Heart: generous allowance, donating money, forgiving debt/loan, benevolent fund, sentimental value, giving money, generous with money, passionate investor, benevolent donor, passionate exchange, heart circulation, grant money

25. Ring: proposed budget, ring/jewelry appraisal, surrounded by stores, wedding money, continuous funding, centralized banking, continuing business activity, ongoing prosperity, ongoing commissions/royalties, alimony payment, continued earnings, deal is profitable, surrounded by water, continuous flow, spin the bottle, gold value, ongoing drinking (alcohol), continued wages

26. Book: smart investment, book value, secret account, book royalties, secret payment, learning to trade stocks, educational loan, secret shopping, book advance, secret drinking, learning to invest, school money, secret commissions, school of fish, secret loan, unknown value

27. Letter: check/paycheck, printing money, writing a check, writing a business plan, advertising costs, writing a financial plan, printing money, paper bond, list of assets, coupon, list of investments

28. Man: materialistic man, business man, male entrepreneur, money man, wealthy man, financially independent man, gold digger (male), man with deep pockets, alcoholic (male), male investor, resourceful man, expensive man, salesman, luring a man, drunk guy, wishy-washy man

29. Woman: material girl, businesswoman, female entrepreneur, money woman, wealthy lady, financially independent woman, a gold digger, woman with a big purse, alcoholic (female), female investor, resourceful woman, expensive woman, saleslady, luring a woman, drunk girl, wishy-washy woman, deep woman

30. Lily: maturing investment, conservative budget, personal resources, discreet drinker, restrained spending, conservative investor, private funding, retirement money, ice water, personal funds, frozen lake, private exchange, discreet shopper, ice fishing, accumulation of wealth, frozen bank account/investments, lifelong wealth

31. Sun: renewing investments, successful, hot water, outcome is profitable, annual earnings, good value, wealthy, truthful exchange, abundance, true wealth, actual cost, tangible resources, hot tub/springs

32. Moon: creators fund, feeling drunk, monthly investment, skilled investor, monthly payment, monthly budget, silver value, emotional drinker, 30-day term deposit, monthly exchange, monthly transactions

33. Key: respected business, key assets, affluent wealth, opulence, key resources, top-shelf alcohol, karmic payment, lucrative wealth, prestigious shopping, access to money/funds, uncovering drinking, open alcohol, revealing spending/shopping, significant value, open bar, key chain (funds), open for business, karmic debt

35. Anchor: staying in business, settlement (money), safety net (money), holding on to investments, insurance premium, savings, insurance payout, saved from drowning, safe exchange, deep waters, bottom-feeder, lasting resources

36. Cross: obligated payments, testing the market, regret drinking (alcohol), disappointing investment, tax payment, difficult exchange, disappointing value, scandalous wealth, regretting a purchase, terrible investment, miserable alcoholic, holy water, disappointing wage/salary

*There are people who have money and
people who are rich.*

—Coco Chanel

35. Anchor

Holding in place, grounded on the bottom of the ocean floor
Securely stable and fixed, ensuring you don't get tossed to shore
Constant and long lasting, a fixed routine makes you feel stuck
Grip of life unchanging, weighty Anchor hanging onto the muck

DESCRIPTION

The sun dips behind the horizon, splashing the twilight sky with hues of sepia, as the coastline lies basking to catch the last drips of golden light. Diffused rays reflect the bright-white caps illuminating the ocean's blues and create stunning shades of tepid turquoise waters. Below all this splendor, the god of the sea stores his bounty in fathomless watery depths; with every steady rise and fall, he exhales a salty swell of breath covering everything with a sheen, leaving a briny aroma in the air as his salty essence clings onto the Anchor washed up onto the shore.

With its sweeping, curving arc embedded into the soft golden sand, the Anchor becomes the quintessential symbol of safety and seamen, and the swirling sea foam tickles its brassy base. A routine fixture on every seafaring vessel is one of the greatest gifts, offering stability and security. The Anchor has a very grounding effect as it settles and grapples into the bottom of the ocean floor, offering a steadfast hold that is enduring, solid, but not permanent, a haven just long enough to keep your boat moored while you rest awhile.

The fronds of palm sway in the air and create a silhouette for the seagulls as they fly against the sienna sky, tossing the gulls against the current of the wind and riding the waves of the salty air. Squawking, they routinely return to the safety of their nests before darkness descends.

All but one brave seagull remains, quietly taking a prideful stance atop the Anchor's brass ring, just wanting to catch your eye to let you in on a secret: ***You are never permanently stuck in any situation; with a little bit of effort, you can hoist the Anchor and be on your way, moving forward once again—you have the power.*** Message delivered; with a nod and a wink, the gull spreads his wings and flies into the darkening sky. At edge of night the only sound heard is the din of the unforgiving turbulent sea, crashing against the rocks, echoing the sound of the waves as they spill forth, and rushing onto the beach, swirling around the steadfast Anchor as the god of the sea continues to thrash and rage on.

The number 35 settles into the Anchor, heralding a flair of creativity by providing a solid building foundation for any enterprise. This number is a magnet to merchants, enabling them to attract riches, while receiving all the blessings the bounty of the sea has to offer.

KEYWORDS

Stability, lasting, settling, fixed, safe, coastal, heavy, bottom, secure, routine, constant, persistent, unchanged, enduring, solid, grounding, steady, hold, stuck, down, foundation, dependable, serious, arranged, hanging, lingering, ties, stay, still, remains, insurance

TIMING

The Anchor denotes something barely moving, stuck for now, but with a bit of effort the Anchor can be hoisted and things will be moving swimmingly once again. If the Mountain is next to the Anchor, this combination adds a note of a greater delay and a touch of permanence to the situation.

MEANING

When the weighty Anchor shows up in a reading, it brings dependability, making you feel safe and secure. Dropped as it grapples itself into the bottom of the ocean, it denotes that something has been lingering for a while, or you are holding on to something for way too long. Even though the Anchor is a neutral card, its meaning is very versatile; it can go from stable and solid to feeling stuck, so its interpretation relies heavily on the context of the question and the surrounding cards.

ANCHOR IN LOVE

When the Anchor appears in love, it can denote a sense of stability in your relationship or a long-lasting love affair; the interpretation is dependent on the context of the question asked. The Anchor can also represent a heaviness of a relationship stuck and going nowhere. If you're single, the Anchor is symbolic of someone who is looking for a solid relationship, finding someone they can truly depend on.

ANCHOR IN CAREER

The Anchor can represent a career involving anything to do with water, boats, or marine life. When it comes to describing your job or a situation involving your career, it can denote either feeling stuck or stability; look to the cards surrounding the Anchor for clarity.

ANCHOR IN WELLNESS

When inquiring about wellness, the Anchor is generally a neutral card: stable and unchanging. Look to surrounding cards for a hint. As a body part, the Anchor resembles the pelvic bone.

Stable and secure finances, fixed investments and rates that are locked in for a while. Can also refer to something being on "hold," such as funds, an account, or a check.

ANCHOR IN MODERN DAY

The Anchor brings grounding: to "feel grounded," or to intentionally "grounding" your energy. Symbolic of being below something, when you drop Anchor, it hits the bottom.

AFFIRMATION

My foundation is strong, and no tempest can ever send me off-kilter; I am safe and secure as long as I hold on . . . all is well.

CARTOMANCY: 9 OF SPADES

A very unlucky card that brings bad tidings, such as an accident, injury, and in some cases death. Adding to daily stresses, the 9 of Spades is connected to karma, bringing ill tidings of sorrows. In the magickal sense, the 9 of Spades indicates intentional harm or being under a spell. As a physical place, it denotes a graveyard. This is a card of endings; be sure that something is coming to an end in your life soon. Similar to the Anchor card in meaning, the 9 of Spades indicates a long-standing problem or situation or hitting rock bottom.

LENORMAND ANCHOR COMBINATIONS

1. Rider: delivery arrangement, other man hangs on, suitor's persistent, acting the same, news is serious, guests stay awhile, other man stays, arrivals on hold, visit arranged, race on hold, young man's dependent

2. Clover: luck holds, temporary arrangement, small opportunity remains, fun lasts, chance remains, brief snag, not so heavy anymore, funny routine, game's tied, briefly on hold, spontaneous

3. Ship: travel arrangements, international security, travel safety, boat insurance, trip on hold, mariner, departure's arranged, goodbye on hold, drive safe, international stay, foreign arrangement, departure from routine, leaving, auto insurance

4. House: real estate suspended, family ties, sanctuary, household, household routine, comfortable arrangement, property ties, brand sustainability, refuge, house remained the same, real estate arrangement, ground floor, family arrangement, house on the coast, housekeeping, place setting

5. Tree: slow down, solid foundation, blood ties, medical insurance, DNA is stable, ancestral ties, medically dependent, spiritual ties, growing endurance, medical condition unchanged/stable, grounding, living arrangement, medical foundation, systematic, medical arrangement, healthful weight, a very long time

6. Clouds: lost footing, head in the clouds (ungrounded), hidden arrangement, behaviors persist, unsure, insecurity, hidden bottom, mind unchanged, hidden ties, troubles last, uncertainty persist, misunderstanding persists, sadness lasts, confusing routine, lost grip of . . .

7. Snake: dark-haired woman holds on, evil ties, needing security, attraction remains, jealousy lingers, toxic arrangement, need grounding, enemy ties, affair lingers, seductive hold, complications last, wanting stability, toxic hold, complicated arrangement, lies persist, spiraling downward, rope/chain

8. Coffin: bad arrangement, dark hold, bad foundation, dreading the routine, nothing stays forever, buried foundation, stop holding on, death grip, emptiness persists, ending ties, final arrangement, not safe/secure, dead weight, badly stuck, releasing the hold, funeral arrangements, ending an arrangement, not settled, released, untied

9. Bouquet: floral arrangement, invitation secured, perfect arrangement, design unchanged, appreciating security, special ties, perfecting the routine, wonderful foundation, invited to the coast, gratitude remains, art insurance, design on hold, presentation lasts long, enjoys routine, gift secured

10. Scythe: severing the arrangement, dangerous ties, unstable, broken down, accident insurance, removing the hold, dangerous hold, obliterating safety, dangerous, unsafe, breaking ground, removing ties, collecting insurance, clearing ground, removing the anchor, cutting out the bottom, on dangerous ground, earthquake (ruptured ground), sudden heaviness, unexpected arrangement

11. Whip: sexual arrangement, aggressive hold, sexual endurance (stamina), sex routine, struck down, sexual ties, anger lingers, disrupting a routine, punishment is serious, habitual routine, hits the coast, patterns hold, debate is tied, repetitive routine, repeatedly stuck, habits persist, intermittent hold, sex restraints (bondage)

12. Bird: partnership ties, two arrangements, flight insurance, flying to the coast, curiosity remains, flight safety, musical arrangement, doubling down, conversation put on hold, negotiating arrangements, ungrounded, flight arranged, conversation lasts, flight grounded, couple settles down, hectic routine, verbal arrangement

13. Child: childhood ties, new arrangement, a bit serious, slightly tied down, child custody arrangement, a bit heavy, insecure, a little bit remains, playing it safe, small arrangement, new foundation, a bit stuck, slightly tied down, starting from the bottom, a bit settled

14. Fox: work arrangement, suspicious routine, vigilance, clever arrangement, mariner, sneakiness persists, pseudo ties, phony arrangement, fraudulent insurance, clever hold, false security, false bottom, untrustworthy insurance agent, guilt lingers, job on the coast, scam persists, mistake sticks, superficial ties, pretending to stay, suspicious arrangement

15. Bear: powerful ties, bearing down, increase security, heavy anchor, increased stability, solid, very persistent, heavy weight, very serious, restaurant insurance, solid arrangement, overbearing heaviness, diet routine, forced arrangement, weighty, maternal ties

16. Star: positive arrangement, high tide, up and down, vast security, expansive hold, future arrangement, extensive routine, vast ties, lifting, expansive hold, heightened security, improving steadily, alleviating heaviness, pulling yourself up from the bottom, floating, enduring, released, extensive ties, lift anchor, lifted weight, wishing for stability, exposed, scientific foundation, famous coast, universal insurance, visible ties, online security, uphold

17. Stork: pregnant pause, changing arrangements, rearrange, evolving routine, changing steadily, moved to safety, pregnancy is stable, changes endured, returning stability, moving/returning to the coast, gentle hold, shifting foundation, moving insurance, long lasting

18. Dog: friendly ties, reliable foundation, watching constantly, following the routine, support lasts, a friend holds on, friendly arrangement, loyalty remains, follow the coast, protective, watch the foundation, observed for a long time, guarding, trustworthy arrangement, familiar hold, dog is safe, protecting the coast, reliable, smell of the coast, "sea and salt"

19. Tower: official ties, formal arrangement, rigid, established routine, standing your ground, self-preservation, established foundation, fixed, government ties, rules stay put, ambition lasts, previous arrangement, prison ties, official hold, defending the coast, institutional ties, governance unchanged, traditions last, established ties, legal arrangement, mandates remain

20. Garden: average hold, public ties, group insurance, common arrangement, event on hold, social media safety, outdoor routine, citizen's security, average weight, general insurance, neighborhood safety

21. Mountain: permanently stuck, interrupted routine, permanent ties, stuck, interrupted insurance, rock/boulder, delays remain, rock/stone foundation, hard bottom, rough/rocky coast, permanent arrangement

22. Paths: path to safety, unusually long lasting, strangely persistent, unusually solid, multiple arrangements, separation remains, choice is heavy, unusual arrangement, between routines, separation arrangement, decision is serious, multiple ties

23. Mice: losing hold, less grounded, crumbling foundation, jeopardizing ties, losing ground, fading endurance, loosening ties, losing grip, ruined stability, low tide, drifting, shaky ground, unsteady, inconsistent, wavering, jeopardizing safety, damaging arrangement, unsettled, low down

24. Heart: romantic ties, giving security, relationship lingers, loving the coast, romantic arrangement, relationship feels stuck, relationship is serious, relationship ties, relationship's foundation, love remains

25. Ring: marital arrangement, continuous hold, marital ties, ongoing arrangement, surrounded by the coast, jewelry insurance, continued stability, marriage hangs on, ongoing, marital stability, contract is solid, deal is arranged, spouse holds on

26. Book: training on hold, secret arrangement, education secured, study routine, secret ties, secrets held, records secured, classes arranged, logical arrangement, memory persists, journaling routine

27. Letter: written in the sand, texting constantly, writing routine, schedule unchanged, texts persist, results are serious, communicating steadily, written arrangement, text/messages kept, documents kept safe, writing constantly, texting routine

28. Man: stable man, settled man, serious man, persistent man, safe man, secure man, grounded man, solid man, stuck man, holding on to a man, lingering man, saving a man, kept man, persistent man, mariner (male), ties to a man, dependable man, arrangement with a man

29. Woman: stable woman, settled female, serious woman, persistent woman, safe woman, secure lady, grounded woman, solid woman, stuck woman, holding on to a woman, lingering woman, saving a woman, kept woman, persistent woman, mariner (female), ties to a woman, dependable woman, arrangement with a woman

30. Lily: experience outlasts everything, paternal ties, old arrangement, personal safety, peace lasts, old but still hanging on, personal insurance, old foundation, personal ties, private insurance, discreet routine, private arrangement

31. Sun: good ties, truly steady, morning routine, vacation/holiday insurance, real ties, yearly routine, successful arrangement, truly settled, good arrangement, truly safe, truth weighs heavily, sunshine coast, fire insurance, truly dependable, real hold, really grounded

32. Moon: emotional ties, feeling anchored, monthly arrangement, feelings unchanged, feeling safe and secure, felling tied down, emotionally stable, magickal knot, feeling emotionally heavy, monthly routine, magickal ties, feeling grounded

33. Key: important arrangement, karmic ties, definitely persistent, significant ties, revealing routine, karmic arrangement, destiny unchanged, definite hold, open bottom, karmic knot

34. Fish: financial arrangement, flood insurance, deep sea, business ties, a safe, payment arrangement, coastal, deep ties, water is safe, resources secured, financial ties, abundance lasts, funds are secure

36. Cross: obligated ties, difficult arrangement, cursed ground, difficult routine, intolerable ties, regret staying, scandalous arrangement, disappointing agreement, religious ties, spirit/entity/ghost hangs around, regretting the arrangement

The anchor holds in spite of the storm.

—Ray Boltz

36. Cross

Burdens bring suffering and hardships, obligations that you want to forget.
Disappointments so exhausting, the harbinger of painful misery and regret
Desperately wanted to believe in salvation but left ashamed and haunted
Suffering waits on the sacred altar; a spirit tested and a sacrifice is wanted.

DESCRIPTION

Reverently walking up the stairs approaching the interior chamber, the smell of beeswax immediately hits your senses. The scent reaches its tentacles deeply into the recess of your mind, triggering memories of something venerable steeped in ecclesiastical mystery. The only sound heard is your footsteps, eerily echoing off the walls amid the sound of silence. A powerful ancient energy, bathing the stone walls in a golden, morning light with hues of desert sand, lies held within these rocks, speaking of an unshakable faith. The ornate, golden Cross displayed on the steps illuminates with an otherworldly glow, pulsing with a powerful presence. This sacred chamber is the perfect place to commune with the gods and contemplate all the hardships that life has dealt you thus far. Many find deep comfort in the Cross symbol, and others get transported into a world of pain, for it is the original symbol of corporal punishment. A spirit swirls around the Cross, bringing suffering and pain—the kind that only human experience can bring. It is this eternal churning of turbulent sorrows that anchors you to this world.

Here, in this sacred space, you get to experience that quiet part of yourself that has faith in something greater than yourself, allowing you a divine moment to connect and commune with the gods.

Holy light filters softly through the doorway, glinting off the Cross, and reflects off the Persian turquoise stones that are acquired from the moon's temple in the watery grave below. The golden color of the Cross holds the spark of the divine masculine, inspiring deep contemplation while fostering the power of communing with a higher power; generous in nature, gold reminds you to be gentle with your soul. The studded turquoise stones bring alignment of your chakras, especially the center of expression, the throat. Refreshing and feminine, she balances out the masculine energy. The Greeks have the belief that turquoise wards off the evil eye; combined with the Christian symbol of the Cross, it offers the greatest protection against all evil entities. The Cross card bears the number 36, facilitating being of service to mankind; as a great humanitarian, 36 is always concerned with the plight of mankind. The number 36 brings a lightness to the burdensome Cross, with a touch of creativity and love of earthly pleasures, because it knows what it means to be human. The number 36 is very similar to the Cross, for both are self-sacrificing, allowing the space for great reflection on a level of global consciousness.

KEYWORDS

Sacred, burdens, despair, sorrows, beliefs, duty, religion, a spirit, suffering, hardships, an altar, pain, intolerance, obligation, regret, ideology, tests, crisis, disappointment, difficulties, responsibility, shame, scandal, tax, anguish, faith, exhausting, burn out, dogma, misery, worship, victim, fatigue, terrible

TIMING

Effects are immediately felt, or on an observed religious holiday.

MEANING

The Cross bears obligations and hardships, bringing with it great difficulty and heralding misery and pain. When this negative card appears, there is no avoiding it, for it is a gate—something you have to go through and experience. The Cross can refer to something sacred, or any organized religion, a hallowed space where spirits and entities can come out and wreak havoc.

CROSS IN LOVE

Just by observing the symbol of the Cross's fragmentation, with lines crossed, demonstrates disruptions in comparison to the Ring, which is round, unbroken, and eternal. It usually denotes a very painful relationship, combined with feelings of obligation and just staying together out of duty. If single, you will remain that way for some time.

CROSS IN CAREER

Causing problems, bringing a sense of hardship and burnout to any career situation. Staying at a job because you need to be there, rather than want to be there. Working in a field that involves some sort of a religious connotation.

CROSS IN WELLNESS

The Cross brings pain and suffering—not a card you want to see, especially when the Coffin or Tree is around.

CROSS IN FINANCES

Difficult financial times ahead bringing misery; remember the saying "death and taxes." This card can indicate a tax burden or a financial crisis.

CROSS IN MODERN DAY

Equally armed Greek Cross predates Christianity and denotes balance. It represents the four seasons, four elements, four cardinal directions, and the unification of the material world with the ethereal world. The Greek Cross blends both masculine and feminine energies. The Cross also stands for a spirit, ghost, or entity.

AFFIRMATION

With every battle I conquer, I become a beacon of inspiration for others.

CARTOMANCY: 6 OF CLUBS

There is a strong feeling of responsibility that surrounds the 6 of Clubs with a sense of either good communication or extreme ignorance. Traditionally seen as a card of movement in all areas of life, the 6 of Clubs has a clear path, giving you a chance to take charge and resolve any lingering burdensome issues. Expressing your thoughts ensures movement after a period of difficult hardship.

LENORMAND CROSS COMBINATIONS

1. Rider: young man in crisis, acting like a victim, coming misery, first test, other man's regretful, coming crisis, quick test, young priest, mobile altar, visiting a church, announcement is terrible, visitation (spirit)

2. Clover: green tax, brief obligation, temporary pain, temporary suffering, wild spirit, lucky altar, short-term crisis, gambling tax, easy victim, briefly disappointed, easing exhaustion, wild scandal, short-term responsibility

3. Ship: traveling spirit, international crisis, foreign curse *mati malocchio*, travel tax, foreign victim, travel obligation, directions crossed, distance causes hardship, travel altar, leaving responsibilities behind, moving with difficulty

4. House: family member spirit, house of worship, family curse, related victim, familiar spirit, housing crisis, property/house disappointment, home chapel, family member is miserable, brand responsibility, house tax

5. Tree: body pain, slowly suffering, deeply rooted ideology/faith, environmental crisis, life of regret, healthcare crisis, a spirit, healthcare system burdened, spiritual crisis, growing pains, ancestral spirit, medical victim, ancestral altar, deeply rooted shame, generational trauma, spiritual beliefs

6. Clouds: lost faith, hidden shame, shadow entity, temperamental spirit, hidden obligations, misplaced beliefs, ashamed, hiding the victim (witness protection), hidden tax, hiding pain, headache (physical), hidden altar, doubting beliefs, hiding disappointment, hiding religious beliefs/ideology

7. Snake: evil spirit/entity, toxic religious beliefs, complicated test, enticing religious cult, lying victim, complicated taxes, unholy, narrow beliefs, toxic ideology, problematic beliefs, wanting to believe, evil, cheating on taxes

8. Coffin: dark entity, black sorrow, spirit/ghost/entity, grief, illness causes pain, cursed, death rites, grave crisis, negative test, skeleton, negative entity/spirit/ghost, final exam, last victim, bad crisis, dark despair, deceased victim, no pain (when death comes, there is no pain), sick and tired, let go the pain, end of obligation, afterlife, death beliefs, ill omen, death crisis, mortified, unmerciful, bad regret

9. Bouquet: pleasant ghost/spirit, wonderful beliefs, special test, nice entity, special ideology, decorating an altar, wonderful religion, special obligation, showing off your religion, Eastern religion

10. Scythe: dangerous ideology, unexpected crisis, emergency drill (test), threatening scandal, dividing responsibilities, dangerous entity, broken faith, exorcist, severing obligations, broken victim, removing a cross, breaking/removing a curse, sudden intolerance, sudden difficulties, vaccine victim, sharp pain, excommunicated from church, removing a spirit attachment, risky test, decimating religion, obliterating an entity, divided by religion/ideology/beliefs, injectable injury crisis, splitting taxes, emergency, urgent obligation

11. Whip: flagellation (religious), intermittent pain, sexually exhausted, sexual victim, aggressive spirit, scourge, sexual pain, pattern of intolerance, angry spirit, hurting (in pain), intermittent testing, sexual abstinence (religious), causing hardship, inflicting pain, sadistic, sexually frustrated, questioning faith/religion

12. Birds: noisy spirit/ghost, talkative spirit, reciting prayers, nervous victim, saying sorry, two altars, scandalous, two spirits/ghosts, confession (speaking your sins), in-fight crisis, double-crosser, nervous affliction, two victims, speech pathology test

13. Child: slight regret, small obligation, new intolerance, small responsibility, new tax, small church, child victim, small crisis, quiz, small altar, weakened spirit/entity, small burden, new obligation

14. Fox: avoiding responsibilities, elusive spirit, work test, pretending to be victimized, avoiding a test, avoiding obligations, elusive pain, sneaky entity, pretending to be tired, tricky test, on-the-job crisis, suspicious religion, employment crisis, suspecting a ghost/spirit is responsible, work obligation, employment tax, job testing, work adverse, avoiding a test, stealthy ghost, pretending to be in pain, feigned responsibly/obligation, pseudo religion, fraudulent taxes, work's terrible, fake crisis, evading taxes, work altar

15. Bear: food intolerance, big test, intense pain, increased fatigue, strong pain, very painful, big crisis, bearing the cross, hunger pains, intense spirit, immense difficulty, food tax, very desperate, increasing taxes, big burden, increased suffering, strong attachment (entity), very intolerant, huge regrets, increased responsibility, heavy anguish, major exhaustion, more difficulties, muscle pain, food crisis, power struggle, big altar, huge tax burden, muscle test

16. Stars: astral being (spirit), star-crossed, alleviating suffering, vision test, angelic being, alien entity, blessings, space crisis, exposed victim, universal tax, electricity crisis, expansive beliefs, sacred, alleviating pain, high altar, lifting obligations, uplifting religion, improving hardships, A+ on a test / acing a test, exposing the crisis, alleviating responsibilities, lifting shame, alleviating tax burden, exposing the cult, uplifting beliefs, technological crisis

17. Stork: recurring pain, evolving beliefs, changing obligations, evolving responsibilities, migrating pain, shifting the burden, seasonal altar, long obligation, moving causes hardships, changing your beliefs, recurring obligations, migration crisis

18. Dog: dog collar (priest), protective spirit, policing crisis, a fetch, hunting ghosts, searching for a victim, investigating a ghost/spirit, searching for something to believe in, watched by a spirit, pet altar

19. Tower: city tax, bar exam, official crisis, self-pity, established beliefs, defending religion, traditional religion, defending beliefs, traditional worship, traditional altar, self-mortification, established ideology

20. Garden: public exhaustion, general pain, societal crisis, congregation, general intolerance, common belief, general test, population tax, shared obligation, social responsibility, common religion, general tax, general fatigue, common intolerance, general disappointment, population crisis, mutual responsibility

21. Mountain: hard test, challenging, tough responsibility, mountain of regrets, restrictive beliefs, interrupted test, border crisis, permanent altar, challenging ideology, deferred taxes, stubborn pain

22. Paths: multiple victims, strange beliefs, unusual pain, strange entity, unusual intolerance, road to misery, crossing, multiple tests, unusual religion, different beliefs, many hardships, strange ideology, unusual obligation, many ghosts

23. Mice: spreading pain, costly ideology, spreading misery, destructive spirit, losing my religion, depleted and exhausted, thinning out responsibilities, irresponsible, worn out, poor spirited, corrupt religion, damaging beliefs, damaging scandal

24. Heart: benevolent spirit, lover's remorse, relationship crisis, to love desperately, relationship tested, given responsibility, donating to a church, lovely spirit, stress test (heart), love altar, heartfelt effort, love comes with pain, relationship obligations

25. Ring: marriage exhaustion, ongoing crisis, continued disappointment, ongoing responsibility, marriage remorse, surrounded by spirits/ghosts, marital obligations, ongoing burden, continuous duty, surrounded by victims, ongoing obligations, continuities difficulties, ongoing fatigue, surrounded by crosses, marriage altar, continual pain

26. Book: unknown entity, secret cult, bible, school test, unknown victim, secret beliefs, secret altar, book of prayers, studying for a test, book on religion, secret responsibility, records in a church, school exam

27. Letter: scheduled religious service, sending a fetch, written exam, communication becomes obligated, written dogma, pamphlet/brochure on religion, written creed, advertising religion, texting/messaging out of duty

28. Man: religious man, miserable man, tormented man, defeated man, afflicted man, needy man, pained man, obligated man, suffering man, burdensome man, remorseful man, difficult man, disappointing man, male in crisis, exhausted man, male spirit/ghost/entity, pious man, worn-out man, male victim, cursed man, intolerable man, scandalous man, disgraceful man, regretful man, terrible man, superstitious man, remorseful man, a priest

29. Woman: religious woman, miserable woman, tormented lady, defeated woman, afflicted woman, needy female, pained woman, obligated woman, suffering woman, burdensome woman, remorseful woman, difficult woman, disappointing woman, female in crisis, exhausted woman, female spirit/ghost/entity, pious woman, worn-out woman, female victim, cursed woman, intolerable woman, scandalous woman, disgraceful woman, regretful woman, terrible woman, superstitious woman, remorseful woman, a nun

30. Lily: lifelong obligation, private tax, personal regret, old priest, elderly victim, personal duty, lifetime responsibility, old tax burden, cold intolerant, renewed suffering, retirement crisis, moral obligation, personal burden, old religion, personal shame, private altar

31. Sun: burnout, annual taxes, happy spirit, true faith, sun altar, southern religion, energy crisis, real victim, heating crisis, success comes with responsibility, daily misery, energetically exhausted, renewed responsibility, positive spirit/entity, conscious obligation, heat intolerant, tangible spirit, really believe it, positive religion, true regret

32. Moon: feeling shame, moon altar, feeling obligated, occult (darker side), feeling burdened, feeling regret, psychic victim, feeling responsible, feeling a spirit/entity (about), feeling disappointed, magickal altar, feeling burned out, magickal responsibility, feeling tired, emotionally exhausted, feeling guilty, manifesting apparition

33. Key: key belief, important responsibility, significant obligation, definite regret, answers to a test, revealing beliefs, uncovering shame, karmic test, way out of a crisis, a portal to hell, way out of responsibility/obligation, definitely disappointed, karmic suffering, freeing a spirit/entity, revealing the scandal, passing a test, revealing shame

34. Fish: financial tax burden, deeply regretful, expensive test, key victim, money shame, buyer's remorse, financial victim, paying penance, tears, financial responsibility, deep remorse, business obligation, deep beliefs, deeply disappointed, deep sorrow, alcohol intolerance, client obligation

35. Anchor: lasting obligation, lingering difficulties, heavy suffering, enduring hardship, lasting burdens, long-lasting fatigue, holding on to shame, enduring obligations, stuck spirit/ghost, heavy pain, serious crisis, lasting intolerance, solid apparition, holding on to pain, keeping the faith, hanging on to misery, enduring shame, holding on to suffering, enduring constant pain

It's during our darkest moments that we must focus to see the light

—Aristotle Onassis

The key to reading the Lenormand is to

"choose words that fit, and you will definitely be on your way!"

The time has finally come to end this magickal tale.
The knowledge I bestow, and the enchantments I share

I am now going to bid you a fond and final "yia sou."

Leaving the rest of this inspiring journey up to you.

All my love,
Kalliope xxx

Yasmeen Westwood is a self-taught photomanipulation artist living in Perthshire in Scotland. Her first deck—*The Tarot of Enchanted Dreams*—was released in December 2019. She was a finalist for her artwork, for the MPower, Mums in Business National Business Awards 2019. For *The Tarot of Enchanted Dreams*, she was runner-up in two categories of the International Tarot Foundation CARTA Awards 2019, for Best Illustrator of a Tarot Deck, and Best Self-Published Tarot Deck, and she won the Bronze for Tarot Decks in the COVR awards in 2020. Her other decks include *Hummingbird Wisdom Oracle* (won Gold, Product of the Year, Industry Choice of the Year and Peoples Choice of the Year and in the COVR 2022 Awards), *Tarot of the Enchanted Soul* (Gold Winner, COVR Awards 2023), *Angels of Healing & Hope* (Silver, COVR Awards 2023), and the recently released *Lenormand of Enchantment*. **www.Enchantedsoulart.co.uk**

Kalliope, named after the Muse of Epic Poetry, possesses an innate connection to magick and divination. Guided by ancestral wisdom, she delves into Tarot's symbolic secrets. Since 1986, she has wholeheartedly embraced its transformative power to profoundly heal and change lives. With over three decades of experience, Kalliope serves as a trusted Earth guide offering soulful insights and guidance worldwide. Her mastery is beautifully showcased in her acclaimed book *Lenormand of Enchantment*. As a sought-after teacher and speaker, she generously shares her wisdom, guiding others on their soul's path. Residing by the tranquil lakeside in southern Ontario, Kalliope finds inspiration in the loving presence of her King of Swords, two beloved boys, and her faithful black cat, Spell. **Visit her at www.musekalliope.com.**

LENORMAND OF ENCHANTMENT
978-0-7643-6378-8

208 pp. | 5 1/2" × 6 1/2" × 1 3/8"
(139 × 165 mm) | Box set
$24.99 USD